Teaching Anticorruption

Teaching Anticorruption

Developing a Foundation for Business Integrity

Agata Stachowicz-Stanusch
Hans Krause Hansen

business**expert**
Press

First published in 2013 by
Business Expert Press, LLC
222 East 46th Street, New York, NY 10017
www.businessexpertpress.com

ISBN-13: 978-1-60649-470-7 (paperback)
ISBN-13: 978-1-60649-471-4 (e-book)

Business Expert Press Principles of Responsible Management Education
(PRME) collection

Collection ISSN: Forthcoming (print)
Collection ISSN: Forthcoming (electronic)

Cover and interior design by Exeter Premedia Services Private Ltd.,
Chennai, India

First edition: 2013

10 9 8 7 6 5 4 3 2 1

Printed in the United States of America.

Abstract

Over the past few years there has been a surge of interest in discussing how university and business school teaching that focuses particularly on anti-corruption can be developed and become linked to the organizational practices of contemporary businesses. The interest in knowing much more about what exactly constitutes anti-corruption practices and how such practices can become meaningfully integrated in the organizational life of companies that operate in multiple contexts reflects a growing awareness amongst experts, teachers and practitioners of management education of the foundational character of anti-corruption for responsible and sustainable business in today's globalizing world.

The movement in management education towards a more serious concern with how corruption can be tackled has occurred in reaction to highly publicized corporate scandals and instances of management misconduct. Widespread scandals have eroded public faith in companies and public authorities as well as fuelled legislative reactions such as the Sarbanes-Oxley and Dodd-Frank acts in the United States, not to forget the recent UK Bribery Act. Concomitantly, management scholars and educators have begun to question the assumptions underlying traditional management education, which in their view not only contributed to the recent financial and moral crisis but also failed to prepare students and executives for coping with the leadership challenges and ethical dilemmas that face any responsible manager in contemporary corporations.

We believe that the statement "a prepared mind favors ethical behavior" carries some important truth to it and have therefore invited a group of world-class scholars with a diversity of backgrounds and perspectives to develop our thinking on how teaching in anti-corruption practices can be conducted today. How to teach anti-corruption in business schools and universities is not an area that has received much scholarly attention so far, and our book is clearly a response to this situation. This book therefore sets out to develop an empirical and theoretical platform for rethinking business school curricula, with a specific view to understanding and meaningfully confronting the challenges of corruption of the second decade of the twenty-first century. In particular, the book will

- offer examples of new tools, teaching methods and case studies for anti corruption teaching
- explore and discuss how particular approaches, such as Giving Voice to Values, may be used worldwide for teaching anticorruption
- explore and discuss how curricula can be streamlined and rejuvenated in order to ensure a high level of integrity in the worlds of business

Keywords

anti corruption teaching, business ethics education, management education, dignity in business world, anti-corruption actions, corporate social irresponsibility.

Contents

List of Contributors

Agata Stachowicz-Stanusch, Silesian University of Technology, Gliwice, Poland

Amy Walburn, American University of Beirut, Lebanon

Andrew E. Michael, Intercollege Larnaca, Cyprus

Dima Jamali, American University of Beirut, Lebanon

Ernestina Giudici, University of Cagliari, Italy

Federica Caboni, University of Cagliari, Italy

Gazi Islam, Grenoble Ecole De Management, France

Hamid H. Kazeroony, Minnesota State Colleges & Universities, USA

Hans Krause Hansen, Copenhagen Business School, Denmark

J. Goosby Smith, Pepperdine University, Malibu, CA, USA

Jodi Detjen, Suffolk University, Boston, MA, USA

Lama Al-Arda, Grenoble Ecole De Management, France

Marco Tavanti, DePaul University, Chicago, IL, USA

Ranjini Swamy, Goa Institute of Management, India

Roberta Atzori, University of Central Florida, USA

Sharon E. Norris, Spring Arbor University, Michigan, USA

Shiv K. Tripathi, Mzumbe University Dar Es Salaam Campus, Tanzania

Susan Schick Case, Case Western Reserve University, Cleveland, Ohio, USA

About the Editors
and Authors

About the Editors

Agata Stachowicz–Stanusch, PhD, DSc, an associate professor of management and the head of the Management and Marketing Department at the Silesian University of Technology, Poland. She is the author of over 80 research papers and has written 14 books: a few of them include *Integrity in Organizations—Building the Foundations for Humanistic Management* (Palgrave Macmillan, 2012), *Academic Ethos Management: Building the Foundation for Integrity in Management Education* (Business Expert Press, 2012), *Education for Integrity: Ethically Educating Tomorrow's Business Leaders* (Emerald, 2011), *Effectively Integrating Ethical Dimensions into Business Education* (IAP, 2011), and *Handbook of Research on Teaching Ethics in Business and Management Education* (IGI Global, 2012). Agata manages an international research team as part of the project "Sensitizing Future Business Leaders: Developing Anti-Corruption Guidelines for Curriculum Change" of the UN Global Compact and the Principles for Responsible Management Education (PRME) initiative. Pro bono she is a member of International Fellows for the World Engagement Institute and International Editorial Board for International Higher Education Teaching and Learning Association. She served as a track chair and track co-organizer during the EURAM conferences (Roma, 2010; Rotterdam, 2012; Istanbul, forthcoming) and was a PDW co-organizer and presenter during the AOM Annual Meeting in San Antonio (2011) and in Boston (2012). She is regularly reviewer of *AOM*, *EURAM* as well as the *Journal of Brand Management* (Palgrave MacMillan) and *Journal of Organizational Change Management* (Emerald). She is associate editor of *Journal of Applied Research in Higher Education* (Emerald), member of editorial board of *Law and Social Change: an International Journal* (Springer), and member of editorial advisory board for *Business Strategy Series* (Emerald). She was thrice doctoral dissertations supervisor and many times doctoral dissertations reviewer.

Hans Krause Hansen, PhD, is Professor of Governance and Culture Studies at Copenhagen Business School. Originally trained in political science and Latin American studies, his current research revolves around the role of private actors in global governance, anti-corruption practices in international business, the surveillance infrastructures and practices of transparency regimes. Hans has published in journals such as *Bulletin of Latin American Studies, Gestíon y Política Pública, Critical Quarterly, Citizenship Studies, Alternatives: Local, Global Political, International Studies Review, Review of International Political Economy, Journal of International Relations and Development* and *International Political Sociology* , just as he has contributed with chapters in a wide range of international anthologies published, amongst others, by Routledge and Oxford University Press. Hans has previously served as Academic Director of the Business, Language and Culture Studies Program at CBS, and he is currently head of the Doctoral School of Organization and Management Studies, CBS. He is also member of the PRME Working Group on Anti-Corruption, as well as a reviewer for several international journals.

About the Authors

Lama Al-Arda is currently full-time Ph.D. student at Grenoble Ecole De Management (GEM) France, with main focus on People, Organizations, and Society, related to that he is involved in research projects as a research assistant. One of the main projects he currently works on is corporate social responsibility (CSR), where a critical analysis approach for the historical emergence of the (CSR) field is taken. His own research project is mainly about social enterprises (SEs) in specific geographical settings, namely Palestine and Jordan, where he attempted to understand the subprocesses enacted in SEs, and link these subprocesses with the transformational change the SEs claim in their missions to achieve.

Roberta Atzori earned her master's degree at the University of Cagliari (Italy) in 2010, where she enrolled as a Ph.D. student in business administration for two years. Presently, she is a graduate teaching associate and Ph.D. student at the University of Central Florida (UCF) where she teaches tourism management at UCF Rosen College of Hospitality Management. She has attended many conferences as a presenter (e.g., EGOS, IABPAD, Academy of Management). She has published many articles: her research interests include sustainability, climate change, and tourism development.

Federica Caboni earned her master's degree at the University of Cagliari (Italy) in 2010, where she currently is a Ph.D. student in business administration (3rd AY). She has attended as a presenter at many conferences (e.g., EGOS, IABPAD, Academy of Marketing, Academy of Management, QMOD). She spent some months at the Stockholm University School of Business as an International research student. She has published several chapters in team books and many articles. Her research interests include storytelling, corporate identity, place branding, and town centre management.

Susan Schick Case is an associate professor of organizational behavior at the Weatherhead School of Management, Case Western Reserve University and associate professor in the College of Arts and Sciences in both Women and Gender Studies and at the Institute of Social Justice. Recent research includes a biopsychosocial lens for persistence of gendered discourse in the workplace, gendered science cultures, the impact of work–family on women's career choices, and religion and business integrity. All focus on valuing differences between and among people and designing systems for effective workplace inclusion. Her newest work draws on Judaism, Christianity, and Islam, providing guidelines for behaving ethically, and with integrity and moral responsibility in business. Based on this work, she was selected as a Kaufman Scholar at the University of Maryland, Center for Financial Policy in 2012–13 for three semesters. An active university professor at all levels (undergraduate, MBA, Ph.D.), consultant, executive coach, and expert witness, all her work intersects organizational integrity issues.

Jodi Detjen has been a professor of management at Suffolk University since 1999. She also is a principal partner of a boutique consulting firm, the InTrinsic Group. The InTrinsic Group guides organizations to leverage their existing people and processes to maximize performance and long-term impact. Jodi writes and teaches in areas of leadership development, systemic and organization change management, and speaking truth to power. Jodi teaches management at the MBA, undergraduate, and corporate education levels both online, in the classroom and abroad in Germany, Africa, and India. Jodi consistently ranks in the top 10% of professors at the Sawyer Business School. Jodi teaches the way adults learn through interaction and application of the concepts. Prior to teaching and independent consulting, Jodi was as an international management consultant based in London, working with Global 1000 clients. Jodi focused on redesigning operations, thereby realizing significant financial benefits.

Ernestina Giudici is a Full Professor of Management and Communication at the University of Cagliari (Italy). She is member of the University of Cagliari Board of Directors, member of the Editorial Advisory Board of the International Journal of Quality and Service Sciences, and member of the Editorial Review Board of the Transnational Marketing Journal. She has published several books, chapters in contributed books, and many articles. Her research interests include innovation, the relationship between organizations and their environment, identity, integrity, humanistic management, creativity, ethic, sustainable development, etc. As a presenter, she has attended many conferences (e.g., EGOS, Academy of Management, QMOD, EURAM, IABE, etc.).

Gazi Islam is associate professor of business administration at Grenoble Ecole de Management and Insper Institute of Education and Research. He teaches undergraduate and graduate courses in leadership and organizational behavior, organizational dynamics, and international management. He completed his Ph.D. in organizational behavior at Tulane University, where his research focused on organizational identity, voice, and power relations. His current research interests include the organizational antecedents and consequences of identity, and the relations between identity, group dynamics, and the production of group and organizational cultures. In addition, he attempts to link identity and organizational culture to wider issues of national culture, ideology, and civil society. His work has been published in journals such as *Organization Studies, Leadership Quarterly, Organization, Human Relations, The American Journal of Public Health, Journal of Business Ethics,* and *American Psychologist.*

Dima Jamali is professor and associate dean at the Suliman S. Olayan School of Business at the American University of Beirut. She is the author of over 40 international publications focusing on different aspects of corporate social responsibility (CSR) and Gender and Careers in the Middle East, all appearing in highly reputed journals including *British Journal of Management, Corporate Governance: An International Review, Journal of Business Ethics,* and *Gender in Management: An International Journal.* Dr. Jamali's research record has won her a number of scientific awards and honors, including the Abdul Hameed Shoman Award for Best Young Arab Researcher for the year 2010, Best Paper Awards at the Irish Academy of Management (2011), and the American Academy of Management (2008), British Academy of Management Fellowship for South Asia and Middle East (2007), and the Best Paper Award by the North American Case Research Association (2003).

Hamid H. Kazeroony's doctoral dissertation, "Organizational Leadership Perception of Change," is based on triangulating Kantian approach to ethics, Hegelian idealism, and Marxist mode of production. For the last 12 years, he has served as administrator, faculty development trainer, curriculum designer, and researcher at for-profit, non-profit, and public institutions, conducting ground, hybrid, and online classes addressing ethics in teaching, the nature of adult education, and higher education strategies. Within the last four years, he has been active organizer, chair, and presenter at the Academy of Management and European Academy of Management. He currently serves as the board member for Higher Education Teaching and Learning (http://hetl.org/boards/) co-chair of editorial board for *Global Management Journal*, and reviewer for *Emerald Management Decision* journal.

Andrew E. Michael is assistant professor and program coordinator at the Intercollege Larnaca Business Department in Cyprus. He is also an adjunct professor and doctoral supervisor at the University of Nicosia in Cyprus. He has a Ph.D. in business administration and an MA in economics. He has published and conducted research in the areas of business ethics, managing diversity in the workplace, person–environment fit, work–life balance, and macroeconomics. He is on the editorial board of the *International Journal of Organizational Analysis* and is conference paper reviewer for the Academy of Management (AOM) and the EuroMed Research Business Institute (EMRBI).

Sharon E. Norris is an assistant professor of business and director of Graduate Studies, MBA Programs, with the Gainey School of Business at Spring Arbor University. She holds a Ph.D. in organizational leadership with a major in human resource development from Regent University's School of Global Leadership and Entrepreneurship. Her recent publications include those on topics of leading change, leadership development, impression management, self-monitoring, and global human resource development. She has presented her research at regional, national, and international conferences and received various awards for her academic achievements. Dr. Norris is a Beta Phi Scholar and recipient of the Gary J. Confessore Award for Significant Contributions to the Advancement of Learner Autonomy presented at Exeter College, University of Oxford, by Dr. Confessore, during the Autonomous Learning World Caucus. Dr. Norris received the Graduate Faculty Scholar Award from Spring Arbor University. She also received an Award of Excellence, Outstanding Doctor of Philosophy in Organizational Leadership Dissertation from Regent University.

J. Goosby Smith is an associate professor of organizational behavior and management at Pepperdine University's Seaver College in Malibu, CA. She previously served in a similar capacity at Butler University and California State University Channel Islands. Her areas of research and consulting practice address diversity education, strategic diversity management, ethical decision-making, and leadership. Smith received her MBA and Ph.D. in organizational behavior from Case Western Reserve

University and her B.S. in Computer Science from Spelman College. She is an active member of the Academy of Management, Alpha Kappa Alpha Sorority, and Mensa America.

Ranjini Swamy, is Professor of Organization Behavior at Goa Institute of Management, Goa, India. She teaches graduate courses in Organizational Behavior, Training & Development, Leadership and Change Management. She completed her Fellow Programme in Management from Indian Institute of Management, Ahmedabad, India. She has since, been writing cases and articles in the field of social entrepreneurship, Ethics (using the Giving Voice to Values approach) and Corporate Social Responsibility. She has published in the *Human Relations*, *Vikalpa* and *Journal of Business Ethics Education*. She has also presented papers in the Academy of HRD Conference and the Eastern Academy of Management (International) Conference. Some of the cases on Ethics are available on the Giving Voice to Values website.

Marco Tavanti is International Public Service professor at DePaul University Chicago and president of World Engagement Institute. He teaches in the field of international sustainable development and global ethics to public service and public administration graduate students. His research looks at the interception of ethical and cultural values with leadership, social movements, and international development. He works and consults for various international development projects with the United Nations Development Program, the World Bank, the US Agency for International Development and numerous NGOs in East Africa, Latin America, and Southeast Asia.

Shiv K. Tripathi is presently professor and head (consultancy and short-courses) at Mzumbe University Dar Es Salaam Campus Business School (Tanzania). He received bachelor's degree in electrical and electronics engineering followed by MBA and a Ph.D. He is the International Faculty Program (IFP) Certificate 2011 alumnus of IESE Business School, Barcelona (Spain). He has served a number of academic institutions and universities in different capacities and has published more than 60 articles, papers, and case studies at international levels, including a book, *Management Education* He has been member of the United Nations Principles for Responsible Management Education (PRME) Working Group on "Anti-Corruption in Management Curricula" and "Poverty Eradication through Management Education." He has been a visiting scholar at ISAE Business School, Curitiba (Brazil) and visiting professor (International Higher Education Management Certificate Program) at the University of Witwatersand, Johannesburg (South Africa).

Amy Walburn holds her MBA from the American University of Beirut (AUB) where she is currently working as a research assistant. Her areas of interest are non-profit management, corporate social responsibility, social enterprise, and cross-sector social partnerships. Before joining AUB, she worked in non-profit management in the United States and the Caribbean.

Acknowledgments

We would like to express our greatest gratitude to the people who have helped and supported us throughout this book project. We extend our sincere thanks to all the chapter authors for their cooperation and hard work on this book. They met the deadlines, engaged the ideas, responded to feedback, and wrote magnificent chapters that made this book outstanding. Thanks to them, the project was extremely enjoyable. We hope to have fruitful collaborations in the future as well.

We would like to thank Dr. Aneta Aleksander who has been very skilful and supportive in moving the book through to publication. To them, and to all others who helped us, many thanks. We especially want to acknowledge David Parker, President, Publishing Business Expert Press, for his professional support and goodwill, Professor Oliver Laasch, Editor of the United Nations Principles for Responsible Management Education Book Collection, for his valuable support and everyone else on Business Expert Press editorial and production team. On a personal note, we thank our families for their undivided support, interest, and encouragement.

Agata Stachowicz-Stanusch

Hans Krause Hansen

Introduction

*I believe, indeed, that overemphasis on the purely intellectual atti-
tude, often directed solely to the practical and factual, in our education, has led directly to the impairment of ethical values.*

                                                            Albert Einstein

While business history is replete with examples of unethical behavior
within and by companies, it is particularly since the 1990s that corruption scandals involving business have come to seriously erode public
faith in companies and public authorities. As a response to this situation
there has been a proliferation of international and national legislative
initiatives addressing various aspects of corruption within and around
business. These legal arrangements include, amongst others, the OECD
Convention on Combating Bribery of Foreign Public Officials in International Business Transactions (1997), the United Nations Convention
against Corruption (2003), the Sarbanes-Oxley (2002) and Dodd-Frank
(2010) acts in the United States, as well as more recently, the UK
Bribery Act (2010), which draws on and extends the US Foreign Corruption Practices Act of 1977, conventionally regarded as the starting
point of what has now become the international regime against corruption. In addition to these more traditional hard law efforts there has
been a surge of soft law initiatives promoted by intergovernmental organizations and hybrid organizational forms and networks operating at
local and transnational levels. Corporations, industries, and nongovernmental organizations (NGOs) have become involved in such boundary-
crossing anticorruption work. Examples include the UN Global
Compact's Principle 10 against Corruption (including the related principles for Responsible Management Education (PRME), see Chapter 1 by
Stachowicz-Stanusch), the Extractive Industries Transparency Initiative
(EITI), the Partnering Against Corruption Initiative, the anticorruption
measures and standards under the novel ISO 26000, in addition to the
pioneering initiatives by the world's foremost NGO in anticorruption,

Transparency International. In other words, in today's globalized political economy the governance of corruption rests not only on the efforts by national governments and intergovernmental actors to regulate business, but also on businesses' voluntary contributions and awareness of their responsibilities in the absence of strong, enforcement mechanisms.[1]

It is in this wider context of global governance that management scholars and educators have begun to question the assumptions underlying traditional management education. In their view, management education not only contributed to the recent financial and moral crisis but also failed to prepare students and executives for coping with the leadership challenges and ethical dilemmas that any responsible manager is faced with in contemporary corporations. These developments are all the more important to keep in mind as the expansion of management education on a global scale over the past decades itself has been massive, if not one of "the greatest success stories in higher education."[2] What characterizes the rapid spread of management education is not only that standardized ideas and frameworks of management education travel with great ease across geographical and institutional boundaries, but also that they come to challenge, coexist with, and even shape the localized dynamics of educational institutions in particular regions.

We believe that the statement "a prepared mind favors ethical behavior" carries some important truth to it and have therefore invited a group of world-class scholars with a diversity of backgrounds and perspectives to develop our thinking on how teaching in anticorruption practices can be conducted today. Widely publicized corporate scandals have pushed public trust in business to an all-time low, just as it has raised questions about the role and effectiveness of university education in developing moral competencies among students and future business leaders. This book is a response to this situation. It sets out to develop an empirical and theoretical platform for rethinking business school curricula, with a specific view to understanding and meaningfully confronting the challenges of corruption of the second decade of the 21st century. In addition to this, the book reflects the engagement of multiple disciplines and scientific languages in the teaching of anticorruption. We regard this diversity to be a strength and thought-provoking at a time where we need to experiment with pedagogical ideas and tools.

Some of our contributors highlight issues relating to the challenge of teaching anticorruption in particular geographical and cultural contexts such as Brazil, the Arab World, India, and Italy, while others focus on more universal, institutional, philosophical, or spiritual matters in moral teaching and learning. Most of the chapters introduce pedagogical models, frameworks, and include questions and practical exercises that teachers might draw practical inspiration from, while other chapters are offering more abstract reflections including diagnoses of contemporary social and cultural orders.

The book opens with Chapter 1, "Alleviating the Malady of Low Ethical Awareness Using PRME as a Tonic Lesson from Europe" by Agata Stachowicz-Stanusch. This chapter sets the stage for our shared concern in the book overall, providing an overview and analysis of the multilateral initiative Principles for Responsible Management Education (PRME). The initiative is itself a product of the global developments briefly sketched in the first sections of this Introduction, providing guidelines for educational programs and giving business schools the opportunity to fulfill ethical objectives. As such, PRME is an instance of soft law, a voluntary initiative spurred by the UN Global Compact with a view to enhancing responsible and sustainable business, not least in the area of anticorruption. In the chapter some solutions proposed by PRME that are implemented in curricula of European PRME signatories—business schools and universities—and published in Sharing Information on Progress reports, are presented and discussed. The analysis is based on more than a hundred reports from 24 countries and was conducted in terms of 7 criteria, such as ethics and/or corporate social responsibility (CSR) courses in curriculum, environmental responsibility issues, financial (and fiscal) responsibility issues, legal responsibility issues in curriculum, special programs for MBA, case studies—understood as an educational method within CSR-related courses and projects for companies (or other organizations) conducted by students.

Chapter 2, titled "Promoting Ethical Behavior in India: An Examination of the Giving Voice to Values (GVV) Approach" and written by Ranjini Swamy and Jodi Detjen, argues that educational institutions, including business schools, can help inculcate the ethical competencies necessary for people to strongly voice their concerns about corruption at the workplace. However, they face challenges in teaching these practices: (a) skepticism among students that ethical approaches are feasible and (b) the lack of learning materials/methodologies to address this skepticism and enable successful voicing of values at the workplace. Drawing on Mary Gentile's GVV framework, the authors address these challenges. They describe the origin and main components of the GVV, its application in developing two case studies, and the experience of piloting one case study in a workshop for faculty from Indian business schools. The tentative implications for GVV case writers, teachers, and researchers are discussed.

Chapter 3, "Business Ethics Education in Brazil: Pedagogical Solutions for Combating Corruption in Brazil" by Gazi Islam and Lama Al-Arda, offers a discussion of the role of ethics education in management as a mechanism for combating corruption in Brazil. The authors argue that ethics education is important for combating endemic corruption. In order to apply this insight to Brazil in such a way as to promote actionable responses by educators, they provide an overview of the Brazilian context. They argue that the historical development of Brazil has led to a culture of administrative personalism, with the cooccurrence of highly formalized systems of administrative bureaucracy and informal personal ties, a combination that allows corrupt practices to spread easily. The authors then turn to the role of higher education in Brazil, noting the challenges faced in this sector, as well as the opportunities posed by recent rapid growth. Finally, they discuss concrete pedagogical practices that can contribute to combating corruption in the classroom, emphasizing the role of participation and dialogue, rather than recipes and codes.

Chapter 4 is titled "Business Schools as Agents of Change: Addressing Systemic Corruption in the Arab World" and authored by Dima Jamali and Amy Walburn. This chapter begins with an analysis of the main characteristics of systemic corruption in the Middle East and North Africa, demonstrating how the phenomenon represents a serious obstacle to business prosperity and economic growth. It then discusses the business case of anticorruption efforts in the region. Finally, it highlights the important contribution that business schools in the Middle East can make to fighting systemic corruption in the region, especially salient as the region faces the historical moment of the Arab Spring. The chapter details the current practices of business schools in the region and then outlines actionable steps that schools can begin to take to tackle this important topic.

In Chapter 5 by Hamid H. Kazeroony, titled "Empowering Learners to Behave Ethically: How Learners Can Find Their Way to Treat Others with Dignity?" a set of recommended guidelines are discussed with a view to educators who want to help their learners create foundations for anticorruptive approaches in treating their organizational stakeholders with dignity. This chapter offers recommendations for designing business curricula that can address ethics through treating learners with dignity with a multicultural lens when creating course objectives, activities, and learning outcomes. The chapter makes the case as to why it is important to address the relationship between learners' dignity, curricula design, and the way we facilitate the conveyance of the ethical decision-making. The chapter also explains the relationship between the learners' dignity, and teaching ethics through curricula design in producing the right outcomes.

Over the years, ethical and unethical behaviors have been described in terms of vices and virtues. Vice-driven misconduct has poisoned organizations around the globe with consequences that are devastating for society. Finding a remedy for the deficit of ethical leadership and organizational corruption holds great importance, and management educators around the world are seeking ways to address these issues. In Chapter 6, "Learner Autonomy, Moral Agency, and Ancient Virtues: A Curative Constellation for the Treatment of Corruption in Modern Workplaces," Sharon E. Norris presents a curative constellation for the treatment of corruption in modern workplaces. *Learner autonomy* refers to the self-regulatory capacity to draw upon both internal and external resources as one chooses to adapt, change, and learn. The salient characteristics of the capacity to learn include initiative, resourcefulness, and persistence. Yet, the capacity to learn and relentless pursuit of goal attainment can be tainted by vices and moral disengagement. As a cure, when the *virtues* of prudence, justice, fortitude, and temperance influence the development of *moral agency*, internalized standards of what constitutes right from wrong behavior, these noble intentions serve as guides and deterrents of behavior. As virtue-based leaders strive toward goals, they are more likely to exercise functional learner autonomy rather than moral disengagement and vice-driven behaviors.

Selection and alignment of a suitable pedagogical tool is critical to ensure impact in anticorruption education. Shiv Tripathi in Chapter 7, titled "Integrating Anti-Corruption Teaching and Research in Management Education: A Framework for Giving Voice to Values (GVV) Based Approach," looks into this dimension by exploring the issue of "fit." Like Chapter 2, this chapter builds on Mary Gentiles's GVV framework. The chapter first establishes the essential requirements for an effective anticorruption education methodology in terms of its learning impact. It analyzes the suitability of GVV in creating and delivering anticorruption contents and discusses how GVV can be integrated in anticorruption teaching and research. The suggested approach aims to facilitate the context-specific and stakeholders' need-driven anticorruption curriculum creation. The focus on the possibility of real-time research-driven cocreation is another important dimension the chapter contributes to. Management educators will find the chapter useful in content and pedagogical mapping for anticorruption education in management.

According to Marco Tavanti, the author of Chapter 8 titled "The Cultural Dimensions of Corruption: Integrating National Cultural Differences in the Teaching of Anti-Corruption in Public Service Management Sector," teaching and training for good governance and culturally effective anticorruption practices are incredibly challenging. In fact, they require a multilevel approach. Based on a review of numerous empirical and theoretical studies on the causes, nature, and correlations of corruption across countries, this chapter introduces an integrated approach to teach and train anticorruption. In doing this the chapter builds on institutional theory, principal–agent theory and cultural dimension theory, which leads the author to suggest a multilevel and multicultural anticorruption model. Through the examination of selected cultural dimensions in relation to corruption, the chapter offers an integrated model for teaching anticorruption in the public service management sector.

In "Understanding and Reducing Business Corruption Through Movies and World Wide Web Videos," Chapter 9 of this volume,

Andrew Michael presents a novel way of teaching anticorruption. The use of audio-visuals and various Web sites dedicated to fighting corruption and promoting a more ethical way of life can be an attractive and lively means of communicating the message that corruption is wrong and must be stopped. Seven movies and seven videos are suggested for viewing along with thought-provoking questions to enhance our understanding of business corruption and encourage reflection regarding its antecedents and consequences. The movies highlight potential ethical dilemmas that arise in the real world. They also include interviews with managers and experts who talk about what businesses can do to reduce corruption in developed and developing countries. The Web sites have a plethora of information regarding the nature and costs of corruption, and what can and is being done to fight different types of corruption. It is hoped that the use of these audio-visuals and Web sites will create a greater awareness of the severity of the problems arising from corruption and also an intrinsic desire to act ethically and in a noncorrupt way in business and in life in general.

Chapter 10, "Applying a Religious Lens to Ethical Decision-Making: My Ten Commandments of Character for the Workplace Exercise," is written by J. Goosby Smith and Susan Schick Case. This chapter argues that there an international crisis in ethical decision-making and a prevalence of cultures of corruption. However, many anticorruption efforts focus mainly on explaining legal requirements rather than connecting to and facilitating the elucidation of individually held ethical standards and tying them to workplace behavior—where much corruption and dishonesty occurs. In order to reduce corruption occurring from individual decision-making and behavior, we need more individual-level anticorruption interventions. In this chapter authors present an exercise designed to elucidate pillars of character by tying them to individuals' most deeply held beliefs: those derived not only from upbringing and culture, but from their religious and spiritual teachings. The authors argue that it is by facilitating individuals' discovery of their most deeply held ethical behavior standards that we can effectively reduce corrupt workplace behavior—one individual at a time.

The book closes with Chapter 11 by Ernestina Giudici, Federica Caboni, and Roberta Atzori: "Testing the Effectiveness of Innovative

Teaching Tools to Train Anti-Corruption Students." This chapter proposes a message that can be summarized with the phrase at the top of the chapter, *The partner of the crime of corruption is often our indifference*. In fact, corruption is so widespread and multifaceted that it sometimes does not receive correct and proper attention. To verify whether and to what extent corruption can be evaluated incorrectly, the authors put at the base of their work the following questions: are students aware of the damages that corruption can cause? Are teachers adequately preparing students to be ethically correct and not corrupt? Which form of communication and teaching tools are more likely to interact with students to create a durable awareness of the corruption damages? The authors involved students from an Italian university to become coproducers of teaching tools, showing that students need to have an active role in their learning activity and that they prefer ironic communication, adopting metaphors, and dealing with serious subjects with joy.

Their evaluation of comics, social network, storytelling, and videos as the most effective objects is irrefutable. This is a big suggestion for each teacher: time has come in which they shall accept the challenge of adopting these and other innovative teaching tools.

To summarize, this book offers examples of new tools, teaching methods, and case studies for anticorruption teaching. It explores and discusses how particular approaches, such as Giving Voice to Values, may be used worldwide for teaching anticorruption. Finally it explores and discusses how curricula can be streamlined and rejuvenated in order to ensure a higher level of integrity in the world of business.

PART I

Teaching Anti-Corruption—A Worldwide Kaleidoscope

CHAPTER 1

Alleviating the Malady of Low Ethical Awareness Using PRME as a Tonic Lesson from Europe

Agata Stachowicz-Stanusch

Integrity has no need of rule.
—Albert Camus

Abstract

The present-day widely discussed ethical concern about the lack of responsibility in the contemporary business world has implicated the necessity of a thorough change, not only of corporate behaviors, but also of academic attitudes toward the process of education of future business leaders.

That is why such initiative as Principles for Responsible Management Education (PRME) has come into existence, which is dedicated to improving the process of education, and is a useful instrument that provides clear guidelines for educational programs, giving business schools the opportunity to fulfill its ethical objectives.

In this chapter, the author presents some solutions compliant with Principles for Responsible Management Education that are implemented in curricula of European PRME signatories and are published in Sharing Information on Progress reports. The analysis was based on more than a hundred reports from 24 countries and was conducted in terms of seven criteria.

Introduction

The present-day ethical challenges of the contemporary business world are not only limited to companies but also include academic society, which constitutes a substantial element of the business environment, and whose members equally need moral reflection. Widely publicized corporate scandals (Enron, WorldCom, Global Crossing, Tyco, Quest, and Adelphia, to name a few) have pushed public trust in business to an all-time low and have raised the question about the role and effectiveness of university education in developing moral competencies among students–future business leaders.[1] Moreover, in recent years new demands have been placed for more active roles of corporations and institutions as citizens within society.[2]

Thus, there has come into existence the necessity of reflection on the role of management education in developing a new generation of leaders capable of managing the complex challenges faced by business and society in the 21st century (as stated by J. Forray and J. Leigh[3]).

The educational system in general, and business education in particular, were immersed in a wave of criticism as being responsible for moral ignorance of the business world and for the failure to inculcate in students the standards of good conduct.[4]

Current thought even suggests that educational systems have actually weakened the moral character of students. Present business education has been criticized for failing to deter and even for encouraging recent executive misconduct through its limited emphasis on student ethical development.[5] Critics of today's educational system (and business education particularly) are not only aimed at the system of higher education, but more frequently at the university as an institution. With alarming frequency, episodes of unethical conduct come from behind the university walls. The examples are cases of plagiarism, master's theses written on request, or the unreliability of conducted research, cheating, and academic dishonesty (such as fabricating or falsifying a bibliography).[6]

The intensive discussion is also provided by scholars.[7] For instance, Mitroff[8] offers a particularly scathing assessment, saying business school faculty are "guilty of having provided an environment where the Enrons and the Andersens of the world could take root and flourish … we delude ourselves seriously if we think we played no part whatsoever."[9] Ghoshal[10] provides one of the most highly discussed critiques of business school education. His primary thesis is that today's business education, with its foundations in agency theory and economic liberalism, contributed significantly to the recent stream of unethical business practices.[11]

The above and widespread concern fueled legislative reactions such as the Sarbanes-Oxley act in the United States.[12] On the other hand it resulted in some initiatives undertaken by academic society, very often in collaboration with business, in order to hinder the negative influence of business education on corporate scandals and on the more recent economic crisis, as well as to foster their graduates' morality. One of such initiatives is the establishment of Principles for Responsible Management Education (PRME),[13] which is a multilateral effort that represents a comprehensive academic collaboration between the United Nations and higher education undertaken to embed corporate responsibility and sustainability in the core mission and learning activities of schools of business. Its aim is to ensure a continuous improvement among institutions of management education in order to develop a new generation of business leaders who will be capable of managing the complex challenges faced by business and society in the 21st century.

In general, the PRME initiative is about promoting responsibility in business education and it provides a framework for academic institutions to advance the broader cause of corporate social responsibility and incorporate universal values into curricula and research. It encourages actions like curriculum development around the corporate responsibility agenda and research in support of sustainable management systems, as well as public advocacy and opinion leadership to advance responsible business practices.

The main objective of this chapter is to identify the ways of implementing the PRME practices incorporated in European schools' curricula in order to significantly improve teaching course content and methods.

Challenges for Implementation of Principles for Responsible Management Education in Educational Programs

The PRME, supported by the United Nations, is a global platform and it makes an urgent call for business schools and universities worldwide to fill the gap and gradually adapt their curricula, research, teaching methodologies and institutional strategies to new business challenges and opportunities.[14] It provides a kind of new "standard" that is a response for questions about the best way of implementing solutions dedicated for effectively teaching responsibility.[15] The PRME are therefore a timely global call for business schools and universities world-wide to gradually adapt their curricula, research, teaching methodologies, and institutional strategies to the new business challenges and opportunities.

The PRME's mission is to inspire and champion responsible management education, research, and thought leadership globally. Its main goal is to promote corporate responsibility and sustainability in business education. Institutions like business schools and other academic institutions, which participate in this initiative, make a commitment to align their mission, strategy, and their core competencies (education, research, and thought leadership) with UN values embodied by so called six principles. Those principles are as follows:[16]

- Principle 1 Purpose: We will develop the capabilities of students to be future generators of sustainable value for business and society at large and to work for an inclusive and sustainable global economy.
- Principle 2 Values: We will incorporate into our academic activities and curricula the values of global social responsibility as portrayed in international initiatives such as the United Nations Global Compact.
- Principle 3 Method: We will create educational frameworks, materials, processes and environments that enable effective learning experiences for responsible leadership.
- Principle 4 Research: We will engage in conceptual and empirical research that advances our understanding about the role, dynamics, and impact of corporations in the creation of sustainable social, environmental and economic value.
- Principle 5 Partnership: We will interact with managers of business corporations to extend our knowledge of their challenges in meeting social and environmental responsibilities and to explore jointly effective approaches to meeting these challenges.

- Principle 6 Dialogue: We will facilitate and support dialog and debate among educators, business, government, consumers, media, civil society organizations, and other interested groups and stakeholders on critical issues related to global social responsibility and sustainability.

The first two principles of the PRME are focused on gaining specific goals of management education such as preparing future leaders to work for a more sustainable global economy, as well as incorporating values of social responsibility into academic activity (including creating of integrity within the university).

The second PRME principle refers to the Global Compact that is perceived as the "moral compass" by many institutions.[17] The four main categories promoted within this initiative (such as human rights, labor issues, environmental issues, and anti-corruption) are being developed into the wider array of values embedded in the organizational cultures of particular institutions.

The third PRME principle concerns teaching responsible leadership. The question arises whether or not ethical problems should be taught in stand-alone courses, or systematically integrated across the curriculum (for example how to better integrate responsible management education into the curriculum, how to convince others that integration is necessary and worthwhile). There are generally two noticeable attitudes to the way of implementing PRME in curricula content (that are contradictory to some extent but not mutually exclusive). The first one assumes that responsibility is something that cannot be taught exclusively through one stand-alone course. The other attitude is that corporate responsibility issues need to be integrated into other courses (such as marketing and finance) to foster their threading across the wider curriculum.[18] That is why great effort is taken by different higher-education schools to apply new teaching techniques supporting educators to reap the full benefits of a business ethics course and make it an experience of great importance for students.

The fourth principle of the PRME is connected with conducting research that has sustainable social, environmental, and economic value. Research and teaching go hand in hand when it comes to responsible management education. This is often reflected in schools that create centers or institutes that specifically address ethical issues, thus attracting scholars to develop their interest in the field of corporate responsibility. It is also a signal for early-career researchers that business ethics related disciplines are worthwhile and desirable these days.[19]

The last two principles of the PRME are connected with collaborative work with business executives and the facilitation of dialogue and debate among business schools and business stakeholders. Such partnerships can help to improve the relevance of both teaching and research. Starting with teaching, inviting practitioners to speak in the classroom is a common technique for making course content more interesting. That is why PRME adopters can facilitate dialogue with a wider set of stakeholders with the use of many channels such as conferences which unite different stakeholder groups, multistakeholder panel discussions, and/or lecture series. The communication process may also be facilitated by modern tools that improve networking education and involve the application of ICT, especially social media.[20] Such new technologies are also used for recruiting world-class speakers.[21]

Manuel Escudero mentions two basic characteristics of PRME that are required for the rethinking of present-day business education, namely the global range of this initiative (as almost all the relevant associations from the United States, Latin America, Europe, and Africa participate) as well as the focus on the crux of the matter (the need to place the new paradigm of sustainable and responsible value creation at the very core of business education).[22]

However, despite the principles being clearly formulated, it is not so easy to implement particular solutions into practice. Just signing onto the PRME as such is not indicative of systemic change or an internal value reflection. For example, the only requirement of PRME participation is to "share information ... on the progress made in implementing the Principles," with approximately 25% of signatory schools failing to produce such a report within set deadlines.[23] Also altering formal curricular goals and content alone is not enough to improve students' sense of social responsibility. Effective PRME implementation requires close attention to the informal ways of developing good management virtues—hidden curriculum, that is, the implicit dimensions of educational experiences.[24] Effort should be taken in order to create synergies between research, teaching, and social initiatives,[25] assess a school's PRME needs and integrate these principles into business school learning environments.[26] Moreover, there is also a necessity to overcome implementation problems such as strategic, structural, and cultural barriers (often being the challenges of political character)[27] as well as to stimulate faculty support that is a critical driver for implementing the United Nations Principles for Responsible Management Education.[28]

Forray and Leigh, preparing the special issue of *Journal of Management Education* that was dedicated to PRME initiative, have indicated the need for affirmative dialog in the 21st century that should help us to[29]

- understand the PRME principles, the evolution of the initiative, and its relationship to corporate citizenship, corporate social responsibility, ethics, and sustainability;
- share knowledge about interdisciplinary course content, pedagogical strategies, and curricular innovations that reflect PRME principles;
- critically question the opportunities and challenges associated with PRME.

Research Results

The research was focused on courses, modules, and tools used for implementation of PRME and was based on reports of Sharing Information on Progress (SIP) submitted by European signatories of the initiative.[30] The analysis was conducted between February 8 and 20, 2013.

The original sample consisted of all of the 427 submitted reports. In some cases a particular organization had submitted the SIP report more than once as it revealed progress in PRME implementation in subsequent years. See Figure 1.1.

Generally, the SIP reports have been submitted by 268 participants, among which 119 come from 24 countries in Europe.[31] Those organizations have prepared a total of 188 reports and its number increases every year. To compare its volume and share of the total number of SIP reports submitted in particular years see Figure 1.2.

Nevertheless, the research sample consisted of only 119 of the most current reports submitted by a particular school (only one prepared SIP

No. of SIP reports submitted by a school

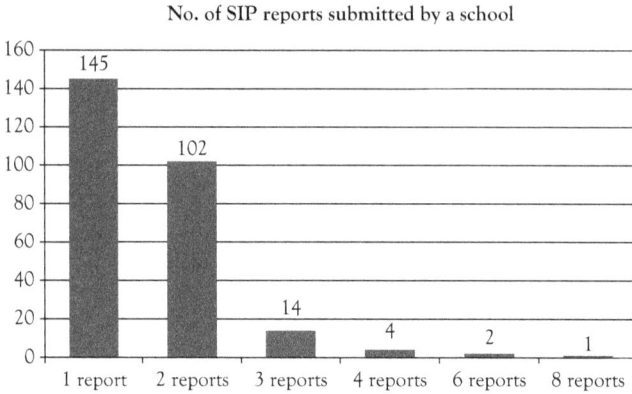

Figure 1.1.

Source: Author's own study based on http://www.unprme.org/sharing-information-on-progress/

No. of SIP reports submitted

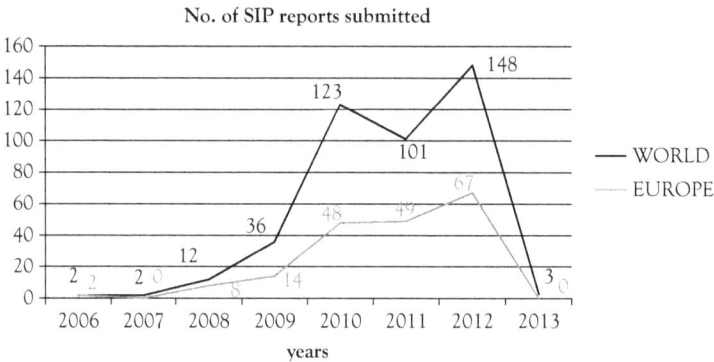

Figure 1.2.

Source: Author's own study based on http://www.unprme.org/sharing-information-on-progress/

report was analyzed for each particular signatory) in order to reflect the structure of participants (see Figure 1.3). Symbols for countries were based on ISO 3166-1 alfa-2 standard.

Ultimately the above number was constrained to 115 as four documents were prepared in the national (non-English) language and they were not subject to study.

The conducted research is the continuation of analysis presented by the author[32] and focuses on 7 of the 54 criteria in the previous study as it relates to the implementation of PRME in curricula. The criteria are presented in Table 1.1.

No. of signatories from Europe that submitted
SIP reports (by countries)

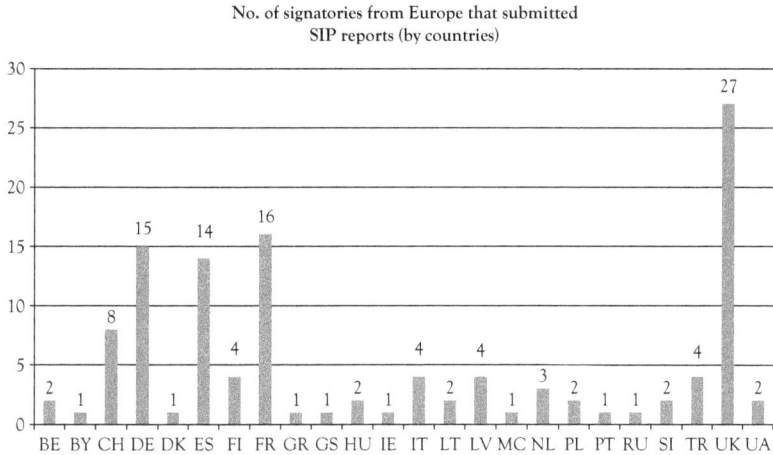

Figure 1.3.

Source: Author's own study based on http://www.unprme.org/sharing-information-on-progress/

Table 1.1. *Criteria for Sharing Information on Progress Reports Analysis*

Criterion of analysis		Description
Curricular content	Ethics and/or CSR courses in curriculum	Signatory that incorporates ethics or CSR issues in its curricula as a separate subject or as an integrated module of the core course
	Environmental responsibility issues	Signatory incorporates environmental problems in core ethical/CSR course or includes ethical dilemmas in courses for environmental management
	Financial (and fiscal) responsibility issues	Signatory incorporates financial/accounting/fiscal problems in core ethical/CSR course or includes ethical dilemmas in courses for finance
	Legal responsibility issues in curriculum	Signatory incorporates legal problems in core ethical/CSR course or includes ethical dilemmas in courses for law
Curricular range	Special programs for MBA	Signatory that incorporates ethics or CSR issues in its curricula especially for MBA course
Curricular methods	Case studies	Signatory uses case studies as an educational method within CSR related courses
	Projects for a company (or other organization)	Signatory's students conduct projects for a company (or other organization) within CSR related courses

Source: Author's own elaboration based on Stachowicz-Stanusch, A. (2011).

The above criteria are usually the integral elements of the first, second, and third PRME elements, namely purpose, values, and method.

The PRME signatories in 102 cases (92%) do include ethics or CSR courses in their curricula but to the different extents. Some of them treat social responsibility as the theme for all the offered courses:

(…) the themes of SD/CSR are becoming more reflexive and embedded in traditional core coursework at GEM (…)

Grenoble Ecole de Management (2012)

IUM is striving to incorporate environmental and social responsibility in the core values of all its programs.

International University of Monaco (2013)

However, more often the additional ethical related subjects are included in some of the existing programs:

Each study programme includes at least one module on Ethics and Social Responsibility. Related topics are also incorporated in other management subjects (modules). The review of study programmes and their modules, both at undergraduate and Master's levels, in 2011 showed some areas for improvement. As a result several modules (courses) on Corporate Social Responsibility were included in some of the Master's level programmes.

Riga International School of Economics and Business Administration (2012)

Specific examples include a dedicated master's level module Corporate Social Responsibility which covers stakeholder theory and practice, green economics and business ethics.

Oxford Brookes Business School (2012)

Quite often the educational courses try to integrate responsibility issues into their traditional management subjects related to environment, finance, and law. Compared to the results gained within the same methodology in 2010 for all the submitted SIP reports, issues of financial

Issues included incurriculum
(comparison)

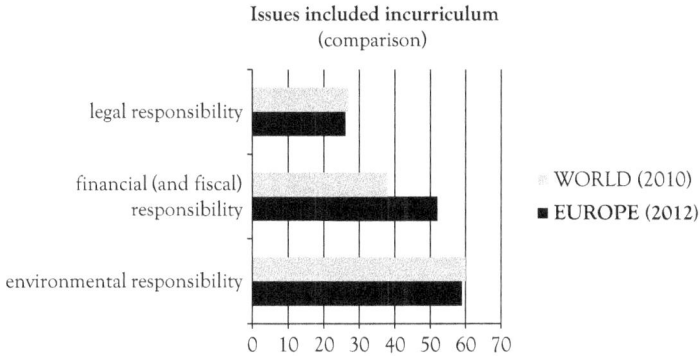

Figure 1.4.
Source: Author's own study based on http://www.unprme.org/sharing-information-on-progress/
and Stachowicz-Stanusch A. (2011).

responsibility seem to be more extensively incorporated in the CSR-related curricula (see Figure 1.4), while the other content seems to be present in educational programs to a similar extent.

The most popular issue (included by over a half of the analyzed schools) is related to environmental management and is incorporated within various modules:

> *Topics and fields of application include (…) environmental economics, renewable energy, (…) public policies on environmental protection, international environmental law (…), to mention a few.*
> Bristol Business School, Faculty of Business and Law (2012)

> *"Environmental Compatibility and Risks" and "Environmental Economics", which explain the impact of business operations on the environment.*
> Faculty of Engineering Economics and Management (2011)

> *In 2010 the Department of Business Environment offered the following modules:*
> *—"Fair Trade" (new)*
> *—Diversity as a Performance Indicator in Enterprises' (new)*
> *—"Environmental Protection and Sustainable Development."*
> ICN Business School (2010)

The field of financing and accounting is also enriched with the responsibility considerations (by 45% of signatories):

Business professionals are invited to deal with specific sustainability-related themes in their courses—the students studying accountancy and tax-law become acquainted with the ethical aspects of banking (…).
Faculty of Economics and Management (2012)

In the summer of 2012 the school also appointed a new professor in accounting and finance with specialization in ethics and sustainability, which will lead to the further development of modules in this area.
Hull University Business School (2012)

The Department of Finance, Audit, and Control offered a (new) module in "Ethical Finance."
ICN Business School (2010)

Also legal aspects are the subject of responsibility management education, despite not being so popular (only 23% of analyzed schools reporting):

—Public Law Two (first year undergraduate law): Human rights law is taught as a central part.
—Criminal and Tort Law (final year undergraduate law): Human rights—the European Convention and the Human Rights Act—are covered.
—Contemporary Employment and Legal Issues (MSc): Ethics and labour law are addressed and the International Labour Organisation is covered in detail.
—International Economic Law (LLM degree): The International Labour Organisation and human rights are taught. Students examine the UN initiatives in this area and cases such as Wiva vs. Shell.
The Business School, Bournemouth University (2012)

Corporate governance addresses the issues surrounding decision making by senior executives and the effects these decisions can have on corporations and their many stakeholders. This separation of decision making and exposure to its consequences creates agency problems. The legal and ethical consequences of conflicts of interest are explored, as is how business ethics practices can contribute to the societal performance of corporations.

Rotterdam School of Management (2012)

In many cases the PRME assumptions are the basis for preparing MBA courses as more than half of signatories (62 out of 115) declare to include ethical modules for those studies:

On the MBA programme, explicit consideration of corporate social responsibility is integrated into the Global Manager theme within the revised curriculum. This was introduced to our full time MBA during 2009/10 and it is now fully rolled out to our part time suite of MBA programmes.

Hull University Business School (2012)

Participation in review and improvement of programme curricula by the International Institute of Business' Committee for Programs and Curriculum Development presenting a new course «Corporate Social Responsibility and Social Entrepreneurship Strategies. Business Ethics» into International MBA and Executive MBA programs.

International Institute of Business (IIB) (2011)

One of the most popular methods used for implementing responsibility management within curricula, enabling to educate and discuss ethical aspects and to relate managerial decision to corporate responsibility is the case study method used by over a half of the analyzed organizations (54%):

(…) students read and participate in class discussions on case studies on what companies can do to minimize their impact on ecological environment.

Istanbul Bilgi University (2012)

The students (…) examine Case studies on CSR-SD themes during their time at the school.

Toulouse Business School (2012)

Moreover, the case study method is not only implemented but quite often developed by the faculties on their own or in cooperation with companies and local society:

Companies can help to shape the course offering in different committees and working groups, while HSBA also gets impetus for research projects from the companies. Case studies are often based on real-life examples from the participating companies.

HSBA Hamburg School of Business Administration (2011)

In addition to widely accepted business education methods, such as case methodology, interactive sessions and simulation games, the School develops its own repository of "live cases."

Kyiv Mohyla Business School (2011)

In a few cases there were also elaborated complex educational programs for implementing the PRME that were outcomes of educational endeavors of particular scholars.[33]

Scrutinized reports also reveal that nearly one-third of PRME signatories from Europe (32 cases) include projects realized by students for external organizations and partners as another educational method:

The Business Project is a consultancy-like project. International student teams solve a real business problem as a one-semester part-time activity tutored by the company and a professor in parallel. These projects reinforce the CEMS partnership between universities and companies in jointly shaping the student learning process in international management.

CEMS (2011)

Student involvement in sustainability projects within HUB (i.e., regarding operations, outreach, etc.), in addition to student projects in collaboration with business partners (i.e., regarding external partners' operations, outreach, etc.) will be critical.

Faculty of Economics and Management (2012)

The Student Buddy Scheme is designed to build collegiality between international and UK students and engage them in crosscultural experiences in the school and externally in the local community. The projects developed by this scheme have involved students in making a contribution to the local community while at the same time enhancing their employability skills.

Hull University Business School (2012)

The presented outcomes of the conducted analysis for the European state of PRME implementation in schools' curricula are quite similar to those presented for all the PRME SIP reports submitted till the end of 2010.[34] The percentage reflection of this implementation is presented in Table 1.2.

Table 1.2. Results for Sharing Information on Progress Reports Analysis

Criterion of analysis		% of reports from all PRME signatories (2010)	% of signatories from Europe (2012)
Curricular content	Ethics and/or CSR courses in curriculum	90%	92%
	Environmental responsibility issues	52%	51%
	Financial (and fiscal) responsibility issues	33%	45%
	Legal responsibility issues in curriculum	23%	23%
Curricular range	Special programs for MBA	52%	54%
Curricular methods	Case studies	39%	54%
	Projects for a company (or other organization)	40%	37%

Source: Author's own study based on http://www.unprme.org/sharing-information-on-progress/

However, when comparing global analysis of SIP contents from 2010 with European declarations from the beginning of 2013, the only noticeable difference (of more than 10%) is connected with the perception of responsible finance as an important element of teaching programs prepared within management courses.

Conclusion

The PRME initiative has attracted many institutions from all over the world and has enabled to set a joint discussion and exchange of experience and best practices in implementing solutions for improving the ethical awareness of present-day business students. The number of signatories is increasing and European schools also seem to be participating in it more intensively.

Integrating PRME into business and management curriculum requires distributing emerging knowledge and best practices, which in turn can promote collective inquiry into associated philosophical, conceptual, empirical, and pragmatic issues[35] and that is why there is a need to diagnose the practices existing within signatories of the PRME.

Key Terms

PRME (Principles for Responsible Management Education): supported by the United Nations, its initiative is to inspire and champion responsible management education, research and thought leadership globally. PRME is aimed at promoting effective practices related to six principles (Purpose, Values, Method, Research, Partnership, and Dialogue) among academic institutions and adapting their curricula, research, teaching methodologies and institutional strategies to new business challenges and opportunities. [*Source*: www.unprme.org]

Integrity: characterizes both the individual and the institutions where he or she works. For individuals, it is an aspect of moral character and experience. For institutions, it is a matter of creating an environment that promotes responsible conduct by embracing standards of excellence, trustworthiness, and lawfulness that inform institutional practices.

[*Source*: Stachowicz-Stanusch A.: The Principles for Responsible Management Education -a pathway to management education for integrity. *Organizacja i Kierowanie*, 2013 (in print)].

CSR (Corporate Social Responsibility): the responsibility of enterprises for their impacts on society. CSR is associated with the process to integrate social, environmental, ethical, human rights, and consumer concerns into their business operations and core strategy in close collaboration with their stakeholders, with the aim of:

- maximizing the creation of shared value for their owners/ shareholders and for their other stakeholders and society at large;
- identifying, preventing and mitigating their possible adverse impacts.

[*Source*: Communication from the Commission to the European Parliament, the Council, the European Economic and Social Committee and the Committee of the Regions: A renewed EU strategy 2011–14 for Corporate Social Responsibility]

Case study: A documented study of a specific real-life situation or imagined scenario, used as a training tool in business schools and firms. Students or trainees are required to analyze the prescribed cases and present their interpretations or solutions, supported by the line of reasoning employed and assumptions made. [*Source*: http://www.businessdictionary .com]

Study Questions

1. What other curricular methods may be effective in terms of raising the ethical awareness of business students?
2. What are the potential barriers of implementing curricular innovation based on six PRME principles?

Additional Reading

Amman W., & Stachowicz-Stanusch A. (Eds.) (2012). *Integrity in organizations— building the foundations for humanistic management*. New York: Palgrave Macmillan.

Amman, W., Pirson, M., Dierksmeier, C., Von Kimakovitz, E., & Spitzeck, H. (Eds.) (2011). *Business schools under fire: Humanistic management education as the way forward*. New York: Palgrave Macmillan.

Caldwell, C. (2012). *Moral leadership: A transformative model for tomorrow's leaders*. New York: Business Expert Press.

Ferrel, O. C., Fraedrich, J., & Ferrel, L. (2011). *Business ethics: Ethical decision making & cases* (9th edition). New York: Cengage Learning.

Palmer, D., & Zakhem, A. (2012). *Managing for ethical-organizational integrity: Principles and processes for promoting good, right, and virtuous conduct*. New York: Business Expert Press.

Stachowicz-Stanusch A., & Amman W. (Eds.) (2012). *Business integrity in practice–insights from international case studies*. New York: Business Expert Press.

Trevino, L. K., & Nelson, K. A. (2011). *Managing business ethics: Straight talk about how to do it right* (5th edition). New York: Wiley.

Wankel Ch., & Stachowicz-Stanusch A. (Eds.) (2011). *Effectively integrating ethical dimensions into business education (HC) (Research in managerial education and development)*. New York: Information Age Publishing.

Wankel Ch., & Stachowicz-Stanusch A. (Eds.) (2011). *Management education for integrity: Ethically educating tomorrow's business leaders*. London: Emerald Group Publishing Limited.

Wankel Ch., & Stachowicz-Stanusch A. (Eds.) (2012). *Handbook of research on teaching ethics in business and management education*. US: Information Science Reference.

CHAPTER 2

Promoting Ethical Behavior in India: An Examination of the Giving Voice to Values (GVV) Approach[1]

Ranjini Swamy and Jodi Detjen

Abstract

Corruption and ethical concerns abound in developing economies. In their 2012 annual ranking, Transparency International rated India 36 on a 100-point scale, indicating that corruption remains high across most sectors of business and government.[2] Containing corruption requires institutional and legislative reform; it also needs a public that is willing to voice its concern about corruption and hold decision-makers accountable for corrupt behavior. This is a challenge, given India's culture of moderate collectivism and high power distance.

Educational institutions, including business schools, can help inculcate the ethical competencies necessary for people to strongly voice their concerns about corruption at the workplace. However, they face challenges in teaching them to students: (a) skepticism among students that ethical approaches are feasible and (b) the lack of learning materials/ methodologies to address this skepticism and enable successful voicing of values at the workplace. The Giving Voice to Values (GVV) framework is an option available to help address these challenges and teach ethical behavior. This chapter describes the GVV framework, its application in developing two case studies, and the experience of piloting one case study in a workshop for faculty from Indian business schools. The tentative implications for GVV case writers, teachers, and researchers have been discussed.

Introduction

Corruption has been studied extensively in the context of developing countries, partly to explain their lack of development despite significant investment. Public sector corruption has attracted more attention because of its greater prevalence and more visible effect on the public welfare. Widespread and endemic corruption in the public sector can have adverse consequences for the public and countries as a whole.[3] Perceptions of corruption among international stakeholders could affect the nation's risk rating and levels of foreign investment.[4] For the public, rampant corruption could reduce access to and effectiveness of services provided. For instance, corruption in the Indian health care sector has led to ineffective delivery of public health care services, increased out-of-pocket expenditure for the public, and inconsistent quality of care.[5] For the corporate sector, endemic corruption in government agencies has meant increased cost of doing business, and possibly reduced competitive advantage relative to players who offer more corruption money.[6]

Therefore, many international agencies identify corruption as one of the single biggest obstacles to economic and social development.[7] They have called for changes in institutional design and the establishment of universal norms that make corruption a criminal offense internationally.[8] Reforms of substantive programs, enhanced accountability measures, and changes in moral and ethical attitudes are seen as critical for containing corruption. Several anti-corruption initiatives have been implemented across countries with debatable success.[9] One learning from these initiatives is the need to factor in the culture of the countries in which they are implemented.[10] People of different countries define and react to corruption differently. In developing countries with a legacy of corruption,[11] there can be more social acceptance for corrupt practices.[12] Efforts to voice concerns over corrupt practices may seem futile, making it appear easier to capitulate instead of fighting the system.

In this chapter, we explore corruption in the Indian context and argue for inculcating ethical and moral attitudes and behavior to contain corruption. Education plays an important role in inculcating such behavior. We discuss gaps in teaching moral and ethical behavior in management education and propose the application of an action framework (the GVV framework) to promote teaching of more ethical behavior. Corruption/unethical behavior is defined here as "the ignoring or manipulation of approved norms/ rules for personal gains or to frustrate public intentions." Examples include bribery and the circumvention of systems or processes for private gain of one or a few stakeholders.

The Indian Context

The extent of perceived corruption in India is evident in its score on Transparency International's annual Corruption Perception Index.[13] In the period 1995–2012, India's score has ranged between 28 and 36 out of 100. India's 2012 ranking is 94, indicating that India is being perceived as more corrupt relative to other countries.[14] Clearly, despite economic liberalization from 1991, corruption in India continues to be high and endemic. India's government recognizes this as well: its annual Central Vigilance Commission report acknowledges that the "current vigilance approach is largely reactive," and the anti-corruption efforts have been ineffective "in containing corruption … [which] has resulted in the citizens losing faith in the system."[15]

In India, as in other developing countries, the opportunity and incentive to engage in corrupt practices is high. The nonimplementation of two important pieces of legislation—the Lok Pal Bill and the National Judicial Council[16]—and the absence of effective controls provide opportunity for people in positions of power to be corrupt. Over time, the corrupt behavior of leaders of several organizations/agencies has led to the institutionalization of corruption. Anand and Joshi highlight how corrupted individuals perpetuate corruption within the organization:

[w]hen newcomers are first exposed to ongoing unethical practices they often experience significant dissonance and apprehension. Individuals may be so uncomfortable that they leave the organization. Ironically, this helps perpetuate the corruption by weeding out those who are most averse to it … there exist potent

socialization tactics by which newcomers are induced to accept corrupt practices. This is often done in conjunction with the rationalizing tactics. Based on a review of white-collar crime in the past century, Ashforth and Anand identified three such processes: (1) cooptation, (2) incrementalism, and (3) compromise.[17]

The legacy and pervasiveness of corruption has generated resignation, even an acceptance of corruption. Surveys suggest that Indians paid bribes worth Rs 21,068 crores ($3,800 million[18]) to avail of one or more public services,[19] indicating a possible acceptance of the practice. Of concern is the trend among youth to value money over honesty and hard work, which makes them susceptible to corrupt behavior. These and other findings suggest that there could be little or no social sanction for acquiring wealth through corrupt means.[20]

Addressing corruption requires considerable institutional reform reinforced by a demand from citizens for noncorrupt/ethical behavior.[21] Citizens need to express their views against corruption and actively hold decision-makers accountable for the decisions and actions taken. This can occur if citizens (a) value longer-term institutional effectiveness over the short term, (b) value the long-term welfare of all stakeholders (not just the in-group), and (c) have the capability to negotiate the social/political context and enact their values.

Some of these requirements are not entirely aligned with the culture of moderate collectivism[22] and high power distance observed in Indian society.[23] According to Hofstede,[24] in relatively collectivistic societies, the interests of the group prevail over interests of the individual; harmonious relationships with group members are valued highly. This is evident in numerous scandals where some Indian politicians set aside rules to favor family members in allocation of public resources.[25] Such a culture could partly explain why managers in India are significantly *less likely* than managers in the United States to consider nepotism and sharing insider information as unethical.[26]

According to Hofstede,[27] high power-distance societies are characterized by an acceptance of unequal distribution of power and related benefits. There is a large psychological distance between those with and without power. Unquestioning obedience and loyalty to those in power is valued.

Such a culture could partly explain the finding that managers in Indian organizations, unlike those in the United States, are *less likely* to see complying with a superior's order (that requires unethical behavior) as unethical.[28]

Clearly, managers in India appear to define unethical behavior differently. Further, when faced with ethical dilemmas, they report experiencing more difficulty in making ethical decisions, due to "competitive pressures." According to them, it is easier to *know* what is right than it is to *do* it.[29] These findings suggest that voicing and enacting concerns about corrupt practices could be challenging.

Role of Management Education

The need: Education is one of the primary mechanisms for cultural change and transmission.[30] By inculcating ethical and moral attitudes and developing ethical competencies, educational institutions could enhance the longer-term accountability of people in positions of power. Clearly business schools have not paid much attention to this responsibility: they see themselves as successful when their students acquire functional competencies, get jobs, and contribute to economic growth. As decision makers, however, MBA holders would be applying their functional knowledge through "cognitions steeped in personal integrity."[31] If they are not made aware of the moral and ethical issues underlying business decisions, they could be making decisions that are technically appropriate but morally inappropriate. The recent business scandals across the world suggest that business schools could be supplying organizations with the "tools of their own destruction—unethical students who could help ruin organizations and the lives of several stakeholders."[32] Therefore business schools need to pay more attention to the inculcation of ethical competencies, whether or not client organizations rate these as important.

The Ideal: How could business schools respond to the new expectations? Apart from reviewing their notions of responsibility (which is to appease the clients' wants or define and pursue the society's and clients' needs), business schools could inculcate ethical behavior through the careful selection of incoming students,[33] creation of forums to report on or review the ethicality of administrative/ student-initiated actions,[34] role-modeling, and rewarding ethical behavior. These administrative initiatives need to be reinforced by mainstreaming the discourse on ethics in the curriculum. Curricular changes require sensitizing students to the need for ethical behavior, improving their analysis of the ethical/moral issues and enabling action.

Business schools in India face skepticism among students about the feasibility of ethical behavior at the workplace.[35] The following excerpt from the students' assignments for the business ethics course in a well-known Business School indicates some of the challenges faced:

> An executive in a public sector firm was asked by his manager to sign a travel expense sheet that presented expenses far in excess of the actual expenditure. The executive did not wish to sign the sheet and explained his predicament to his mentor. He was told that the client group had encouraged the company to recover additional expenses (incurred due to frequent design changes) in this way as it did not want to publicize the frequent design changes to its management. If the executive blew the whistle, the team working on the project would be sacked and the company would lose the project. The executive was uneasy but went along with his mentor.

The executive appears to have felt dissonance about following through on the requested action. He experienced pressure to act unethically and succumbed to it despite his discomfort, either because he did not know how to resolve the issue or because of the threat of personal or professional repercussions.

The Gaps: The curriculum of business schools needs to address these problems in an actionable manner. However, presently, ethics courses tend to focus on inculcating critical thinking and analysis. There is limited attention to creating actionable plans for a specific ethical dilemma. The attitudes and skills required to effectively navigate the diverse (often conflicting) interests and values of multiple stakeholders are not addressed. Learning materials/methodologies to enable successful voicing of values in the workplace are lacking. It is in this context that the GVV[36] framework attains significance.

The Giving Voice to Values Approach to Teaching Ethics

The GVV is an action framework that helps individuals develop strategies to voice and act on their values[37] in the face of countervailing pressure. It acknowledges that "value conflicts" are a reality at the workplace, occurring when two competing values coexist in a situation and adhering to one compromises the other. Value conflicts typically characterize corrupt or unethical behavior. Compromising strongly held personal/professional values in the face of such conflicts could adversely affect an individual's productivity, satisfaction, and involvement in their organizations. Individuals are often unprepared to face these value conflicts; they need to be better prepared for expressing their values at the workplace in ways that are aligned with their identities and the circumstances they confront.

The GVV approach presumes that individuals want to behave ethically in most situations. They know what the right thing to do is but do not know/are not confident about translating this knowledge into action. Unlike the high-risk approach of whistleblowing, GVV helps individuals develop a "script" detailing whom to contact, what to say, when to approach them, and how to present the value conflict for effective resolution. The script is then rehearsed and strengthened through feedback from a supportive audience (peer coaching). By practicing scripting and peer coaching, individuals could enhance the effectiveness of attempts to voice (and enact) their values at the workplace.

The GVV approach requires an individual to answer the following questions:[38]

1. What action is the decision maker contemplating? What values could conflict?
2. What reasons and rationalizations can be offered against the expression of values inherent in such action?
3. Who are the affected constituents? What is at stake for each of them?
4. What can the respondent say or do to respond persuasively to each reason/rationalization?
5. If the decision maker has to interact with others to ensure he does the right thing, what legitimate mechanisms can be used to influence them?

The contemplated action: In this first step, the protagonists in a situation initially express the action they want to take in the given situation. Individuals become conscious of the value conflict inherent in the situation by identifying the underlying values being challenged and the areas of concern.[39]

The value conflict may initially present itself as a feeling or emotion: uneasiness, guilt, anger, frustration, worry. From this feeling, individuals can tease out the underlying areas of concern and understand which values are being challenged. By exploring the conflict one feels, the conflict then becomes "speakable" in a different way, opening the possibility of exploring the conflict further.[40]

Reasons and rationalizations: Most requests for unethical behavior have a standard reason or rationalization that purportedly justifies the need to compromise individuals' values. Gentile identifies four of the most common arguments:

- Expected or standard practice: "Everyone takes bribes in my culture."
- Assuming no impact: "It doesn't really hurt anyone."
- Not my responsibility: "I'm just following orders."
- Locus of loyalty: "I know this isn't quite fair to the customer but I don't want to hurt my reports/team/boss/company."[41]

These standard rationalizations are powerful; they are repeated consistently and promote self-silencing. Identifying these helps one to identify from where the resistance will arise. Some may assume that these rationalizations will be stronger in India, given the high power-distance scores relative to those in the United States.[42] However, recent research suggests that its influence may be offset by the attitudinal commitment of individual employees even in the high power-distance context prevalent in India.[43]

Understanding stakeholders: The next stage is to identify the various stakeholders and what they have at stake by examining their underlying interests. The following framework, adapted from Fisher et al.,[44] enables understanding of the interests of the stakeholders:

Who's involved	Their interests and goals	Their challenges	Their fears and concerns

This analysis enables one to consider multiple reasons for a stakeholder's response and reaction toward the actions/decisions of the decision-maker. For example, a sales executive (a stakeholder) paying a bribe to a government official may be concerned that if the contract is lost, he or she will lose his/her job. This analysis fosters empathy in the decision maker, enabling more options to be recognized. The decision maker begins to see opportunities for change or common ground with the stakeholders. This widens his/her perspective, forming the basis for framing the issue to the stakeholders and suggesting opportunities for possible coalitions.

How to respond persuasively: Building on the above analysis, the decision maker can start to identify levers for change. This may require reframing the rationalization (unpacking the beliefs/assumptions underlying the request to behave unethically and testing their validity) so that long-term implications can be identified. Typically, rationalization is viewed as a "dichotomy:" either the reasoning is right or wrong. Simply identifying a belief as an assumption (versus fact) enables an individual to see the situation from a different perspective.[45] By examining the validity of this belief, the decision maker can search for and persuasively present evidence that this may not be true.

For example, when discussing business in India, a common assumption made is "pay the bribe or lose the business." However, Infosys, a leading Indian information-technology company, has chosen to test this assumption by strictly complying with national laws and implementing a high degree of transparency.[46] Partly as a result of this, it has become an internationally competitive, global company with a reputation for fair practices.

How to influence others: After preparing the responses to potential rationalizations, the decision maker has to plan effective communication of the same to relevant stakeholders. This could require interaction with important stakeholders. The decision maker has to develop and analyze multiple strategies for enhancing the chances of success during such interactions. Generally, the strategies need to be aligned with the profile of the decision-maker (e.g., risk orientation) and the relevant stake-holder. Answering the following questions can help the decision maker prepare:

a. Who can be approached? In what sequence?
b. When and where to meet them to increase the comfort level of those involved?
c. How can the issue be framed?
d. What mode of communication will be appropriate and most useful?
e. What role can be adopted by the decision maker in the interaction?

This process helps the decision-maker develop a script in response to the decision problem. He or she could then rehearse it before a supportive audience (peer coaching) to strengthen it. Rehearsal before peers can take the decision-maker a step closer to the emotions he or she can potentially experience during action; in the process, the potential emotional blocks become apparent and can be managed as part of the planning process. Rehearsal also builds confidence and the ability to express values in different circumstances.[47]

Applying the GVV Approach in India

From the description above, the GVV approach appears to have the potential to address the gaps in teaching ethical behavior. In the next two sections, we describe the application of the GVV approach to the development of two case studies and share the experience of piloting one of them in a GVV workshop for faculty members from Indian business schools.[48] Later, we describe the potential challenges of teaching ethical behavior using the GVV approach and how these could be addressed.

Case Studies Using the GVV Approach

The cases were based on the real-life experiences of two civil servants who were students of the Executive MBA program in India.[49] Civil servants, like managers in business organizations, are expected to deliver valued outcomes aligned with their organization's objectives (e.g., equitable development). In doing so, they are expected to adhere to an imperfectly articulated code of conduct[50] and manage the interests of multiple stakeholders in a context that is reportedly very corrupt. Consequently, they are called upon to exercise considerable judgment in making decisions. Cases that depict ethical behavior in such challenging decision contexts could (a) address the skepticism among students about whether ethical behavior is feasible and (b) provide ideas about how values conflicts could be negotiated in challenging local contexts. This could in turn enhance the transfer of ethical behavior to the workplace. Therefore we see no problem in the adoption of such cases in business schools.

Both respondents were asked to recollect a situation when they had experienced a value conflict and successfully resolved it. A list of questions[51] was sent to the respondents in advance, to prepare them for an interview. The subsequent interviews were transcribed and written up as cases. Each case was presented in two parts: Part A described the decision problem faced by the civil servant, with the alternatives and possible fallouts of each alternative for the various stakeholders. It ended with questions about *how to* ensure that institutional concerns were met in a manner aligned with the protagonist's values.[52] Part B of the case described how the protagonist resolved the problem.

A brief synopsis of the cases is provided below:

Case 1: "The Indent for Machines: A sugary finale (Part A)."

Viraj had joined the state government as a civil servant. Within a few years, he was made managing director of a loss-making sugar cooperative that was being propped up by the state government through grants. To reduce the dependence on the state government and the consequent political interference, the cooperative needed to improve productivity. Toward this end, Viraj obtained permission from the minister in charge of cooperatives, to float a tender for purchase of new equipment. Equipment suppliers were invited to bid for the contract within a timeframe; the supplier quoting the lowest price would win the contract. A few days later, the minister asked Viraj to award the contract to one of the suppliers, independent of the price quoted. Viraj was uncomfortable doing this. He believed that the contract should be awarded fairly, on the basis of the criteria specified. At the same time, he did not want to jeopardize his relationship with the politician. It was a challenge to express his values to the politician in a way that did not attract reprisals.

He explored the options before him and the possible consequences of each. He was clear he wanted to award the contract on a fair and transparent basis. He needed to develop strategies to voice his values to the minister in a way that did not antagonize him. Part B of the case describes how he went about doing this. It provides details of his script and how he implemented it. The outcome of his actions was that the supplier who quoted the lowest price won the contract. (This was not the minister's well-wisher.) There was no apparent ill-will from the minister's side.

Case 2: "The Temple Encroachment Issue: Part A."

A civil servant served as the Additional Collector of a state district. His responsibilities included collection of revenue and securing the property rights of the public. During assembly elections, his responsibilities additionally included ensuring free and fair elections in his district. This was a challenge, as any event (especially communally sensitive events) could be exploited by political parties to garner votes, with little cognizance of its implications for others.

During one such election year, he received a complaint from a builder that his land had been encroached upon and that he had been warned of dire consequences if he reported the encroachment. On exploring the matter, the civil servant gathered that the builder, a wealthy Muslim, had recently purchased property from a Christian owner in an area populated by Hindus. The property was contiguous with an ancient temple revered locally. The temple was clandestinely constructing an annex, which clearly encroached upon the property of the builder. When confronted, the temple committee members had told the builder that the property demarcation was not clear and threatened him if he complained.

The civil servant saw that the temple's annex was clearly illegal. He wanted to be just to the builder without compromising the interests of the locals and the fairness of the election process. The question was how to achieve this. Considerable pressure was being exercised to ensure that the temple construction continued.

Part B of the case describes how he went about accomplishing this goal. It provides details of his script and how he implemented it. As a result, the temple encroachment was successfully dealt with. The civil servant did not experience any negative fallout.

Use of One of the Case Studies in the NEN Workshops

The cases provided a means to apply the GVV framework to the Indian context. They were distributed as learning materials to participants of two workshops on GVV, sponsored by the National Entrepreneurship Network (NEN), India and conducted during 2011. The objective of the NEN workshops was to create awareness about the GVV approach among faculty members and to enable application of the same within the existing curriculum. These workshops provided an opportunity to test the application of the GVV approach and identify the potential challenges in its use.

Day one of both workshops focused on the salient features of the GVV framework for teaching ethics. The participants shared examples of unethical behavior that they experienced at their workplace and the impact of being ethical or unethical. At the end of the first day, participants in one of the workshops[53] were asked to read Part A of the case "The Temple Encroachment Issue" and prepare responses to the questions.[54]

Day two had two sessions devoted to the application of the GVV framework using the case. Participants spent the first part of the sessions developing a script in small groups. The script illustrated how they would meet institutional objectives in a manner aligned with the concerns of the stakeholders. Questions drawn from the GVV framework aided the participants in developing a script. One group then presented its script to the class and participants jointly explored how the script could be strengthened (made more workable), based on their experiences. Following discussion, Part B of the case was briefly presented to the participants. The participants thus got to experience the GVV framework in action.

Lessons Learned

It is difficult to generalize from the experiences with a small sample of faculty members. Nevertheless, as the sample was fairly representative of publicly funded and autonomous institutions, there could be useful pointers to the application of GVV approach.

Early discussions with participants across the two workshops highlighted skepticism among faculty about whether ethical approaches could actually work in India. This was addressed to an extent through the two case studies, as they depicted real-life situations wherein civil servants had been ethical and effectively voiced their values in challenging circumstances. In one of the workshops, some participants said they had experienced a similar situation but the response of the civil servant to the situation was instructive.

Potential Challenges in classroom use of GVV case-studies:

A few of the potential challenges to the classroom use of the case study were gleaned from the reactions and queries of the participants:

- *Difficulty in identifying ethical issues in the decision situation.*
  Participants took time to identify the value conflicts in the case. Some saw the case as a legal problem and found it difficult to identify the values at stake. It is possible that the case did not highlight the ethical issues prominently enough or the instructor did not adequately prepare the participants for identifying value conflicts. Alternately, this could partly be a result of "ethical fading," whereby unethical behavior escapes attention as it is often seen as "being practical."
- *Reluctance to deal with emotionally charged topics.* Before the case discussion, some participants expressed reservations about discussing the case as it explored a sensitive topic (conflict between two religious communities) and could evoke strong emotions. The participants discussed the issue and decided to continue with the discussion. The case generated heated discourse among the participants. A major challenge for the instructor was guiding the discussion sensitively, so that the focus continued to be on process issues. The strong reluctance among a few participants to discuss the case raised an important issue: could there be some value conflicts

that should not be explored in a classroom setting? How can instructors be prepared to deal sensitively with the emotions arising from value conflicts? Can this be captured in a teaching note?

- *Difficulty in focusing on process issues.* During the presentation of a script, workshop participants tended to focus on "what should be done" not on how. If this reflects their preferred focus, how can process issues obtain more attention in case discussions?

Implications for teaching and writing GVV case-studies:

These challenges could have implications for teaching and writing cases on value conflicts underlying unethical behavior. For case writers, choosing less sensitive value conflicts and clearly bringing out the value conflicts could enable more frequent usage of the case. If they choose to write about sensitive or emotionally charged issues, the teaching note needs to suggest ways of sensitively handling emotional issues in the class. (Many teaching notes focus on the content of the responses and the sequence of discussion, not on handling emotionally charged issues.)

For instructors in India, the following session outline (based on the GVV pedagogy and the case study experiences) could help students learn how to voice value conflicts at the workplace in an ethical manner:

- Distribute the case-study, along with readings on value conflicts, in the previous class, to help students identify value conflicts experienced by the decision maker in the case. Also, ask the students to individually prepare a script in response to the case questions.
- Start the session by exploring the value conflicts in the case-study. The instructor could then lead the *stepwise* application of the GVV approach to plan an ethical response aligned with the values of the protagonist and the circumstances faced. Ensure that the concerns of *all* stakeholders are identified and addressed.
- During the class, have students form small groups and finalize a script collectively. Faculty members could circulate among the groups and help them focus on process issues, especially on when to voice value conflicts and how to persuade those who are more powerful.

- Invite groups to present their script to the rest of the class. The class needs to help the group ensure the script is better aligned with the requirements of the situation and the profile of the protagonist.

For researchers, an intriguing question is whether there are distinct, culturally appropriate approaches to voicing values in the Indian context. The cases described by civil servants in India indicate that there could be distinct patterns in when and how they express their values at the workplace:

- ***When*** *they voice values*: Both cases occurred when elections were due and the election code of conduct was in force. It appears that circumstances characterized by reduced political interference provide more opportunities for being ethical. This could be specific to public sector context.
- ***How*** *they voice values*: While persuading an authority-figure to behave differently, the protagonists tended to ensure that they overtly *respected the former's position/"face."* They tended to frame the problem in terms of the former's *short-term concerns* such as gain/ loss of power, money and/or prestige.

In sum, given the experiences of using a GVV case in workshops for business school faculty, some guidelines for writing cases/teaching notes and using the cases in class are proposed. Substantial practice may be needed before the framework begins to guide action at the workplace. Some research questions emerging from the development of the two case-studies are also presented.

Summary and Conclusion

This chapter describes the level of corruption in India and the need for contextually relevant approaches to manage it. Besides institutional and legislative reform, there is need for enhanced accountability from people in positions of power. Citizens need to voice their concerns about unethical behavior and demand action in response to these unethical behaviors. This requires changes in the competencies of people, which educational institutions (including Business Schools) can help inculcate.

Indian business schools face at least two challenges in teaching ethical behavior: (a) skepticism among students that ethical approaches are feasible at the workplace and (b) the lack of learning materials/methodologies to address this skepticism and enable successful voicing of values in the workplace. The GVV framework is an option available to help address these challenges and teach ethical behavior. The chapter describes the application of the GVV framework to developing two case studies and the experience of piloting one in a workshop for faculty from Indian business schools. The pilot provided glimpses into the potential challenges in using the GVV approach to teach ethics. The tentative implications for GVV case writers, teachers, and researchers have been discussed. With sufficient practice, the GVV approach could better prepare students in India to behave ethically at the workplace.

Key Terms and Definitions

Attitudinal commitment: "A psychological attachment to the organizations driven by an employee's identification and involvement with the organization."[55]

Collectivist society: People belong to "in groups" that take care of them in exchange for loyalty.[56]

Corruption/unethical behavior: The ignoring or manipulation of approved norms/rules for personal gains or to frustrate public intentions.[57]

Ethical fading: The process whereby situations that once evoked strong ethical responses fail to do so later (akin to the "slippery slope phenomenon").[58]

Masculinity: The society is driven by competition, achievement, and success, with success being defined by the winner/best in field.[59]

Power distance: "The extent to which the less powerful members of institutions and organizations within a country expect and accept that power is distributed unequally."[60]

Psychological distance: An event removed from direct experience is said to be "psychologically distant." There are multiple dimensions along which an event could be far from direct experience, such as the social distance between the actors in that event.[61]

Psychological safety: People's perception of the consequences of taking interpersonal risks. Safe environments allow people to contribute without fear of reprisal.[62]

Stakeholders: Stakeholders are groups or individuals who affect and/ or are affected by the decision of the protagonist.

Study Questions

1. How might you explore the possibility of negotiating "instructions" with superiors or others with more "power?"
2. How might the assumptions based on cultural norms be explored and tested to determine their validity in the situation?
3. What are ways in which difficult topics can be discussed (e.g., religion, politics, etc.) in order to help participants manage a situation with these characteristics?
4. What kind of values conflicts might typically present themselves in ethically ambiguous instances?
5. Brainstorm and expand the identification of stakeholders beyond the ones that immediately are present in the situation. Often possible alliances can occur at the edges of those involved, for example, a civil society group or NGO with a particular interest in the situation.
6. What about this approach that feels comfortable? What seems challenging? Discuss.
7. What are ways to minimize the challenges?
8. What are the benefits to using this approach in ethical compromised situations you have been party to?
9. Culture is multifaceted. What is the interrelationship between organizational and country culture?
10. How do laws such as the US accountability law affect companies when they work abroad in relation to making ethical decisions?

Additional Reading

For a useful discussion on the role of religious/spiritual beliefs on Indian Ethics see:

Bilimoria, P. (2007). *Indian ethics: Classical traditions and contemporary challenges.* Ashgate, UK: Ashgate Publishing.

Gentile, M. (2010). *Giving voice to values: How to speak your mind when you know what's right.* Ann Arbor, MI: McGraw-Hill.

Kusyk, S. (2010). Unmasking The Myths: Learning to Navigate the Rough Seas of Ethics. *IESE Insight*, (5), 31–37.

Learning and teaching materials related to the Giving Voice to Values approach can be found on the websites: http://www.babson.edu/faculty/teaching-learning/gvv/Pages/home.aspx and http://www.caseplace.org/d.asp?d=3371

CHAPTER 3

Business Ethics Education in Brazil: Pedagogical Solutions for Combating Corruption in Brazil

Lama Al-Arda and Gazi Islam

Abstract

This chapter offers a discussion of the role of ethics education in management as a mechanism for combating corruption in Brazil. We argue that ethics education is important for combating endemic corruption. In order to apply this insight to Brazil in such a way to promote actionable responses by educators, we begin by an overview of the Brazilian context. Following much literature, we argue that the historical development of Brazil has led to a culture of administrative personalism, with the co-occurrence of highly formalized systems of administrative bureaucracy and informal personal ties, a combination that allows corrupt practices to spread easily. We then turn to the role of higher education in Brazil, noting the challenges faced in this sector, as well as the opportunities posed by recent rapid growth. Finally, we turn to concrete pedagogical practices that can contribute to combating corruption in the classroom, emphasizing the role of participation and dialogue, rather than recipes and codes.

Introduction

International attention on corruption, from scholars and international agencies, has been increasing in recent years.[1] Defined as "the misuse of public office, trust or power for private gain,"[2] corruption may be associated with the lack of optimal use of national resources and equal distribution among populations and thus creates social disparity and inequity, resulting in negative psychological and social consequences.[3] The importance of addressing corruption is partly to understand its causes in order to derive practical and equitable solutions to combat corruption.

Educational institutions and programs can be an important vehicle for reducing corruption through ethics education. Scholars recently have realized that "ethics education matters."[4] Some empirical research has suggested that ethics education can play a significant role in affecting ethical decision making[5] and can enable learners increase their "ethical awareness and moral reasoning." Emphasizing ethics in the education of potential future business leaders will imbue them with the essential foundations to ethically deal with complex managerial situations, dilemmas, or questionable situations.

Although the value of ethics education has been recognized, there has been little discussion of how to tailor ethics education to diverse global contexts, particularly regarding the issue of corruption.[6] In an era of globalized commerce, where managers will have to work across different cultural and ethical value systems, such discussions are overdue. Because corruption arises out of particular social, political, and cultural contexts, education toward combating corruption must take such contexts into account. Even countries at relatively similar levels of economic development may have different notions and perceptions of what constitutes corruptions, and what is appropriate in business ethics education. The five BRICS economies (Brazil, Russia, India, China, and South Africa), for example, have relatively different notions of ethics education.[7] In order to best design programs that speak to the problems and practices of the wider society, it is therefore necessary to place ethics education in its cultural context.

The current chapter addresses the link between higher education and corruption in Brazil. It highlights some of the advantages of introducing ethics into higher education in one of the world's largest emerging economies. We first move from broader perspectives on Brazilian culture to the more specific context of ethics education in Brazil. We pay special attention to the concept of *jeitinho*,[8,9] a key cultural notion with regards to corruption issues in Brazil. Then, we briefly describe higher education in

Brazil, providing a general overview of this sector. Based on this overview, we provide insights and recommendations regarding teaching ethics in Brazil, along with some pedagogical issues relevant to the Brazilian context.

Overview of Brazilian Context

Brazil is the world's sixth largest economy and has been historically marked by vast economical inequalities, with wealth "concentrated in the hands of a small portion of the population."[10] Furthermore, Brazil has been "known as a place of vast potential,"[11] possessing valuable resources, such as freshwater, tropical forests, fertile land, and huge mineral and hydrocarbon wealth. However, despite being a wealthy land, and despite a growing middle class in recent years, Brazil is still a country of large economic and social disparities. One of the main reasons often noted is the "inadequate education system,"[12] which calls for renewed attention to education in such a context, and precisely education involving the important social issues faced by Brazil. Teaching ethics in Brazil can be considered a step in reducing the huge disparity amongst the population and can be part of the enabling environment for sustainable economic development, and very important for developing business principles that emphasize human and social well-being.

As mentioned earlier, Brazil is a country of inequalities. This can be explained by various factors, for example, long period of colonialism.[13] The postcolonial period has been marked by periods of military intervention, foreign dependency and debt, and a history of institutional corruption.[14] Before, during, and after colonial periods, the economic elite was central in creating the political, social, and economic hierarchy,[15] allowing personalist ties between powerful actors to become central to the organization of society.

The costs of social exclusion, however, have prevented Brazil from realizing its economic potential in the long run. Human capital, as a core engine of advancing political and social change, suffered due to long-standing exclusions from quality education. Perhaps as a result, Brazil has long adopted "a debt-driven developmental model, that heavily relies on loans from international bodies."[16] The debt model gave Brazil the fiscal basis to accelerate its economical growth and led to the "Brazilian miracle."[17] However, this economic model further concentrated income in the hands of the upper class, while it enforced "regressive wage policies and repressive measures for the underclass."[18]

Despite the high concentration of power and resources in Brazil, the democratic opening of Brazil over the last 25 years has led to increased awareness of the need to include larger segment of the population into economic and social activity. This growing social consciousness makes Brazil a good candidate for educational innovations in teaching ethics and social responsibility. Such initiatives, linked to national education, could replace the current culture of compliance that affect primarily larger, transnational institutions based or operating in Brazil. As Griesse (2007, p. 20) puts it, "only large transnational firms are pressured by the international marketplace and international organizations to comply."

Related to this opening, recent political openings have allowed for the creation of a third sector in Brazil, which is corporate social responsibility (CSR). This is promising especially since this sector has evolved as a response to the disparity that distinguishes Brazil.[19] CSR in the Brazilian context is meant to install citizenship to "allow full participation of all citizens in national space, and strengthen the collective decision making process."[20] Following the wave of interest in CSR, corporations in Brazil have started to humanize their business activities through integrating ethics in their business activities and introducing a code of conduct in their operations, as well as adopting training strategies to build their employees' capacities to ethically deal with workplace situations.[21]

The challenge of such initiatives in business education is to imbue a sense of anti-corruption and social conscience into Brazilian business culture. As the main arms of this emerging economy, business organizations function as vehicles of "promoting change."[22] Some studies of Brazilian business ethics have identified a culture based on maintaining harmony and coherence among group members, with loyalty to the group leader.[23] While a focus on social harmony may be consistent with anti-corruption initiatives, in cultures where loyalty to leaders is high, it stands to reason that the ethical practices and values of leaders are of particular importance.

The above point implies that the institutional and economic history of Brazil does not only make itself felt in resulting structural inequalities, but also in cultural and value systems that reinforce hierarchical relationships, loyalty, and personalism.[24] Such cultural aspects have developed from a system of patronage based around fixed hierarchies in a colonial, then a land-owning economy.[25] However, transplanted into a modern political and economic scenario, they may be precursors to institutional corruption and understanding how such cultural practices work may be key to understanding business in Brazil.[26]

For example, the notion of *jeitinho* (little way) has been central to understanding hierarchical, including corrupt, relations in Brazilian society.[27–29] *Jeitinho* has been defined as "an informal problem-solving strategy, social mechanism that entails bending or breaking the rules in order to deal with difficult or forbidding situations. It is a useful strategy to get things done in work organizations."[30] It involves interpersonal favors or rule-bending in order to avoid complex protocols that have proliferated in highly bureaucratized contexts. While such rule bending have the effect of smoothing social relations and creating social harmony in the short run, it leads to widespread economic inefficiencies and difficulties in the long run, notwithstanding the perpetuation of social inequities.[31]

Jeitinho and the tendency toward personalism, as a "hermeneutic key" of Brazilian society,[32] give Brazilians a sense of cultural identity, and also include friendly and gentle behaviors that would not always be considered clearly unethical.[33] Thus, it is an important part of culture, and as a driver of corruption and unethical behaviors, such phenomena are not clearly resolved through implementing codes of conduct or top-down enforcement of rules. Rather it requires the kind of sustained dialogue around ethical dilemmas that takes place in ethics classrooms, and thus are an issue for discussion, rather than legislation.

Having thus given a brief overview of the historical and cultural issues involved in corruption in Brazil, that indicates social disparity, institutionalized informal relations, we may now turn to the area of education, to see how classroom treatments of these topics can be conceptualized, and how solutions to corruption can be imagined by educators.

Overview of Education and Social Issues in Brazil

We argue that higher education is a potential driver of change in Brazil. We begin by discussing the distinguishing characteristics of this sector, enabling us to derive some insights regarding teaching ethics in Brazil, in terms of content and pedagogy. By providing such overview we will be in a better position to propose pedagogical recommendations and insights as well as learning activities that would be effective enough to maximize and achieve the desired results.

Higher education, from a sociological perspective, can be considered as an "incubator for the development of competent social actors, and temples for legitimating official knowledge."[34] Higher education thus grants the legitimacy of certain domains of knowledge. As such, it is one of the main pillars of state building and for the formation of an accepted body of administrative knowledge, practice, and values[35] (p. 15). Additionally, higher education acts as a "hub" by which key social actors are connected with each other, as well as with the institutional structures of society.[36] Higher education serves as a mechanism that can produce the human capital required for social and economic stability. Education in Brazil can significantly influence the effectiveness of political participation, and as some have argued, growth in educational attainment can pose a challenge for corruption practices by elites.[37]

Brazil has been highlighted for the key role that education can play in development,[38] and as has been stated in many studies higher education in Brazil has the highest return on education among the 17 Latin American countries, demonstrating the potential for education to improve social conditions in Brazil. As such, managing the emerging educational structures of Brazilian higher education is especially pressing.

Education in Brazil is composed of public and private, profit-making and nonprofit institutions, as well as diverse community institutions. The latter encourage community participation and philanthropic institutions that require a separate eligibility, the "certificate of social assistance from the national council for social assistance."[39] New institutions and courses are regulated by the national council of education (CNE), first established in Brazil in 1995.[40] This administrative entity can be possibly seen as an enabling institution to ease the promotion of new courses in teaching ethics without rigid complications or going through dealing with many administrative channels.

The diversity of forms of higher education in Brazil, between autonomous universities, private foundations, and less regulated educational centers,[41] pose both challenge and an opportunity for designers of curricula, since the academic background, interests, and need of potential students might change quite markedly across different forms of institutions. Popular areas of study across institutional forms, however, include social science, business and law, humanities, which belong to the so-called soft science.[42] This is another avenue that teaching ethics would be effectively incorporated into, since the vast majority of entrants enroll in such fields, then the learning outcomes of these courses would be intensified and diversified largely.

A key issue in Brazilian higher education systems is quality, with cause for concern at various levels. Pisa, the international evaluation, highlighted the poor quality of higher education in Brazil, giving Brazil one of the lowest positions in terms of student achievement.[43] Such results may be a result of the poor quality of basic education, which perhaps consequently led to high rates of dropouts and repetition. Quality is also most likely to intersect with the unequal educational opportunities, especially for those who live in poor areas and accordingly educational opportunity on the national level is deeply undemocratic.

Focusing on the student populations, higher education enrollments are relatively low, at 17%, with students concentrated at the upper socio-economic levels. Seventy-one percent of students come from the top 20% of household incomes, with a low representation of Afro-Brazilian students, and a concentration in the wealthier South and South-Eastern.[44]

Notwithstanding all these problems that distinguishes education in Brazil in general, some progress and improvement has taken place, such as recruiting better qualified teachers or even upgrading their qualifications and competences. Nationally, specific curriculum parameters have been put in place to improve the quality of higher education. Efforts to improve education in Brazil have been also steered toward improving and changing the content of curriculum especially for basic education, with a special focus on the importance of developing competences and skills in problem solving and logical thinking. Based on these changes in curriculum content, the overall educational system in Brazil started to change from memorization-based systems to reasoning, and building knowledge and competences and behaviors rather than quantity of information.[45] "Learning to learn and to think"[46] has also been one of the slogans for improving education. This has more effective implications, especially when it comes to relating knowledge to real-life experience, giving meaning to what has been learned, or interpreting these real daily examples through knowledge and concepts students acquire.

Higher education in Brazil is based on three main functions/forms: teaching, research, and extension. The latter form of education, extension courses, refers to the continued education of working populations and is particularly extensive in Brazil.[47] The core essence of these courses is that they have a social character but they can be offered in the higher education institutions. These courses are not academic degrees but can potentially have a positive impact.[48] This allows a convergence of theory and practice that is important in ethical decisions.

The extension courses can be used as the major vehicles to teach business ethics in higher education institutions. These courses can be a very active forum for reflecting on the daily lives of practitioners through bringing real-life examples, and combining such examples with the conceptual and theoretical understanding of course content. Thus, extension courses can enhance and institutionalize continuing education in Brazil, which is once again necessary for such an emerging economy.

One of the main trends with potential to improve education in Brazil is the growth of private institutions of higher education. This growth has been based on the fact that private providers of educational services increase relatively low enrollments and create the potential to enhance positive competition among education institutions.[49] Unfortunately, despite World Bank predictions that increases in private education would facilitate the inclusion of socially disadvantaged groups, most families, with average incomes around $600 per month, cannot afford tuitions and thus remain excluded from the majority of the sector.[50] Compounding this problem, private institutions are concentrated mainly in the richer South and South-East regions. On the other hand, the decentralization of education from the federal public university system could potentially create the heterogeneity in educational offerings that drive innovations. It remains to be seen whether such adoptions can adopt a socially and environmentally responsible approach while being purely driven by a market model.[51]

The situation presented so far about higher education in Brazil suggests that the education system in Brazil has critical implications in excluding a very large majority of the population from educational opportunities, and deprives them of this right, and therefore forces them in a way to resort to other possible ways to survive and earn their living regardless of it being ethical or not. One possible way out is the inclusion of these groups, by including them in educational opportunities, or at least include them in education partly through introducing ad hoc courses, or through the extension courses that are already in the structure of higher education in Brazil, so as to raise the ethical awareness of this group and to retain a social awareness necessary to understand the implications of corruption. This may be one possible precautionary measure to reduce corruption in Brazil.

The majority of this education is for-profit, private education, and nonresearch-oriented. Most people who enter these schools take it as a way to further their careers. On the other hand, public education is mainly based on a classical European view of education, focusing on theoretical rigor, academic publication, and autonomy from outside pressures. This view is more humanistic and research-oriented, and internally recognized as having generally higher academic legitimacy as compared to the private sector.[52] We argue, in the next section, that a sharp division between "academic" and "professional" education is not a positive trend for anticorruption education; rather, such divisions tend to isolate ethical theory from practice, and at the same time, lead to theory that does not understand the needs and demands made for managers.

To summarize, higher education in Brazil takes varied forms, and is in a recent and relatively fundamental period of change. Brazil's emerging middle class, as it encounters the new educational forms springing around it, will be affected by the kinds of alternative curricula and visions of management that are promulgated in these centers of learning. In a very real sense, therefore, the new forms of higher education, are often based on extension courses, night courses, and other alternative formats, that can serve as training grounds upon which a new generation of Brazilian managers will develop knowledge required for ethical management. As such, they provide a key front on which the struggle against corruption must be carried out, and socially conscious values can be promoted. In the next section, we will discuss practical ideas for engaging in this educational initiative.

Business Ethics Education: Pedagogical Tools for Addressing Corruption

Although business ethics education has tended to underplay issues of systemic corruption and society-wide ills,[53] it is impossible to discuss ethics in Brazil only at the level of individual behaviors. While it is true that corruption occurs by people's individual choices, in specific situations, and individuals must ultimately be held responsible for their actions, these actions must also be understood in the context of a society that has maintained social disparities, personalism, and corrupt practices for centuries. In such a situation, individual acts of corruption may not take on the illegitimacy that is suggested by looking at codes of ethics; rather they may exist in an informal but "permissible" way, in order to navigate the daily lives of actors.

Among the key goals of promoting ethical teaching in Brazil is to provide a platform by which students can engage with prevailing social disparities, eventually promoting a national dialogue around how to develop an equitable way. Because economic power in Brazil has circulated among relatively closed minority segments of the population, consciousness rising at this level is necessary for such dialogue to occur. As the current government of Brazil has emphasized, addressing and combating corruption is a major goal for social policy.[54] As the government has itself been accused of corrupt practices such as payoffs and support buying, it suggests that change needs to occur at the deeper level of educational and cultural transformation for such gains to be realized.

Having a reasonable background in ethics should be considered a key prerequisite in higher education curricula across the diverse types of programs. Below we suggest some pedagogical tools that could help the design of ethics pedagogy in the Brazilian context.

For example, promoting ethical awareness, as recognition of the moral nature of a situation, allows students to recognize that certain situations constitute an ethical dilemma with conflicting ethical standards. In situations where "getting the job done" contradicts organizational codes or ethical principles, the use of such dilemmas could allow students to openly share their feelings about rule-bending and discuss possible alternatives with their peers. Rather than simply giving recipes for correct action, such discussion could develop moral reasoning, defined as the ability to analyze and evaluate certain actions taking into account ethical principles.[55]

Such discussions could be promoted via critical incident methods,[56] which bring real-life scenarios to the classes that constitute an effective pedagogical approach in teaching corruption related issues. These real-life scenarios would provide very good platforms to blend real life with the concepts and theories. Referring to critical incidents also enables students to understand such incidents, analyze them, and perhaps suggest ways to deal with some of these issues or ethical dilemmas that confront the real world. Class discussions could also be led by practitioners who might attend courses in business ethics especially in the case of extension courses tailored to specific business groups.

The extensive involvement of practitioners in higher education in Brazil, a function both of the historical lack of doctoral programs and the rapid increase in higher education programs provides an opportunity to link theory and practice, and emphasize real-world situations in the classroom. The practitioners' involvement can promote debate and discussion amongst the students, practitioners, and the academic staff and it is likely to be closer to the kinds of real-world situations that students can expect to encounter in the labor market.

On the other hand, having business ethics courses taught largely by business practitioners also poses challenges. While these actors may be more in tune with the exigencies of the market, they may not have the critical distance from business necessary to reflectively critique, question, and challenge current "business as usual" assumptions, and thus risk perpetuating status quo corrupt practices. It is thus imperative for practitioners, academics, and students to interact and participate in ethical discussions in the classroom. Such discussions become moments for true dialogue, rather than simply training in current corporate practices.

Such interaction might take the form of team-taught classes between academically qualified and professionally qualified instructors, enabling students to encounter different points of view in the classroom. The team teaching format would be useful on several fronts. First, it would "decenter" the authority of the professor from a single individual, promoting participation in a more collaborative environment. Second, it would, on the one hand, force the academically qualified professors to engage with real-world issues while forcing the professionally qualified faculty to step back and reflect on the conceptual bases of business action. Third, it would allow students to see that many of the situations that they encounter at work are not straightforward in meaning, and engage a search process in which they are forced to consider different points of view on a topic.

The extensive use of ethical business cases would be a key element in an anti-corruption pedagogy within management education. Cases put students within an experiential setting where they can in classrooms experience certain ethical dilemmas or situations to see what they can do accordingly.

Pedagogically, ethical discussions should involve "experimental" simulations, such as role reversals, where instructors surprise the participants in reversing roles on the spot, asking students to assume that such incidents they themselves encountered, will they handle or perceive it in the same way they suggested before. This way the instructors can verify immediately whether the students were candid in their responses about the incidents reflecting upon their experience in different roles and social positions.

Because of the ethical issues surrounding personalism in Brazil, ethics instructors could design cases to challenge the students/participants on how will they react in an ethical dilemma if a friend is involved, or an acquaintance or a relative. The point of such cases would be for the students to internalize potential situations, where the students would be directly asked how they will handle a situation with their friends or relatives. The cases should be carefully designed to refer to how they relate or interpret their reactions to such dilemmas to the values of friendship, loyalty, professionalism, kindness, and favor.

Similarly, extreme scenarios are of particular use, where students are exposed to two extreme ethical scenarios. Such situations could involve issue of public or private safety, or situations that risk the firm's survival, or seriously impact social well-being. Such cases would force the students to look into their foundational values, and decide whether expediency is worth compromising core normative beliefs.

Case discussions surrounding the *jeitinho* might look critically both at the behaviours that subvert organizational rule structures and also at those rule structures themselves. In a first phase, the class might take an "actor's view" perspective on an organizational situation. For example, burdened by an arcane and complex tax system, organizational managers might have the opportunity to avert taxes by recategorizing expenses, hiding key information, or paying off local officials. These activities could be discussed both as responses that arise from the understandable difficulties of managing a difficult system, and also as socially destructive behaviors that, in the long run, erode the power of the state to administer its economy. The ability to see both sides of such behaviours, while not providing easy answers, could better equip students to face the situations that they are likely to encounter as managers.

Conversely, the same kind of exercise could be reframed from the "social engineer's point of view." That is, students could take the role of a strategist designing organizational policies, or a government official drafting legislative plans. From this point of view, the focus would be on how to create systems that allow corruption to be avoided. The discussion could go in several directions. First, students and teachers could debate ways in which administrative structures could be streamlined to avoid the bureaucratic bottlenecks that often lead to bypassing the system. Second, they could discuss the design of auditing and monitoring systems that would disincentivize corrupt behavior, and, importantly, incentivize correct behavior. Such "institutional design" perspectives would allow students and professionals to step back from the day-to-day exigencies of their professional lives to look at the big picture of how organizational behaviors both arise from and affect wider institutional structures.

The key take away point from each of these suggestions is that a traditional lecture mode of pedagogy may be inappropriate to the specific topic of anti-corruption in management classrooms, because the content of such a course is likely to challenge fundamental cultural practices that occur in the economy. Such modes of teaching, by focusing attention on a single authority, and forcing student to learn what that authority wants in order to pass an exam, may paradoxically reinforce the same kinds of top-down and leader-focused dynamic, which, we argued above, is associated with widespread corruption. Rather, pedagogy can model forms of relationality that stress mutual respect, participation, and creative problem solving, thus creating an experiential basis for democratic, egalitarian interactions in the public sphere. Beyond course content per se, modeling such forms of social interaction might in itself be a step against corrupt and antisocial business practice.

Conclusion

Brazil, as musician Tom Jobim pointed out, "is not for beginners." As such, teaching management in a way that is sensitive to local contexts is essential to make ethics education meaningful for Brazilian audiences. Dealing with local complexities can be both a challenge and an opportunity for educators. This chapter has provided insights, tools, and ideas for pedagogy against corruption.

Curricula should be sensitive to context, especially in the case of teaching ethics. We have argued that teaching ethics is one of the effective means to fight corruption. However, education programs must be grounded on the causes of corruption in Brazil. Understanding those causes allows us to create more pedagogically effective tools.

Brazil emerged out of particular political, social, and cultural conditions that have led to problems with corruption. Despite its great potential, the political, social, and economic hierarchy and a history of institutionalized corruption, beginning from the colonial period, have hindered Brazil's development.

The institutionalized corruption described above not only exists at the political level through maintaining power, authority, and wealth in the hands of elites, but also extends to include social values and practices. The notion of *jeitinho*, for example, reflects the personal ties that prevail in many Brazilian administrative settings.

A lack of quality education characterizes the Brazilian educational system. As such, student achievement in Brazil has been reported by Pisa as among the lowest positions worldwide. The problems in the education system start from basic education and trickle upward in the higher education, resulting in, among other problems, very low enrolment of students.

In sum, corruption has been historically ingrained in Brazilian society at many levels, leading to myriad social difficulties. Despite its historical difficulties, however, we have argued that many aspects of higher education in Brazil show cause for optimism in terms of its ability to resolve corruption, despite deeply engrained difficulties.

First, the autonomy enjoyed by the main educational institutions is one of the most attractive features that give such institutions the flexibility to introduce new courses such as business ethics. An important feature of education system in Brazil is that it is mainly based on teaching, research, and extension. The latter is the most suitable and malleable form for widespread change. This is because it can act as a hub to reach out various actors who can play main roles to incrementally combat corruption. Extension courses are also of importance to include the population that has been deprived of education opportunities for different reasons.

Based on the features attributed to the Brazilian context in general and educational system in particular, we provided few pedagogical insights that we argued can reap huge benefits in fighting corruption systematically and incrementally.

The critical incident method is a key tool in this regard. It is based on bringing to classrooms real-life scenarios, where learners simulate, interact, exchange, and reflect on their own experiences, merging practice and theory to enhance learning outcomes. As part of this method, practitioners can also be invited in some sessions to talk about their experiences, creating a solid debate platform amongst learners. Similarly, some experimental simulations, role reversals should enable learners to closely assess their capabilities and reactions in ethical reasoning. Because of the widespread nature of corruption historically, there are many cases that can be brought to classroom for discussion that can further and strengthen the conceptual and theoretical concepts.

In short, Brazil's emergence on the world stage can best be supported by an educational strategy that attempts to combat corruption while taking local history into account. The present time is a ripe moment for change, in a country that is rapidly changing in many ways.

Key Terms and Definitions

Corruption: The use of social or public position or authority for private or illegitimate ends.

Higher education: Education above the secondary or high school level.

Study Questions

1. What are the ways in which corruption is evident in the Brazilian context?
2. What is the role of higher education in combating corruption?
3. What classroom techniques can be used to make this role effective?

Additional Reading

Barbosa, L. (1995). The Brazilian jeitinho: An exercise in national identity. In David Hess and Roberto DaMatta (Eds.), *The Brazilian puzzle: Culture on the borderlands of the western world*, pp. 35–48. New York: Columbia University Press.

Brown, E., & Cloke, J. (2011). Critical perspectives on corruption: an overview. *Critical perspectives on International Business, 7*(2), 116–124.

Vizeu, F. (2011). Rural Heritage of early Brazilian Industrialists?: Its impact on managerial orientation. *Brazilian Adminstration Review, 8*(1), 68–85.

Business Schools as Agents of Change: Addressing Systemic Corruption in the Arab World

Dima Jamali and Amy Walburn

Abstract

Systemic corruption in the Middle East and North Africa (MENA) region is a serious hindrance to economic growth and business prosperity. Not only does it result in millions of dollars in lost revenue and productivity ever year, but it further slows growth by detracting foreign investment. This chapter argues that business schools in the MENA face a unique opportunity and challenge to serve as agents of change through offering a platform from which to teach integrity, responsibility, and anti-corruption. The chapter begins with a documentation of corruption practices and their peculiar expressions in the Arab World. From there, we present an analysis of the role of business and business education in the fight against corruption and document the "business case" against corruption. Finally, some regional higher education institutions are sampled and documented to highlight current trends in business school education in the Arab region in regard to topics relating to business ethics, corporate social responsibility (CSR), integrity, and anti-corruption. Recommendations are made in light of the findings revolving around the need for universities in the Arab region to introduce courses that sensitize future managers and leaders to the complexities of ethical decision-making.

Opportunities and challenges for business schools serving as agents of change in this context will be discussed and a roadmap for action presented for those business schools ready to embark on the journey.

Introduction

We have witnessed over the past 30 years a significant improvement in research and policies aimed at addressing corruption, yet the latter continues to be a subject that is difficult, if not risky, for scholars to pursue. This chapter contributes to the literature on the subject by addressing the intersection of education and corruption. In doing so, it seeks to examine the role that business schools might play in the fight against corruption through relevant education, an anti-corruption platform that has scant mention in the literature. Taking the Middle East and North Africa (MENA) region as a case in point, the chapter sheds light on corruption in MENA and makes recommendations for business schools in the region to address corruption through appropriately tailored curricula and pedagogical techniques.

In analyzing the literature on corruption, especially as it relates to business, the chapter tackles two questions that are likely to be relevant to readers of this book. The first pertains to the business case for adopting an anti-corruption platform and the second one relates to the role of educational institutions in providing the needed cognitive infrastructure to support the fight against corruption. Using the example of corruption in MENA, the book chapter offers numerous examples of pedagogical techniques appropriately suited for buttressing the fight against corruption across the globe.

At a time of critical historical importance for the MENA region, the Arab Spring has heightened citizens' concerns about fair and representative government, equality and access to opportunity. Corruption is a concern that has been loudly voiced by Arab constituents since the uprisings in Tunisia began in December 2010. The Arab Spring no doubt presents a potent opportunity for the business community to heed the demands of the public at large and respond in-kind with more ethical and fair practices. It is also an opportunity for business schools to reconsider the relevance of their offerings and think about how to more systematically realign their curricula with expressed issues and needs around them.

The book chapter begins by focusing on corruption in the MENA. We document the entrenched and widespread corruption across the region. Then we proceed to examine the relationship between business and corruption. As this edited volume entitled, "Teaching Anti-Corruption—Developing a Foundation for Business Dignity," suggests the private sector is inherently implicated in the fight against corruption. We show this relationship, first for its own sake, and second, as a value-added for open and transparent society-building and sustainable development. We move from there to address the parallel important role for business schools in the fight against corruption, and then finally back to the MENA region to offer useful suggestions with innovative ideas for relevant classroom instruction to address the corruption epidemic in the region and beyond.

Corruption in MENA

The Arab states[1] suffer from pronounced levels of corruption. Indexes such as Transparency International's Corruption Perception Index (CPI) measuring levels of corruption in the world give a good indication of corruption in the region.[2] Total scores range on a scale from 0 to 10, 10 being least corrupt, 1 being most corrupt. While only measurements of perception are used, over time, the CPI has shown to be a rather accurate measure of actual corruption levels in a given country.[3]

According to a report of Transparency International issued at the end of 2010, 36% of the population of the Arab world had to pay a bribe to government officials in different positions.[4] From obtaining drivers' licenses, to employment to permits, to job placement through wasta and bribery, corruption permeates the culture of the MENA region.[5] Looney notes that both grand and petty corruption are manifest in MENA. The former describes ways in which autocratic rulers steal from the state, in systematic ways such as economic models, awarding state contracts and facilitating private enterprise on their behalf. The latter describes ways that smaller scale corruption manifests in offices and bureaucracies throughout MENA countries. This might entail taking small bribes to expedite government services, falsifying government papers or government officials favoring their family and friends in the distribution of official services.

Table 4.1. *Transparency International Corruption Perception Index Scores 2011*[6]

Country	CPI Score	Country rank
Qatar	7.2	22
UAE	6.8	28
Israel/Palestine	5.8	36
Bahrain	5.1	46
Oman	4.8	50
Kuwait	4.6	54
Jordan	4.5	56
Saudi Arabia	4.4	57
Tunisia	3.8	73
Morocco	3.4	80
Djibouti	3	100
Algeria	2.9	112
Egypt	2.9	112
Syria	2.6	129
Lebanon	2.5	134
Comoros	2.4	143
Mauritania	2.4	143
Yemen	2.1	164
Libya	2	168
Iraq	1.8	175
Sudan	1.6	177

While a comprehensive description of the causes of corruption in the region is beyond the scope of this book chapter, Table 4.2 compiles some of the most important and commonly invoked causes.

Business and The Business of Corruption

Business is implicated in the fight against corruption, as it sometimes plays a role in catalyzing corruption and also suffers from its consequences. Business acts on the supply side of public–private corruption in numerous ways, and economists and development specialists alike have been keen to

Table 4.2. Main Causes of Corruption in MENA

Cause	Description
Rentier Economies	An economic model in which nothing is produced, but something is rented, such as assets like land or oil. This is a defining characteristic of the MENA, which is rich in oil, minerals and metals, as well as remittances from abroad, foreign military, and economic aid, and international tourism.[7] These types of economic transactions constitute more than one-third of the MENA economies.[8] As with all economic models, rentierism has implications for governance and politics, most notably as international rents decrease the need of tax collection and therefore accountability in government.[9] "The culture of rent has negative effects in Arab countries. It is a culture that denigrates effort and prefers intermediation rather than the direct production of real wealth."[10] This thesis is compatible with the existing theories of corruption in developing countries made by scholars such as Rose-Ackerman[11] and Shleifer and Vishny[12] that show corruption is greater in economic models where bribes can be extracted from rent producing activities.
Autocratic Regimes	Theories on the prevalence of corruption show that democratic regimes provide more safeguards against corruption.[13] Arab states, since decolonization in the mid-20th century have had a tradition of autrocratic rule.[14] This has only recently been challenged in a substantial way, with the Arab Spring protests. "Arab states' political institutions have been non-representative and non-democratic. In some instances, they are monarchical, and in others they are republics where, in most cases, power was assumed by military-turned civilian rulers via orchestrated elections."[15] Appendix A highlights democracy/freedom scores in the Arab world.
Quasi Economic Liberalization Welfare States	The literature on corruption and its causes shows that in times of economic liberalization, opportunities for significant corruption and collusion exist and when corruption occurs in these contexts, growth and the rate of technological change and growth is debased.[16] The quasi-economic liberalization facilitated corruption in the Arab states, which in turn has had a negative correlation to innovation, growth, and sustainable development.
Poverty	Poverty is a reality of the MENA region for most countries (see Appendix A). GDP per capita in some of the most populous countries is well below levels that contribute to adequate human development. Prominent economic development scholar Jeffrey Sachs notes poverty is a contributing factor to corruption[17] and the MENA region is no exception. In a similar vein, low salaries of civil servants, a cause of corruption in emerging markets has been identified by Salem as a root cause of corruption in MENA.[18]

(*Continued*)

Table 4.2. Main Causes of Corruption in MENA (Continued).

Cause	Description
Culture	A culture of "wasta" and bribery and corruption is endemic to the region.[19] Wasta, which at its root meaning roughly translates to "middle," describes the act of a mediation or go-between to influence decisions or bestow favor.[20] This intercession is used to facilitate daily transactions in the life of most Arabs. Salem identifies the historical rule of the Ottoman administration for inculcating a culture of corruption of the civil service in the Arab world.[21] Furthermore, the region is diverse economically, politically, ethnically, and religiously which creates factionalsim in society that often gives way to sectarian and religious strife characterizing the region.[22] This sectarianism helps a culture of corruption to thrive as civil servants are more apt to help their family or clan than to feel obliged by national identity to serve everyone equally under the law.

show the severe socioeconomic side effects of such involvement. In the sections below, we provide evidence that corruption significantly increases the cost of doing business, but also has detrimental effects at the level of society at large, which come back to haunt a business in its basic operations.

Starting with the negative externalities that corruption has on business itself, the World Economic Forum (WEF) has created a platform for business to address corruption in an initiative known as Partnering against Corruption Initiative (PACI). In mobilizing the business community in the anti-corruption platform, PACI has put together a business case against corruption. Using the simple and practical language of business, the PACI business case against corruption makes the platform for business to combat corruption easily accessible to any manager or director. See Figure 4.1.

Figure 4.1 provides a sense that corruption raises the cost of doing business both in time and money and therefore decreases profitability. In a report to the World Bank in 1997, Rose-Ackerman offers two pieces of advice regarding the debate about corruption "greasing or sanding" the wheel of economic development.[23] She states emphatically that corruption is always a second best option. While it may grease the wheel, its

Financial	Legal	Ethical	Socio-economic
• Corruption increases of doing business by up to 10% on average • Maintain good standing for public bidding • Avoid substantial fines and penalities	• Due to strengthening of legal infrasturcture, corruption law enforcement has increased • Companies, CEOs and board members more likely to be held liable for their actions	• Doing business with integrity attracts and retains principled, motivated employees and ethically-oriented investors	• Estimated that more than US$ 1 trillion is paid in bribes annually • Corruption is a collective action problem, which distorts markets, stifles growth, debases democracy and undermines the rule of law

Figure 4.1. PACI business case against corruption.[24]

negative externalities will eventually outweigh the grease it can provide and start "sanding" the wheel. Corruption is not a sustainable strategy. When businesses engage in corruption, there are serious financial costs, as well as costs in terms of time and productivity. Moreover, with enhanced legislation and enforcement, the cost of getting caught looms large.

At the societal level, there is little doubt and accumulating evidence that the negative externalities of corruption far outweigh its potential greasing effect in the short term. Corruption has indeed been shown to negatively affect the following indicators:

- *Economic growth*: Aggregate levels of economic growth are negatively affected by corruption because it decreases efficiency of the marketplace and inhibits or detracts investment activity and acts as a barrier to trade.[25] In parallel with slowed growth comes lower GDP per capita.
- *GDP per capita* studies that show a negative correlation to corruption.[26] It is relevant to note that despite the overwhelming evidence that corruption negatively affects growth, the Asian Tigers of Singapore, Malaysia, Indonesia, and South Korea have been outliers to this evidence.[27]
- *Biased composition of government expenditures*: Mauro produced for the first time quantitative empirical evidence that corruption diverts government spending away from issues of national importance, such as health care or education.[28] In his particular study, he proved that

for every one standard deviation point of additional corruption, GDP spending per capita on education was reduced by 0.05%.

- *Political stability*, including undermining trust in public institutions and legitimacy.[29] This concept is pronounced in the Arab Spring context, where highly corrupt countries such as Libya, Syria, Bahrain, Egypt, and Tunisia have witnessed extreme political instability as a result of people demanding less corruption, more transparency and more freedom. The Arab context will be given more attention in the following sections.

Given the findings above, it is apparent that there is a viable business case to be made for anti-corruption; moreover, it becomes a business imperative to fight corruption. This implicates business in the fight against corruption, first for its own sake, and secondly, as an avenue for open and transparent society-building and sustainable development. Many businesses have taken heed of this information and started recreating policies and procedures to combat corruption. Many have introduced these changes within an agenda of corporate social responsibility (CSR). A 2005 survey by the University of Hong Kong compiled a list of the most salient CSR priorities for business and their stakeholders.[30] Telling results ranked corruption as a top priority in a survey of over 15 issues. Addressing anti-corruption should therefore be integrated within the CSR and strategy framework of business firms globally. While business is starting to realize the business case for transparency and fair practice, it is imperative that business schools also start to integrate these relevant and important topics into their curricula. The following section tackles in turn the role of business schools in the fight against corruption.

Business Schools in The Fight Against Corruption

Do business schools have a role to play in addressing corruption? Illustrative and compelling empirical, as well as contemporary anecdotal evidence show that corruption is a tremendous societal problem with huge economic and political costs, as well as a salient business issue. Why then are business schools not addressing this issue more explicitly? Education gets to the root cause of many of these corrupt behaviors and offers hope and potential to address the inception of the problem, rather than law enforcement or compliance programs. Raging debates about the role of business schools in nurturing integrity and fighting corruption continue to unfold with the main axes of the controversy summarized as follows: (1) To teach or not to teach business ethics; (2) If one is convinced of the argument that business integrity should be taught then there are further debates in which to engage regarding teaching business ethics in the classroom: (A) Should it be taught as a stand-alone course, or should it be integrated into all courses? (B) Should the methodology of focus be on ethics or compliance?

The first argument is that "you can't teach ethics, so you should not even try." There are many arguments on this side of the debate. They can be summarized as such: First, the "Milton Friedman" argument, which posits that the private sector is only obligated to engage in activities geared toward profit maximization. If one uses this argument, it typically implies that students should only study what increases their technical prowess, and in this case, ethics courses would be a waste of time. The second argument relates to incentives and states that even if there are duties beyond profit maximization, the only practical way to encourage ethical behavior is through appropriate incentives, because business people usually respond to these, not ethics lectures. In this case, it isn't necessary to teach ethics, but simply to teach compliance. The third argument pertains to moral development, pointing out that ethical behavior is related to personal moral development, which is not easily molded in a classroom setting.

On the other side of the teaching ethics debate, Von Weltzien Høivik argues that despite the fact that teaching ethics is admittedly difficult, we have also learned through research that a course about ethics in a business school can be effective in developing moral awareness and reasoning.[31] Moreover, the business community itself has given a compelling call to action for business schools. In a 2010 UN Global Compact survey of over 750 CEOs, 88% of CEOs surveyed said that they believe it is important that educational systems in general and business schools in specific equip future leaders with the mindsets and skills needed to manage sustainability.[32] If anti-corruption can be viewed in the context of a sustainability framework then it seems a pressing business imperative that students learn about corruption as a sustainability issue in the classroom.

Regarding the debate about how to institutionalize ethics in the curriculum, the first position argues for a stand-alone course to be made mandatory for students and the second position argues for integration. This controversy came to light in 2002 when AACSB stated that mandatory ethics courses would not be required for accreditation. Many professors were furious, recognizing that AACSB failed to enact a policy about teaching ethics that could have had a substantial impact on student education. Recognizing that AACSB has considerable impact on the curricular decisions of thousands of universities across the globe, Windsor and Swanson drafted a letter to AACSB in 2002, which was signed by over 200 professors, making the case for the importance of stand-alone ethics courses. They conclude their argument for the importance of stand-alone ethics course mandated by AACSB Accreditation by saying, "Although one ethics course won't solve all ills, it could be the only opportunity some students have to grasp a saner view. It might also keep some of them out of jail."[33] It is this strategic concept that we believe should drive education about corruption especially given that AACSB Accreditation is being widely sought after in the MENA region.

Whatever side of the debate one finds most compelling, the practical challenge of implementation and institutionalization within the business school context looms large for most sustainability advocates. Jamali and Abdallah provide a useful framework to use in institutionalizing corporate responsibility teaching and practice within a business school context.[34] They refer to this process as "mainstreaming CSR" and provide a helpful roadmap for business schools looking to implement a sustainability approach. This roadmap will be a useful tool for designing appropriately paced recommendations for MENA business schools looking to institutionalize anti-corruption teaching. The three-step framework is illustrated in Figure 4.2 and sample activities are provided within each stage of the model.

MENA Business Schools in The Fight Against Corruption

Given the significance of corruption, the systemic nature of its causes in the MENA, and the business case to be made for anti-corruption,

Stage 1: Experimenting with CSR mainstreaming
- Identification of a core group of interested faculty
- Experiment with offering Ethics/CSR as elective
- Supplement course offerings through guest speaker lectures and events

Stage 2: Expanding the boundaries
- Solicit partnerships and funding
- Include Ethics/CSR as a mandatory course offering
- Identify faculty across different discipline areas, for CSR integration
- Supplement teaching with inter-disciplinary research

Stage 3: Institutionalization and anchoring
- Sign the UN PRME and consider its operationalization
- Establish a net impact student chapter in the School
- Establish an inter-disciplinary group from across the university with an interest in social issues

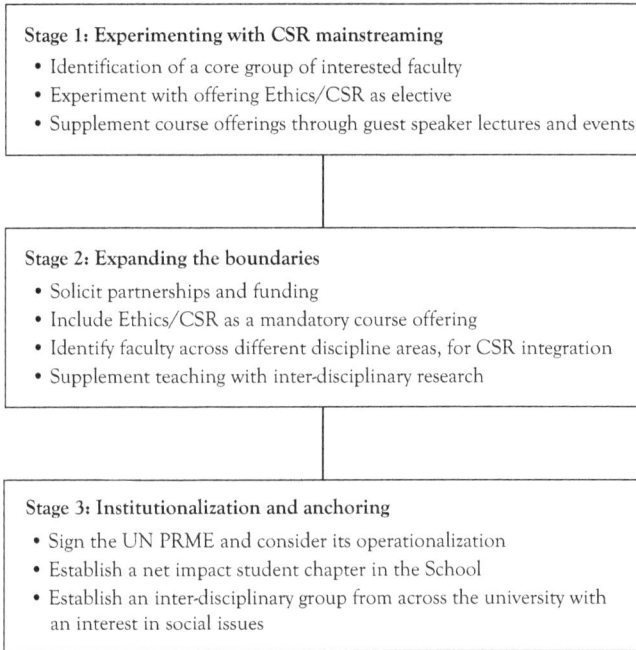

Figure 4.2. A typical CSR mainstreaming process.[35]

businesses in the MENA have begun to take a stand. There are over 250 companies in the MENA region that are active signatories to the UN Global Compact, which includes a principle to combat corruption.[36] "The United Nations Global Compact is a strategic policy initiative for businesses that are committed to aligning their operations and strategies with ten universally accepted principles in the areas of human rights, labor, environment and anti-corruption." Since its official launch in 2000, the initiative has grown to more than 8,000 participants, including over 6,000 businesses in 135 countries around the world.

Regional business schools are also starting to understand the importance of teaching business transparency. In a recent survey of MENA business schools, we garnered the following results.[37] The objective of the data compilation and analysis was to generate a report on what schools in MENA were teaching regarding the subject of corruption. The methodology undertaken for the secondary data collection was to use publically available information on the Internet to find out if and how MENA business schools are addressing the subject of integrity and anti-corruption in their curricula. Whenever possible, personal contact with schools was made directly, via email or a telephone call. Business school websites were used to get information about faculty and curricula. When the curriculum was not posted online, data was then compiled from email exchange, and the use of a questionnaire (Appendix A).

The first phase of the methodology was to compile a sample of schools. A list of business schools in the MENA was derived from Eduniversal, a French-based consulting company and a rating agency specializing in higher education. The Eduniversal ranking agency establishes an official selection of the Best 1000 Business Schools in more than 150 countries in the world, annually. Schools get rated and ranked in the Eduniversal study. We took the ratings for each school in our sample and marked them qualitatively as per Eduniversal's codes: Local Reference (1), Good Business School (2), Excellent Business School (3), Top Business School (4), Universal Business School (5). None of the schools in the Arab MENA were ranked in the 5th category. Only two were given a number 4 ranking, as "top business schools." The sample attempted to take at least one university from each of the 21 countries in the study. The only countries not represented in the sample are Libya and the Comoros Islands. University of Baghdad was used for Iraq, but not listed in the Eduniversal survey for 2011.

To analyze the responses from the website searches, questionnaires, and email conversations, Microsoft Excel was used. We first listed all the schools and then noted their country, their Eduniversal score, whether or not business ethics was taught, whether it was integrated or stand-alone, and made any additional notes given. We then sorted these responses with the data sort function in excel to tally the number of schools per sample that taught business ethics. Nine schools out of the 30 in the sample, or 30% of the sample teach some form of business integrity coursework. We then further classified those 10 programs accordingly to the Jamali/Abadallah (2011) "Mainstreaming CSR" framework and identified, based on the framework, what stage of mainstreaming each program was in. See Appendix B.

- Number of Schools in Eduniveral study, 2011: 48
- Number of Schools in Sample: n = 30, 63% of Eduniversal survey

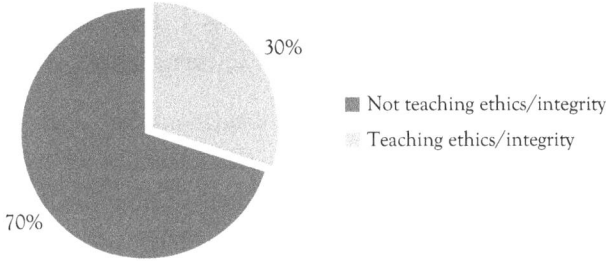

Figure 4.3. MENA schools teaching business ethics.

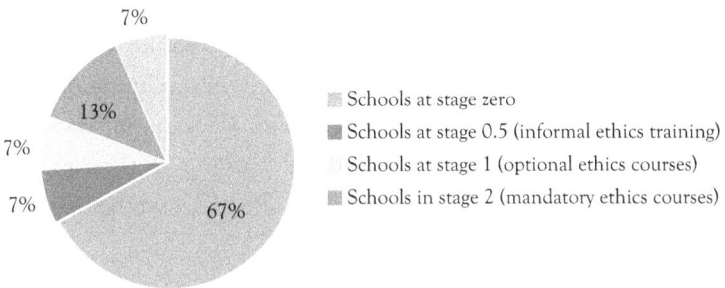

Figure 4.4. Mainstreaming stages of anti-corruption teaching.

- MENA Countries Represented: 20/22, 90% of Arab States
- Questionnaires Sent: 23/30, 76% of sample
- Questionnaires Completed: 6/23, 26% response rate
- Information taken exclusively from website: 18/30, 60% of sample

Below are the aggregate results of the schools in the sample.

- 30% of schools surveyed were teaching ethics or corporate governance in some manner, either integrated or stand-alone
- 44% of schools teaching ethics responded that the curriculum deals directly with teaching anti-corruption
- Number of faculty teaching ethics and currently engaged in the teaching of business ethics from this survey equates to less than 1 per MENA country
- Only one school in the sample is a signatory to the UN PRME (American University of Cairo)

Recommendations—A Business Ethics Pedagogy to Address MENA Corruption

The following section outlines recommendations for MENA business schools to implement curricula that adequately address the topic of corruption. These recommendations are synthesized from the business case against corruption, global best practices in teaching integrity and ethics in business schools, and account for the peculiar characteristics of corruption in MENA. We make a number of relevant suggestions that are likely to be useful for business schools around the globe in terms of tailoring their curricula to buttress the fight against corruption. These include: (1) mandatory exposure to business ethics; (2) mandatory exposure to compliance frameworks; (3) contextual and experiential learning about anti-corruption; (4) gradual mainstreaming of ethics, CSR and anti-corruption offerings, and (5) a five P framework of teaching anti-corruption in MENA: "Pilot, Partner, Practice, Promote, PRME," synthesized at the end of this table.

Conclusion

This chapter compiles the literature on corruption that is specific to the MENA region and specific to the private sector to attempt to construct a relevant, high-impact pedagogy for teaching business ethics in MENA classrooms. This effort is both timely and relevant. The time is ripe in the Arab states to introduce change. From Egypt to Bahrain, citizens are demanding and expecting change. The region is dynamic in a way not seen for decades. Free and fair elections are being held and the people for the first time in years are choosing their representatives. Now is the right moment to introduce a new paradigm of business ethics, integrity, and anti-corruption education to the region. People want democracy in government and transparency in the private sector as well. As indicated by the Corruption Perceptions Index scores from Transparency International, the region stands to improve the transparency with which it operates, both within the private and public spheres. If the private sector seeks to act strategically, it will harness the current zeitgeist sweeping across the region and build on existing anti-corruption platforms in the region. Moreover,

Recommendation	Justification/Actionable steps
1. Mandatory exposure to business ethics	Teaching integrity and anti-corruption is an imperative for business schools across the globe. Business professionals wield a tremendous amount of power, both to generate positive and negative externalities from their work. When business professionals act without integrity, they can cause significant harm to society and the environment.[38] Moreover, it is especially critical to teach business students about integrity, as they have been shown in numerous studies to be on average less concerned about ethical decision-making than their peers in other disciplines, and more motivated by financial gain.[39] Finally, if business schools want to remain relevant and competitive, they must train students on these contemporary, business-critical issues.
2. Mandatory exposure to compliance frameworks	Compliance frameworks are necessary to teach because trends in global business indicate a need for business leaders to think about issues of sustainability.[40] As demonstrated, corruption is a business compliance issue that can have serious legal and financial consequences. An anti-corruption agenda should be fully realized in the classroom as strategic business issue. This can be achieved by teaching it in line with strategic corporate governance, Strategic CSR or as a stand-alone course. Placing these topics inside a strategic management or in a stand-alone course gives them attention to pertinent business trends in CSR and anti-corruption, which are gaining momentum in institutional practice and in enforcement.
3. Contextual and experiential learning about anti-corruption	Instructors of ethics and integrity in MENA business schools should be concerned with contextualizing anti-corruption to the region, as corruption has its own peculiarities in the MENA. Currently, many of the resources that are used to teach anti-corruption in the classroom come from a Western context, where manifestations and prevalence of corruption are different than in the MENA. It was noted in 30% of the completed questionnaires to MENA business schools that relevant, regional, contextual material needs to be developed for the region. The literature on teaching business ethics is full of examples of the power of exposure to ethical issues via experiential models.[41] Regarding experiential learning, Sanyal reminds the reader of a popular quote attributed to Confucius, "I hear and I forget, I see and I remember, I do and I understand." This quote has been referenced numerous times to explain why it is that students respond better when they are actively engaged in the learning. Studies show that experiential learning helps students retain the material longer and participate more actively in the learning process.[42]

(Continued)

Recommendation	Justification/Actionable steps
4. Gradual mainstreaming	For the majority of MENA business schools that find themselves in Stage 0 or 0.5 of sustainability mainstreaming, placing anti-corruption curriculum inside the context of strategic management courses, which are required in all BBA and MBA curriculum, gives the subject required "air-time," without having to introduce new courses. To address anti-corruption in an academically rigorous manner using this framework, professors can use literature regarding strategic CSR.[43] Additional tools that can be useful are the business cases that have been made for anti-corruption such as the WEF PACI, the World Bank, and the United Nations. The *Journal of Teaching Business Ethics* is another great resource for instructors to use in forming relevant pedagogy and learning best practices. Since 2004, it has published over 24 articles that deal explicitly with teaching anti-corruption in the business school setting. For schools in Stage 1 and moving to Stage 2, a more rigorous pedagogy is recommended. Below are concrete examples of how schools can implement such curriculum. We refer to these recommendations as the five P's of teaching anti-corruption in MENA, "Pilot, Partner, Practice, Promote, PRME."
5. The Five P's	*Pilot Innovative Approaches and A Reality-Based Curriculum:* Case studies on corruption are plentiful and are a great starting point for trying to bring reality into the classroom. In addition to case studies, numerous anti-corruption resources can also be found from institutions such as: Ethical Corporation, Transparency International, Center for Private Enterprise (CIPE), World Economic Forum, United Nations, and the Organization for Economic Cooperation and Development (OECD). *Partner with Regional Business Leaders and Anti-Corruption Specialists:* Partnerships offer the opportunity for both experiential and contextual learning that is integrative in framework and approach. There are over 250 businesses and organizations that are UN Global Compact signatories in the MENA with which schools could partner. *Practice Transparency and Anti-Corruption:* It is important that students see these behaviors modeled and applied. The university settings should be modeling the way forward both in practicing and teaching transparency methodologies. If the business school is encased in a larger university structure, it can act as an advisor to the university about sustainability practices, transparency, and anti-corruption.

(*Continued*)

Recommendation	Justification/Actionable steps
	Promote Scholarship in Corruption: Business ethics as a scholarly field depends critically on the research of its leading scholars. If business schools make a commitment to teach business ethics, they must also accept an obligation to support scholarship in the field. As was mentioned in the notes of 30% of the completed questionnaires relevant, regional, contextual material needs to be developed for the region. *Join the UN PRME Network:* The value proposition for schools joining UN PRME is that it provides a framework for business schools to position themselves as innovators in integrating sustainability into management curricula and research. It also recognizes an organization's efforts to incorporate sustainability and corporate responsibility issues in teaching, research, and internal systems.

business schools should join this movement and introduce more ethical leadership in the classroom to educate the next generation of business leaders that can further an anti-corruption agenda. They can do this in a way that specifically addresses the contemporary needs of business and the needs of the MENA at the same time in an effort to be powerful agents of change in a region that is brimming with the seeds of transformation and revolution.

Key Terms and Definitions

Corporate Social Responsibility (CSR): The commitment of business to managing and improving the economic, environmental, and social implications of its activities at the firm, local, regional, and global levels. (World Bank)

Corruption Perception Index (CPI): The CPI ranks countries/territories based on how corrupt their public sector is perceived to be. It is a composite index, a combination of polls, drawing on corruption-related data collected by a variety of reputable institutions. The CPI reflects the views of observers from around the world, including experts living and working in the countries/territories evaluated. (Transparency International).

Rentier state: A state as one that extracts a significant share of its revenues from rents extracted from international transactions, such as oil/mineral extraction, tourism, remittances, etc.

Wasta: At its root meaning roughly translates to "middle," wasta describes the act of a mediation or go-between to influence decisions or bestow favor.[44]

Study Questions

1. How is corruption manifest in the Middle East?
2. What are its root causes?
3. Are business ethics courses in the region addressing these issues? If so, how?
4. What does the author recommend for the region?
5. Given the authors' recommendations and the practical application tools from the other chapters in the book, if you were to be a consultant for a MENA business school, what steps would you recommend the business ethics curriculum take to combat regional corruption?

Additional Reading

Arab Human Development Report (2009). *Challenges to human security in the Arab countries.* New York: United Nations Publications.

Beblawi, H. (1990). The rentier state in the Arab world. In Luciano, G. (Ed.), *The Arab state* (pp. 85–94). London: Routlege.

Doh, J., Rodriguez, P., Uhlenbruck, K., Collins, J., & Eden, L. (2003). Coping with corruption in foreign markets. *Academy of Management Executive, 17*(3), 114–127.

El-Din Haseeb, K. (2011). On the Arab "democratic spring": Lessons derived. *Contemporary Arab Affairs, 4*(2), 113–122.

El Badawi, I., & Makdisi, S. (2011). *Democracy in the Arab world: Explaining the deficit.* London: Routledge.

Hills, G., Fiske, L., & Mahmoud, A. (2009). Anti-Corruption as Strategic CSR: A Call to Action for Corporations. *FSG Social Impact Advisors.* http://www.fsg-impact.org/ideas/item/Anti-Corruption_as_Strategic_CSR.html

Hooker, J. (2004). The case against business ethics education: A study in bad arguments. *Journal of Business Ethics Education 1*(1), 73–86.

Kolb, D. A. (1984). *Experiential learning: Experience as the source of learning and development.* Englewood Cliffs, NJ: Prentice Hall.

Appendix A: Arab States: Summary Statistics, 2011

Country	Population estimates 2012[45]	Percentage of Arab world by population	GDP in USD 2011[46]	HDI rank 2011[47]	TI CPI rank 2011	Polity IV score	Freedom in the world
Algeria	35,400,000	11.16%	7,200	96	112	2	Not free
Bahrain	1,240,000	0.39%	27,300	42	46	8	Not free
Comoros	737,000	0.23%	1,200	163	143	9	Partly free
Djibouti	774,000	0.24%	2,600	165	100	2	Not free
Egypt	83,600,000	26.35%	6,500	113	112	3	Not free
Iraq	31,100,000	9.80%	3,900	132	175	3	Not free
Palestine	4,200,000	1.32%	5,848[48]	114	36	Not given	Not free
Jordan	6,500,000	2.05%	5,900	95	56	3	Not Free
Kuwait	2,600,000	0.82%	40,700	63	54	7	Partly free
Lebanon	4,100,000	1.29%	15,600	71	134	7	Partly free
Libya	6,700,000	2.11%	14,100	64	168	7	Not free
Mauritania	3,350,000	1.06%	2,200	159	143	2	Not free
Morocco	32,300,000	10.18%	5,100	130	80	6	Partly Free
Oman	3,000,000	0.95%	26,200	89	50	8	Not free
Qatar	1,950,000	0.61%	102,700	37	22	10	Not free
Saudi Arabia	26,500,000	8.35%	24,000	56	57	10	Not free
Somalia	10,000,000	3.15%	600	Not given	Not given	77[49]	Not free
Sudan	26,000,000[50]	8.20%	3,000	169	177	2	Not free
Syria	22,500,000	7.09%	5,100	119	129	7	Not free
Tunisia	10,700,000	3.37%	9,500	94	73	4	Partly free
UAE	5,300,000	1.67%	48,500	30	28	8	Not free
Yemen	24,700,000	7.79%	2,500	154	164	2	Not free

Appendix B: Summary of Research Findings

Business school	Country	Ranking per Eduniversal 2011	Main-streaming stage
American University of Beirut: Suliman S. Olayan School of Business (OSB)	Lebanon	Top business school	Stage 3
The American University in Cairo: School of Business	Egypt	Top business school	Stage 3
Kuwait University: College of Business Administration (CBA)	Kuwait	Excellent	Stage 2
University of Dubai: College of Business Administration	UAE	Excellent	Stage 1
King Saud University: College of Business Administration	Saudi Arabia	Good	Stage 1
Qatar University: College of Business and Economics	Qatar	Good	Stage 1
Sultan Qaboos University: College of Commerce and Economics	Oman	Good	Stage 1
United Arab Emirates University (UAEU): College of Business and Economics	UAE	Excellent	Stage 0.5
Ecole Supérieure des Affaires	Lebanon	Good	Stage 0.5
Queen Arwa University: College of Commercial Sciences and Administration	Yemen	Local reference	Stage 0
ESSEC Tunis	Tunisia	Excellent	Stage 0
IHEC Carthage	Tunisia	Excellent	Stage 0
Institut Supérieur de Gestion de Tunis (ISG)	Tunisia	Excellent	Stage 0
HIBA:Higher Institute of Business Administration	Syria	Good	Stage 0
University of Khartoum:School of Management Studies	Sudan	Local reference	Stage 0
Mogadishu University: Faculty of Economics & Management Sciences	Somalia	Local reference	Stage 0
CBA: College of Business Administration	Saudi Arabia	Good	Stage 0

(Continued)

Business school	Country	Ranking per Eduniversal 2011	Main-streaming stage
King Fahd University of Petroleum and Minerals: College of Industrial Management	Saudi Arabia	Excellent	Stage 0
Al-Quds University: Faculty of Business & Economics	Palestine	Local reference	Stage 0
Groupe ISCAE	Morocco	Excellent	Stage 0
HEM: Institut des Hautes Etudes de Management	Morocco	Excellent	Stage 0
Université de Nouakchott: Faculté des Sciences Juridiques et Economiques (FSJE)	Mauritania	Local reference	Stage 0
Universite Saint Joseph	Lebanon	Excellent	Stage 0
The University of Jordan: Faculty of Business	Jordan	Excellent	Stage 0
University of Baghdad	Iraq	Not listed	Stage 0
Ain Shams University: Faculty of Commerce	Egypt	Excellent	Stage 0
Université de Djibouti: Faculté de Droit Economie Gestion (FDEG)	Djibouti	Local reference	Stage 0
University College of Bahrain (UCB): School of Business	Bahrain	Excellent	Stage 0
Ecole Supérieure des Affaires d'Alger (ESAA)	Algeria	Excellent	Stage 0
MDI Alger Business School	Algeria	Excellent	Stage 0

PART II

Ensuring Dignity Thought
Business Ethics Education

CHAPTER 5

Empowering Learners to Behave Ethically: How Learners Can Find Their Way to Treat Others with Dignity?

Hamid H. Kazeroony

Abstract

This chapter provides recommended guidelines for educators who want to help their learners create foundations for anti-corruptive approaches in treating their organizational stakeholders with dignity. The chapter provides practices that can help learners find their own way to treat others with dignity. This chapter will review the background and urgency of the issue, ways that ethics-based curriculums can connect to learners' behavior through streamlining syllabi objectives, outcomes, and assessments. Finally, this chapter will provide recommendations for designing business curricula that can address ethics and treat learners with dignity through a multicultural lens with appropriate an approach to creating course objectives, activities, and learning outcomes.

Introduction

The 21st century ushered in a new era of teaching challenges for business educators in preparing higher education graduates with the necessary tools to ethically function in a multicultural and globalized context irrespective of the economic sector and country in which they serve. This chapter will provide recommended guidelines for educators who want to help their learners create foundations for anti-corruptive approaches in treating their organizational stakeholders with dignity. This chapter will review the background and urgency of the issue, ways that ethics-based curriculums can produce behavioral outcomes leading to ethical decisions by learners through streamlining syllabi objectives, outcomes, and assessments. Finally, this chapter will provide recommendations for designing business curricula that can address ethics and treat learners with dignity through a multicultural lens with an appropriate approach to creating course objectives, activities, and learning outcomes.

Thus, this chapter argues that it is important to uncover the reasons for addressing the relationship between learners' dignity, curricula design with an eye on ethics, and the way we teach or facilitate the conveyance of the ethical decision making. To establish the connection and explain the relationship between the learners' dignity, and teaching ethics through curricula design in producing the right outcomes (i.e., helping learners to become ethical decision makers), this chapter will (1) explain the terms, (2) scan the literature to explain why it is urgent to address the issue now, and (3) it will explore the relationship between the teacher and the learner (i.e., teacher approach in treating the learners with dignity while constructing the nature of ethics with respect to the learners' culture). Finally, through tying dignity, ethics, and ethical curricula design, this chapter will provide recommendations as to how one may proceed in implementing the process.

Operational Definitions

Defining terms, as the first step, will help us examine the topics from the same perspective with the same understanding and hence, eliminating the challenge of discerning the meaning of intended statements. As higher education evolves within the 21st century and technology can provide plethora of information to learners, *educators* are facilitators who help learners make sense of information and move from describing a phenomenon to evaluate its impact on how they use/apply the phenomenon on their own. In this context, educators are no longer the givers of knowledge or source of information but rather guides who help learners make sense of what they acquire—through class environment or other sources. *Dignity* is the appreciative approach, when interacting with others, to recognize and reconcile one's own values with others to assure the conveyance of idea is respectful of the receiving/intended parties. Dignity can be characterized as (1) fair treatment of others with respect to social justice as norms dictate[1] and (2) autonomy of the learners with respect to their human value and the nature of interaction[2] as they engage in the process of learning. However, the degree of latitude that guides (teachers) possess will provide the contextual framework for treating learners with due dignity in conveying the learning[3] of ethics in the proper paradigm so that the learner can correctly interpret each case and arrive at higher levels of analytical and evaluative understanding of it. *Ethics* is the practical application of right and wrong when interacting with others, to be respectful of others' values, treating others with dignity. Therefore, these ethical standards should be applicable to various cases where a reasonable person, irrespective of culture (or subsets) can distinguish between right and wrong and act on it based on a set of moral principles which keeps the good of others in mind. Teaching ethics like any other topic requires sensitivity and care in guiding learners to arrive at their own conclusion and; hence, we should be mindful of the level of dignity that is used when interacting with learners. *Ethical decisions* are those that are respectful of others' values. Ethics and law may not coincide and in some cases what may appear unethical may be legal and; therefore, it is important to follow ethics. Curricula design, for the purpose of this writing, includes any part of a course design, the course of study, and/or any part of the aggregate program design within a given domain of inquiry, which produces an academic outcome for learners. *Syllabi objectives, outcomes, and assessments* can be defined as the document/s which outlines intended topics of discussion for a given course/s (objectives), the synthesized knowledge gained by learners (outcome), through evaluative tools that can determine the degree of learning by each learner (assessment).

Background and the Urgency

A number of factors has contributed to the urgency for reexamination of the role of ethics in professional fields such as business and accounting.

A range of elements, from changing environment within which organizations operate to outcome of programmatic changes, within the last 20 years have provided higher level of awareness in addressing the need for a closer look at the role of ethical integration in business teaching in higher education institutions.

First, social responses to organizational behavior have acted as catalysts in the creation of urgency for integration of ethics in teaching. A recent study commissioned by European commission for Education and Training (2011) outlined ethics as a required training. Also, the need for leadership in global organizations and differences in cultural orientations have required addressing ethical dilemmas through integration of ethical teaching in business and accounting curricula.[4,5] Additionally, organizations, indirectly, might have been contributing to the rise of unethical behavior by accepting resumes from perspective employees who through manipulation of words have been providing unqualified statements about themselves.[6] Therefore, the ethical decision making process, as argued by Buchholz and Rosenthal (2008) has been left open to interpretation due to the fact that

> Science is reductionistic and has to reduce the factors that are considered into something that can be quantified and observed in some mechanistic sense. But most decisions facing business management are matters of judgment and cannot be reduced to a scientific equation (p. 203).

Therefore, integration of ethics in the decision-making process becomes important in addressing behaviors and highlighting its importance.

Second, the arguments and evidence have provided the necessary connection between the emphasis on ethics in teaching business programs, accelerating the urgency of the issue. The irresponsiveness of MBA programs to stricter legal business environment concerning ethics,[7] based on the observed unethical behavior within the last several years in the corporate world, has led to business schools to take on the responsibility of preparing their graduates to act ethically when entering workforce[8] to better grasp the impact of their actions as global citizens.[9] Empirical evidence suggests that once ethical training is integrated into business curricula, learners can benefit from better ethical decision making.[10] However, a review of some professional programs such as strategic management in tourism and hospitality courses indicates lack of sufficient attention to the topic of ethics[11] as of five years ago. Therefore, the need for closer scrutiny of the integration of ethics and teaching is required by academicians to make sure the issue is addressed at every level of postsecondary education.

The Learners

Few points can be established about learners. Ethical behavior, as learners' attributes, must be carefully screened at the outset of entry to any educational program, shifting the burden of addressing ethics from institutions to individual learners.[12] Despite skepticism by some that learners can and/or are interested in ethics at higher education institutions, the learners have generally expressed high degree of interest in honing their skills in dealing with ethical behavior.[13] Therefore, one can suggest that although ethical behavior may be viewed as learners' responsibility, by integrating ethical cases, business schools can help students improve their skills in dealing with complex ethical issues.[14]

The established points lead a reasonable educator to believe that although learners carry their own burden of acting ethically from the outset, based on their values, one should act on behalf of an educational institution to create a conducive environment through the creation of curricula (encompassing the programmatic, course, and lesson plans within each course) that can help learners examine the values and circumstances of various severities in different contexts as a way of practicing their skills. Such an approach by educators would enable learners to reexamine their own values when making decisions to make sure that such decisions can lead to the right thing for all concerned in a particular situation.

Connecting the Learner to Ethics-Based Curriculum

To instill ethical competency (skills, knowledge, and ability) in each learner requires understanding learners' values, beliefs, and possible ways that they can arrive at differentiating various scenarios, generating alternative courses of action, appraising each alternative consequence, and identifying the optimal ethical action. Through understanding learner's needs for tools and pathways in arriving at ethical decisions, academicians must change higher learning institutions to positively impact society at large[15] and build a bridge between learners' needs and regulatory requirements to make sure learners are successful in performing their job after graduation.[16,17] For example, simulations, scenarios, and cases can be used to help learners explore, examine, and reflect on different sets of circumstances and review the possible outcomes to better equip themselves with appropriate tools for identifying ethical concerns, examining each case from the recipient point of view, making better decisions that can treat others with dignity when rendering ethical decisions. Some educators and institutions may have already developed ethical curricula to address such pathway suggested here. However, one should be aware of the nature of changes.

When making changes in curricula, the focus should be on creating a cadre of virtuous students rather than simply teaching them to avoid the bad.[18] Therefore, as guides, educators must help learners, by using various andragogical facilitation techniques, develop their own tools in resolving the fundamental issues such as fairness, justice, correctness, and appropriateness that arise in solving ethical problems. Essentially, educators, as guides, must be able to design the process for connecting the dots for learners.

In response for the call to action, there is an increasing interest by business and accounting departments to integrate teaching ethics into each course.[19] The process of connecting learners to ethics-based curricula can begin with the thought that ethics should serve as the basis for the decision making in all economic transactions as a universal principle[20] and focus on helping learners appreciate fortitude, prudence, temperance, and justice as a way of introducing them to ethical behavior.[21] To illustrate the qualities required for ethical decision making, a scan of business environment can provide plethora of examples for learners' examination of the issues and they can be assessed for their ability to develop the mental models in dealing with such challenges at the beginning points and gradually shifting to the rationale for the process, and finally the reasoning provided to continually improve each learner's skills. In addition, colleagues have already explored other means of helping learners with ethical decision making and treating others with dignity as well.

Numerous avenues have been explored in connecting learners to ethics-based curricula. Integration of ethics into business curricula can be achieved through socialization with the concept of ethics, which may actually shift students' approach to be less lenient with unethical actions.[22] Changing MBA programs to integrate public management market efficiency with market failure can prepare graduates to better address unethical behavior.[23] The presence and consistency between institutional ethical standards, faculty engagement in ethical teaching, and course ethical design can help improve graduates' ethical behavior.[24] Developing assessment tools in conjunction with specific computerized presentation to increase students' awareness about the importance of ethical decision making in accounting profession in different countries has been suggested as a way to increase recognition of the importance of ethical behavior;[25–27] and incorporating it into social responsibilities in business education curricula to help remedy unethical behavior in the corporate world. Also, adding particular courses in the final stages of any business/management programs can help improve graduates' reflective thinking in making better ethical decisions.[28] In some programs, such as hospitality management programs, more rigorous ethical integration into curriculum has been advocated to prepare graduates who can respond to the industry needs.[29] Connecting learners to ethics-based training has been pronounced in recent years. Currently, *Financial Times* top 50 business schools include ethics, corporate social responsibility, and sustainability in their curricula.[30]

Various methods have been offered in connecting learners to ethics-based training. Some have suggested that including service learning in the curriculum can enhance students' positive perception of doing good and therefore acting more with ethical consideration when making decisions.[31,32] In addition, case studies with reflective journaling can lead learners to become entrenched in behaving ethically when making real-life decisions.[33,34] It has also been pointed out that using video case studies, presenting realistic work environment, supplemented with discussions would allow learners formulate appropriate ethical responses and practice the way each individual would take action to correct unethical behavior.[35] Some, such as Fleming, Pearson, and Riley Jr. (2008) have added experiential learning as a requirement for learners to become better equipped with practicing ethical behavior and identifying unethical behavior in professions such as accounting. It has also been argued that integrating cases at the beginning of each course can provide more reflective time for learners to examine, grasp, and follow ethical behavior when graduating and serving public institutions.[36] Therefore, there is sufficient evidence about the availability methods to connect learners to ethics-based training. However, the question arises as to how do we know that learners have successfully internalized ethical decision making and what evidence can we have as individual faculty and institutions that our learners would actually behave ethically once they leave our institutions; how can we assess the outcomes?

Connecting Objectives, Outcomes, and Assessments

Professional accrediting bodies such as Accreditation Council for Business Schools and Programs (ACBSP) and The Association to Advance Collegiate Schools of Business (AACSB) have created the underlying requirements in leading the way for integration of ethics into business and accounting curricula. ACBSP, in its Article II, Section I, item 3, delineates, as a part of its objectives, "to promote lawful and ethical practices" (p. 1). AACSB steps 1 through 5 standards, aligns desirable ethical learning objective with outcomes, which can be assessed and results can be improved through analysis over time (Rexeisen and Al-Khatib, 2009). At institutional and programmatic level,[37] using Ignatian pedagogical paradigm, constructed an approach to teaching ethics by applying "context, experience, reflection, action, and evaluation" (p. 453), which can serve to connect course and programmatic objectives to outcomes while allowing assessment and evaluation of outcomes.

In addition to accrediting bodies' requirements, colleagues have advanced ideas such as film viewing and discussions, role playing, guest speakers who are practitioners, journaling, adding moral reasoning to non-business courses as a part of graduation requirement, adjusting and integrating students' diverse value systems into universities' curricula, creation of overarching ethical consideration and assessment of its understanding with pre and post-tests, coping, modeling, problem solving (CSPS), simulations, relating ethical behavior to larger social needs within curricula context, and service learning have been put forth.[38–45] Natale and Sora

(2010) suggested creation of a link between ethics and all courses offered in a degree program, linking ethics to creation of knowledge by learners within a wide spectrum of learning. However, one should be mindful that efforts to help learners with ethical decision making should also allow for learners' own values and beliefs to be integrated in the process to assure lasting results by those who are learning rather than catering to the wishful ideas of educators.

Designing Business Curricula with Ethics and Dignity

Cultural context within which learning takes place, learning objectives are communicated, and activities are conducted must consider learners' cultural perceptions and orientation about the process and stakeholder expectations about the outcome transnationally and relationally. Cultural perception of the learner should be evaluated as one begins constructing the andragogical method of pedagogy for ethics. For example, in some cultures, it is customary to tip individulas involved in business transactions from government offices to expedite interactions and produce results. However, such behavior is considered unethical in most Western countries. Therefore, the curricula construct should be observant of the prevailing values underlying learners' culture. Consequently, learners' dignity takes the center stage.

Three factors should be considered to make sure learners are treated with appropriate dignity in integrating ethics into business curricula. First, curricula should be created based on a grading process which validates outcomes where learners, irrespective of their cultural orientation, can perceive values associated with grades in the same way; hence, the legitimacy of learning process differently, leading to different understanding of ethics, pertains to justice.[46] Second, depending on the supervisory nature of faculty who may simply attempt to seek faults rather than helping to improve learners' ability to improve himself/herself, learners can be treated with different level of dignity as they attempt to proceed through learning ethics.[47] Third, the process of teaching ethics should consider the rights of the learner and the teacher equally and as mutual relationship to be considered dignified.[48] The three principles can act as relational agents for treating learners with dignity. However, business curricula design should

also be capable of providing sufficient latitude to address cultural variation, experiences, epistemological underpinning, and the rationale for the
process of ethical decision making.

A Road Map for Integrating Ethics into Business Curricula

A roadmap for integrating ethics should consider five principles. First,
within global context, instructors must help students to follow experimentation, reflection, and conceptualization to recognize the necessary cultural intelligence required in realistically and correctly assessing each
stage in the cycle to arrive at the correct ethical decision.[49] Second, a new
epistemological framework to synthesize experiences and theories helping
learners evaluate ethical challenges with a more retrospective lens is essential.[50] Third, pedagogical approaches should frame teaching to inspire students by disengaging them from materialism and enabling them to see the
consequences of greed which lead to unethical behavior.[51] Fourth, curricula should enhance rigor in helping students make critical inquiry and to
conduct analysis and evaluation of alternatives to enable them develop a
better framework for making ethical choices after graduation.[52] Fifth, educators should be held accountable to effectively teach their students the
organizational context of practicing ethics and the organizational subtlety
that could lead to ethical players losing momentum and getting discour-
aged.[53] Based on the principles discussed, various techniques, as already
discussed throughout the chapter such as case examination, journaling,
simulations (just to name a few) can be used to help learners internalize
and practice ethical decision making.

In a discussion, at the academy of management conference in 2012[54]
the following emerged as techniques that one can employ to help learners
frame, reflect on, and move their thoughts to ethical action:

1. Storytelling: Providing consequences of each action, to help learners
   realize how decisions can yield different outcomes.
2. Engaging students in the process of thinking about changing their
   behaviors to make the right decisions by appealing to those students

who can act as cheer leaders encouraging other students to become engaged.

3. Provide exercises where learners have few seconds to respond. Once they provide the response, they should be given adequate time to reflect on their decision, analyze the rationale for their actionable thoughts, allowing them to begin reframing/refining their thought process to make the best ethical decisions under the set of circumstances.

4. When appropriate (i.e., when students are adults with experiences), use reflective exercises to reexamine their experiences to optimize their ethical decision making retrospectively and learn from the past errors to be better ethical decision makers in the future. Such an approach provides live examples and allows learning from failures.

5. Connect students to real situations such as current political, social, environmental, and other issues, and allow them to formulate appropriate ethical responses based on reflection and analysis while providing them the opportunity to think critically.

6. Connect students to real situation by incorporating community service, internship, and other such methods, providing practical experiences where students are faced firsthand with ethical dilemmas and can think through them with instructors to arrive at the most optimal decisions and develop the necessary mental tools to better address future ethical challenges.

7. Provide institutional level cases where learners can examine ethical issues from various stakeholders' perspectives to better grasp, holistically, the challenges with different ethical decisions.

Conclusion

This chapter examined (1) the importance of connecting educators and learners in a dignified manner, (2) making changes in curricula to afford learners opportunities to examine ethics from their own perspective and formulate solutions with educators' guidance, (3) role of academicians in advancing the case for such approaches, (4) role of accrediting bodies to promote changes to empower learners with new ethical tools for operating in their respective future organization, and (5) various tools that are available to help learners earn the necessary competencies to be effective ethical decision makers. However, ethics is inherently organic in its relationship with social, cultural, and technological changes and; therefore, tools and approaches require occasional refinement in education to adapt new ways of examining the changes.

Key Terms and Definitions

Educators: Facilitators who help learners make sense of information and move from describing a phenomenon to evaluate its impact on how they use/apply the phenomenon on their own. In this context, educators are no longer the givers of knowledge or source of information but rather guides who help learners make sense of what they acquire—through class environment or other sources.

Dignity: An appreciative approach, when interacting with others, to recognize and reconcile one's own values with others to assure the conveyance of idea is respectful of the receiving/intended parties.

Ethics: Practical application of right and wrong when interacting with others, to be respectful of others' values, treating others with dignity. Therefore, these ethical standards should be applicable to various cases where a reasonable person, irrespective of cultural (or subsets) can distinguish between right and wrong and act on it based on a set of moral principles which keeps the good of others in mind.

Ethical decisions: Those respectful of others' values. Ethics and law may not coincide and in some cases what may appear unethical may be legal and therefore, it is important to follow ethics.

Curricula design: Any part of a course design, the course of study, and/ or any part of the aggregate program design within a given domain of inquiry which produces an academic outcome for learners.

Syllabi objectives, outcomes, and assessments: The document(s) that outlines intended topics of discussion for a given course(s) (objectives), the synthesized knowledge gained by learners (outcome), through evaluative tools that can determine the degree of learning by each learner (assessment).

Study Questions

1. What forces have led educators to see the need for integration of ethics in teaching?
2. Explain some of the arguments in favor of integrating ethics into teaching.
3. How can educators connect learners to ethical decision making process and its importance?
4. How should curricula be changed to address ethical decision making for learners?
5. What are some methods that can be utilized in familiarizing learners with ethical decision making under different circumstances?
6. Explain the road map for educators to helping learners understand the concept of dignified treatment of others.

Additional Reading

Cam, P. (2012). *Teaching ethics in schools: A new approach to moral education.* Camberwell, Australia: ACER Press.

CHAPTER 6

Learner Autonomy, Moral Agency, and Ancient Virtues: A Curative Constellation for the Treatment of Corruption in Modern Workplaces

Sharon E. Norris

Abstract

Over the years, ethical and unethical behaviors have been "delineated in terms of vices and virtues."[1] The ancient virtues of prudence, justice, fortitude, and temperance have been connected with ethical leadership, and vices such as deceiving, lying, selfishness, narcissism, arrogance, hubris, abusiveness, document falsification, malevolence, and masked intentions have been linked with unethical conduct and destructive and corrupt leadership.[2] Virtue-based leaders create socially responsible organizations whereas vice-driven leaders sow seeds of discord and organizational corruption. Vice-driven misconduct has poisoned organizations around the globe with "devastating consequences for the entire social fabric."[3] Finding a remedy for the deficit of ethical leadership and organizational corruption is a paramount consideration.[4] In this chapter, learner autonomy, moral agency, and the ancient virtues are presented as a curative constellation for the treatment of corruption in modern workplaces.

Introduction

Over the years, ethical and unethical behaviors have been "delineated in terms of vices and virtues."[5] The ancient virtues of prudence, justice, fortitude, and temperance have been connected with ethical leadership, and vices such as deceiving, lying, selfishness, narcissism, arrogance, hubris, abusiveness, document falsification, malevolence, and masked intentions have been linked with unethical conduct, destructive, and corrupt leadership.[6] Virtue-based leaders create socially responsible organizations whereas vice-driven leaders sow seeds of discord and organizational corruption.

Vice-driven misconduct has poisoned organizations around the globe with "devastating consequences for the entire social fabric."[7] Waples and Antes posited, "whether organizational leaders perpetrate misbehavior or foster an environment permitting unethical conduct, scholars are left asking how to remedy what appears to be a deficit of ethical leadership in organizations."[8]

It was once believed that corporate leaders were the social elite who looked after the success of the organization with a commitment to the common good. Today, corporate leaders are viewed as narcissistic impression managers, who con their way to the top through self-promotion and care little about others. The image of the CEO with pop star, superhero, and celebrity status has given way to anger, frustration, and feelings of betrayal as reports of corporate scandals now dominate the business news.[9] In the 21st century, many people view corporate leaders as suspicious, dishonest, unethical, and corrupt.

Vice-driven and unethical leaders, especially when coupled with susceptible followers, create corrupt organizational environments. Organizational corruption has been described as the abuse and misuse of authority within organizations for private gain.[10] Where the abuse and misuse of authority occurs, unethical conduct spreads like wildfire. Corrupt leaders create conformers and colluders who either "go along to get along" or "go along to get ahead." In their research on acceptance and perpetuation of corruption in organizations, Anand, Ashforth, and Joshi[11] observed a notable and disturbing feature of corrupt organizations: employees knowingly go along with the unethical conduct of destructive leaders. This confluence of leader, follower, and environmental factors has been described as the toxic triangle.[12]

Recovering from the refractory disease of organizational corruption is more difficult than preventing its onset. Organizational disease disrupts normal functioning, and it is difficult to restore the system to functionality after such breaches have occurred. For this reason, it is paramount for corporate executives to establish and maintain ethical environments. Because the formal economy in the world's most advanced countries have become the breeding grounds for corruption, the time has come for business educators around the globe to respond to this crisis of leadership by promoting responsible management through business education and development. In this chapter, it is proposed that ethical conduct and ethical leadership requires the development of learner autonomy, moral agency, and the virtues of prudence, justice, fortitude, and temperance as a curative constellation for the treatment of corruption in modern workplaces.

Learner Autonomy

Leaders are expected to do what is right, promote good, and act justly.[13] Leaders are also expected to possess the capacity to learn and assess outcomes in terms of rightness, goodness, and justice. Personal evaluation and moral appraisals of options, action choices, and subsequent behavioral consequences are based upon feedback, which play an important function in the adult learning process. Effective leaders are efficacious learners.

Adult educators have long recognized the linkages between effective learning and self-evaluation skills, and adult learning is most powerful when individuals possess learner autonomy.

Learner autonomy refers to the self-regulatory capacity to draw upon both internal and external resources, as one chooses to adapt, change, and learn. The self-directed capacity to learn, or the notion of efficacious learner autonomy, shares characteristics with what Carl Rogers described as the educated man: "the man who has learned how to learn; the man who has learned how to adapt and change."[14]

Effective adult learners draw upon a wide range of information to formulate internalized standards, monitor their behavior, and evaluate the consistency between their personal standards and conduct. Using this information, they either decide to continue on the present course of action or make course corrections. Evers posited the "principle of learner autonomy seems to be required to balance error feedback."[15] The capacity for self-examination, self-evaluation, and self-directedness are characteristics of efficacious autonomous learners. Efficacious people believe they possess the capacity to perform tasks, can utilize performance feedback to make improvements, and have the ingenuity to surmount obstacles.

Efficacious learner autonomy represents a behavioral construct that can be enhanced with interventions such as through education and training.[16] In other words, people can learn how to learn. Personal responsibility, autonomy, flexibility, and adaptability are key characteristics of self-directedness among adult learners.[17] These same qualities are necessary for people who are facing unique challenges and making important decisions in the workplace. The capacity to learn may be one of the most vital ingredients for organizational success in today's knowledge era.

The salient characteristics of the capacity to learn, or behavioral intention to learn, include initiative, resourcefulness, and persistence.[18] A person who takes *initiative* is goal-oriented and self-starting. Once moving toward a goal, the person may encounter new situations or problems. *Resourcefulness* is needed in handling difficulties that arise. The autonomous learner is also persistent. As roadblocks or obstacles are encountered, there can be a temptation to give in or give up. Autonomous learners are not easily deterred from their course of action and will be *persistent* in the pursuit of goals. The efficacious autonomous learner takes initiative, is resourceful, and persistent in pursuit of goals.

Ongoing, continual lifelong learning is needed for business people to survive in the permanent white water conditions of the 21st century.[19] Without the capacity to muster the requisite cognitive inducements of learner self-directedness, people are ill equipped to withstand pressures of the modern workplace.

Tapping into the conative factors of efficacious autonomous learning (i.e., initiative, resourcefulness, persistence) is necessary for achieving goals, yet people with selfish ambitions and inhumane intentions can be persistent, resourceful self-starters who doggedly pursue self-interest at others' expense. Without the exercise of moral agency, individuals may stray from the path of ethical behavior. For this reason, it is important for effective autonomous learners to put goal-oriented, learner autonomy to work toward noble intentions and pursue them ethically.

Moral Agency

Moral agency is the "regulation of humane conduct."[20] People develop a set of internalized standards of what constitutes right and wrong behavior, and those standards serve as guides and deterrents of behavior.[21] When a workplace dilemma occurs, these self-sanctions regulate conduct.

Internalized standards and self-monitoring processes provide useful information for making self-evaluations that individuals respond to with either self-approval or disapproval and then these factors serve as incentives for further action.[22] When people engage in behaviors that violate their internalized standards, they experience *cognitive dissonance*. The theory of cognitive dissonance explains that people experience distress when there is a lack of consistency between what they believe and what they do.[23] People then attempt to reduce the dissonance by changing their behaviors so there is alignment between internalized standards of conduct and actual behaviors. Therefore, there are dual aspects of moral agency: *inhibitive moral agency* deters inhumane conduct and *proactive moral agency* guides benevolent behaviors.[24]

Moral disengagement refers to the process of deactivating moral self-regulation through cognitive mechanisms that remove the self-sanctions that would deter people from violating internalized standards and behaving unethically.[25] In toxic environments, both leaders and followers are susceptible to moral disengagement. When business people are morally disengaged, they are more likely to commit corporate transgressions and act reprehensibly without experiencing personal distress.[26]

Moral disengagement occurs through eight psychosocial maneuvers that include moral justification, euphemistic labeling, advantageous comparison, displacement of responsibility, diffusion of responsibility, distortion of consequences, dehumanization, and attribution of blame.[27] Research has shown that the propensity to disengage morally is malleable to external influences;[28] therefore, training employees to be on the lookout for modes of thinking that deactivate moral self-regulation may help individuals avoid the type of thinking that initiates, facilitates, and perpetuates unethical behavior and organizational corruption.[29]

It has been argued that people who morally disengage are also likely to quickly climb the corporate ladder. If individuals with the propensity to morally disengage rise through the corporate ranks faster than others, then it stands to reason that the individuals at the highest ranks of an organization may have the greatest propensity to commit corporate crimes and corrupt their organizations without experiencing duress over their misdeeds. These morally disengaged executives perpetuate organizational corruption by rewarding underlings who have a similar capacity to cognitively reframe issues, leave moral considerations out of their deliberations, and downplay ethical impact of actions.[30]

When unethical leaders use deceptive behaviors to push their personal agendas, they mask their true intentions by feigning concern for the organization. When they succeed in making short-term improvements, these destructive leaders create conditions where employees may be tempted to replace personal responsibility with conformance. Displacement of responsibility has been linked to unethical work behavior.[31] Anand, Ashforth, and Joshi described denial of responsibility as "a rationalization tactic where individuals convince themselves that they are participating in corrupt acts because of circumstances—they have no real choice."[32]

Employees at all levels need to become aware of the human capacity to morally disengage, and they need to be cognizant of how corrupt corporate executives are highly skilled at manipulating others into either colluding with or conforming to their unethical standards. Unethical and destructive leader tactics include emphasizing the importance of advancing the organization as the highest good, instilling fear over the failure to advance organizational goals, and rewarding those who place the advancement of the organization over every other priority in life including personal, professional, and spiritual well-being.

One way to cleanse the organization of corruption is to create an environment where moral agents thrive and moral disengagement cannot take hold as a dominant paradigm. Moral agents measure their actual behavior against internalized standards. When presented with a challenging situation, their internalized values and beliefs serve as behavioral guides and deterrents.[33] When the consequences of their behavior fail to achieve anticipated outcomes, moral agents reassess the situation, take responsibility for the consequences of their actions, and modify their future conduct.

As individuals resourcefully take initiative and persist in their pursuits, they also take stock in what they are achieving and evaluate the congruity of their actual behavior with internalized values. People who established noble intentions and pursue their goals ethically are strengthened by their virtues. They are sensitive to the temptation of their vices.

Ancient Virtues

Great thinkers across the centuries have discussed the positive influence of virtues on human behavior. In medieval times, the ancient virtues of prudence, justice, fortitude, and temperance were believed to elevate individuals toward good while vices contributed to human demise.[34] The virtues have been characterized metaphorically as a road that ascends to heaven and vices a road that descends to the depths of hell.[35]

Prudence

The exercise of prudence represents a distinct mode of intelligence that individuals draw upon as they deliberate and choose their actions.[36] Exercising prudence draws upon the cognitive power of the mind to deliberate.[37] Individuals bring their deliberations to bear on contingent matters through the exercise of human agency, or the capacity to choose, which represents an action of the will. The mind and will, deliberation and choice, operate together to exercise prudence.[38] Mensing explained, "prudence perfects the intellect and inclines man to act in all things according to right reason."[39]

The process of thoughtful consideration and choice of action represents the exercise of prudence, and this exercise is not a one-time deliberation that ensures ethical behavior. Prudent individuals continually develop their cognitive power of reasoning by deliberating over universal considerations and applying them to specific things.[40] Prudent leaders understand the importance of helping organizational members develop their capacity to deliberate well and make appropriate choices because no rule, policy, or procedure will answer all of the complexities involved in carrying out the daily work in organizations. According to Aquinas, "Prudence involves three acts of reason: deliberate will, judging rightly, and commanding what one should do or not do."[41]

When the essential function of top management is viewed as controlling the organization, their primary work activities revolve around organizational decision-making. Mintzberg[42] defined the organizational decision-making process as the work of defining problems, developing courses of action, and deciding on outcomes. Once decisions are made, policies and procedures are established to ensure the work is carried out according to plan. Unfortunately, policies and procedures alone fail to address every possible contingency and cannot solely guarantee right action. New circumstances arise that continually require thoughtful consideration and prudence in choice of action. Hariman stated, "Prudence is the mode of reasoning about contingent matters in order to select the best course of action."[43]

In contrast to top-down control, when the essential function of top management is viewed as nurturing the capacities of organizational members to collaboratively control the organization, the leader's primary work activities involve developing employees' problem-solving and decision-making skills. Such leaders know that prudent people conscientiously seek counsel from wise individuals with diversified perspectives as they search for the truth; they possess genuineness, openness, farsightedness, and a teachable spirit.[44] Effective leaders model the exercise of prudence and encourage organizational learning. Bass and Bass stated, "prudence is recognizing and making the right choices in specific contexts."[45]

Imprudent leaders feign deliberation in pursuit of disordered self-interests; they possess exaggerated egoism and exhaust human systems as they socially undermine the workforce.[46] Imprudent leaders fear looking like failures and endlessly deliberate over appropriate courses of action because they are more concerned with appearances than with truth. Their inordinate focus on their own interest creates distrust among their underlings. When leaders are imprudent, their behaviors are motivated by their vices. Without prudence, they also lack the self-control (temperance) and fortitude to do what is right and just. Imprudent leaders justify their vice-driven decisions by claiming that the situation demanded such maneuvering because the issue was political or their decisions were forced by economic conditions. It is evident when working with unethical, vice-driven leaders that their bottom line is not the financial statement but rather protecting themselves, and they will do so at the expense of others. Unethical leaders lack prudence and they contribute to organizational corruption.

Justice

"Justice is fairness."[47] The perfect act of justice requires doing what is good, rendering to another what is due, avoiding evil, and inflicting no injury upon another.[48] When vice-driven, unethical leaders take actions that satisfy self-interests at the expense of others, their deeds are unjust. In contrast, virtue-based ethical leaders who take thoughtful actions that give others their due and inflict no harm are just. Duska explained, "justice demands a person go beyond self-interest."[49]

In their book titled, *Ethical Leadership*, Mendonca and Kanungo contended that giving others their due goes beyond a legalistic concept of contractual rights and "includes whatever others might need in order to fulfill their duties and exercise their rights as persons."[50] The unethical, vice-driven leader deals unfairly with people and withholds needed help and support.[51] Baron stated, "injustice destroys people and deconstructs organizations."[52]

In an organizational context, justice "means to exercise a sense of responsibility and balance, in a fair manner, the rights of all the stakeholders."[53] Where there are organizational injustices, people are treated disrespectfully. Mensing reported that where distributive justice is lacking, there is also improper respect for certain persons.[54] For example, some unethical leaders treat employees at the lowest levels of the organization as though they are dispensable objects, and they show favoritism to lackeys.

Most corporate executives will proclaim a commitment to doing what is right and just, but the extent to which they actually exercise justice is evidenced by their actions. Havard stated, "justice emphasizes the need for good will, which is reflected not in mere desires or intensions but in the constant determination to give everyone his due."[55] Each person has the right to just treatment because justice is a natural right. Pope stated, "what is right constitutes the deepest intelligibility of human laws, and it is the task of human law to render specific formulations of what is right in particular contexts."[56]

Fortitude

Fortitude is "the courage to take great risks for an ideal which is worthwhile. A courageous person faces difficult situations and strives to act positively to overcome obstacles in order to do what is good and noble."[57] In the contemporary marketplace, leaders experience strong situational pressures that can make it difficult to maintain their commitment to do the right thing.[58] The person who possesses fortitude perseveres and exhibits "endurance against odds."[59] Bass and Bass stated, "fortitude is the courage to pursue the right path despite the risks."[60] When pursuing a difficult good, a person with fortitude has a confident tendency to continue forward rather than succumb to fear and despair.[61]

Lack of fortitude has been characterized as the "disruptive nature of the extreme emotions."[62] Titus identified these extreme emotions as (1) fear, anxiety, fright, terror, cowardice, timidity, and the pathologies of hypochondria, panic, and phobia; and (2) fearlessness, aggression, audacity, rashness, recklessness, and indifference.[63]

In situations where people are vulnerable, people sometimes experience emotions such as fear or anxiety.[64] Tillich argued, "anxiety and fear have the same ontological root but they are not the same in actuality."[65] According to Tillich, fear can be faced and acted upon whereas anxiety represents "fear of the unknown."[66] Whether the source of fear is known or unknown, fortitude is the capacity to continue toward the pursuit of some good in the face of difficulties.[67] When a person possesses fortitude, he has a greater capacity to persist toward goals.

People lacking fortitude are driven by vices, which have been discussed as cowardice and foolhardiness. The vices opposed to fortitude are fear and fearlessness.[68] Cowardice and foolhardiness are distortions of fortitude. The opposite of fortitude is cowardice, according to Newman.[70] Mattison stated, "the coward cuts and runs in the face of difficulty."[69] Another distortion of fortitude is foolhardiness. Mattison further explained that foolhardiness looks like fortitude because one continues to pursue an end in the face of difficulty but does so in a manner that disregards real dangers.[71]

Temperance

Temperance has been described as self-control[72] and moderation.[73] Mensing stated, "the vice of intemperance is directly opposed to the virtue of temperance by way of excess."[74] In other words, intemperance weakens the inner order of man whereas temperance strengthens him.[75] The person who possesses the virtue of temperance closely monitors both extremes of rigid restriction and indulgence because the manifestation of both indicates some dysfunction is present.

In the 21st century, some of the most egregious corporate crimes have been associated with a failure to live contently with enough and instead irrationally pursuing more and more. According to Mendonca and Kanungo, the practice of temperance "involves distinguishing between what is reasonable and necessary, and what is self-indulgent."[76] Baron posited, "immoderate appetites lead to greed, the modern day crisis for corporations and individuals."[77] Bass and Bass stated, "temperance is self-discipline and moderation of emotions and indulgences."[78]

Cooper noted, "temperance in the true sense of the word means moderation and keeping to the virtuous middle path, while avoiding *both* extremes."[79] In the organizational context, the moderation of ambition may be a difficult middle path to walk. On the one hand, an overly ambitious executive may push his or her agenda to get what he or she wants; at other times, the same person may refuse to lift a finger when others need help. These extreme swings between over ambition and refusal to act indicate a lack of temperance. Peterson and Seligman explained that in psychological terms, temperance has been described as self-efficacy[80] and self-regulation[81]—the ability to monitor and manage one's emotions, motivations, and behavior.[82]

Conclusion

Given the challenges that people face today, a foundation of virtues is necessary in order for individuals to act as moral agents and autonomous learners. Vice-driven conduct has crippled individuals, poisoned communities, and contributed to widespread organizational corruption. The development of learner autonomy, moral agency, and the ancient virtues, is a curative constellation for the treatment of corruption in modern workplaces.

The way many business schools have attempted to develop the ethical behavior of future leaders is through the addition of business ethics courses in their curriculum. Unfortunately, assigning readings and administering examinations on philosophical perspective have not been sufficient for immunizing individuals from succumbing to unethical behavior. Similarly, many businesses have created corporate codes of conduct to articulate organizational values and expectations but have proven ineffective in safeguarding against organizational corruption.

In order to remedy the deficit of ethical behavior and organizational corruptions, both business schools and business organizations will benefit by helping individuals develop learner autonomy, moral agency, and the virtues through reflective experiential learning. Experiential learning activities place individuals in learning contexts that mirror the real-world environment with all of its contradictions and conflicting priorities. When individuals experience the pressure to both follow their internalized standards and meet imposed performance targets, these experiences afford the opportunity for applied ethical training.

Reflective exercises embedded within these programs can also be designed to encourage individuals to openly share experiences of cognitive dissonance. Participants can personally assess their exhibition of learner autonomy (i.e., initiative, resourcefulness, persistence) as well as the extent to which their goal-directed behaviors are driven by vices and virtues. When they experience temptations to morally disengage, they can ponder what occurred, how they responded, and develop action plans to strengthen their capacity to work toward noble ends.

Learner autonomy, moral agency, and the ancient virtues are a curative constellation for the treatment of corruption in modern workplaces. Developing these psychosocial dimensions of human functioning and social interacting are vital ingredients for remedying unethical behavior and organizational corruption.

Key Terms and Definitions

Efficacious: Belief in personal capability to perform

Fortitude: Inner strength to face and overcome obstacles; endurance.

Justice: Rendering to others what is due.

Learner autonomy: The capacity to learn.

Moral agency: Self-regulating processes that guide or deter conduct

Moral disengagement: The process of deactivating moral self-regulation

Prudence: Deliberate reasoning to select appropriate actions

Temperance: The virtuous middle path; moderation

Virtue: Inner strength or power

Study Questions

1. What are the conative factors of an efficacious autonomous learner? Why are these attributes valuable for individuals in the 21st century environment?

2. Self-directed individuals who exhibit learner autonomy may be functional or dysfunctional in their use of the conative factors of learner autonomy as they pursue goals. What role does moral agency play in the process of moving along the path of goal pursuit?

3. How does each of the ancient virtues strengthen and preserve an individual's capacity to achieve the highest levels of human functioning and contribute to the development and maintenance of a thriving organization?

4. Complex problem-solving through experiential learning activities provide individuals with the opportunity to exhibit learner autonomy in the pursuit of individual and collective goals. During such activities, why is it important for people to reflect upon their attitudes and actions? How can people use this information to make personal improvement?

Additional Reading

Brief, A. P., Buttram, R. T., & Dukerich, J. M. (2001). Collective corruption in the corporate world: Toward a process model. In M. E. Turner (Ed.), *Groups at rork: Theory and research* (pp. 471–499). Mahwah, NJ: Erlbaum.

Butterfield, K. D., Trevino, L. K., & Weaver, G. R. (2000). Moral awareness in business organizations: Influence of issue-related and social context factors. *Human relations, 53*, 981–1018.

Confessore, G. J. (2009). *The role of learner autonomy in the reconciliation of cognitive dissonance.* In M. G. Derrick and M. K. Ponton (Eds.), *Emerging Directions in Self-Directed Learning* (pp. 77–98). Chicago, IL: Discovery Association Publishing House.

Havard, A. (2007). *Virtuous leadership: An agenda for personal excellence.* New York: Scepter.

Johnson, C. E. (2009). *Meeting the ethical challenges of leadership: casting light or shadow.* Lost Angeles, CA: Sage Publications.

Moore, C. (2008). Moral disengagement processes or organizational corruption. *Journal of business ethics, 80*(1), 129–239.

Rego, A., Pina e Cunha, M., & Clegg, S. R. (2012). *The virtues of leadership: Contemporary challenges for global managers.* Oxford: Oxford University Press.

CHAPTER 7

Integrating Anti-Corruption Teaching and Research in Management Education: A Framework for Giving Voice to Values Based Approach

Shiv K. Tripathi

Abstract

Teaching of anti-corruption in management and business education programs presents a challenge in the design and delivery of the contents. The varying requirements of teaching and research integration across the course value chain make the process further complex. The studies show that the teaching of "anti-corruption" should focus on the value transformation process in order to realize the desired outcomes. The situation triggers the need for innovation, not only in terms of content or pedagogy but also across the broader spectrum of education, including the adjustment of teaching and research subsystems. The chapter explores the need for value-focused anti-corruption education in graduate level management and business programs and shows how Giving Voice to Values (GVV) methodology could be utilized in research-teaching requirements of anti-corruption courses. The relevant literature has been reviewed to develop conceptual framework of the chapter. The chapter also captures author's experiences with the use of GVV framework.

Introduction

Corruption is often seen as an outcome of ethical failure, both at the individual as well as at the organizational level. The last decade witnessed ethical failure in many leading corporations of the world, questioning the relevance of the management models, practices, and behavior. Despite a strong written code of ethics, derived from sound stated values of respect, integrity, communication, and excellence,[1] Enron collapsed. The examples of Siemens or Volkswagen in Germany reveal that those who engage in bribery to win contracts, for instance, oftentimes devise elaborate side-systems of kickback schemes or front companies through which they personally profit to the financial detriment of the company.[2] The situation indicates the origin of the managerial corruption from the managerial behavior perspective, which in turn, is a product of the value system. It implies that the managerial education and training should focus not only on the desired skill-knowledge set but on wider dimensions of managing the business–society interface and its far-reaching impact. This, undoubtedly, requires B-schools to engage in continuous experimentation with novel teaching-learning interventions in developing relevant content and methods for teaching of applied ethics and anti-corruption-related issues. Despite the repeated need realization, unfortunately, most of the B-schools appear not to place much importance to mainstreaming of such social issues in MBA education. A survey of 1,850 MBA students in United States[3] indicated that majority of the students perceive the need for greater focus on social issues and business–society linkages in their respective programs of study.

Corruption, in its different degrees and forms, has been identified as a major cause of most of the social and economic problems, irrespective of region, country, and continent.[4,5] The businesses, if not done ethically, can be a catalyst for fueling corruption, thus adversely impacting its sustainability in the long run. Looking into the emergent need for mainstreaming anti-corruption issues in business and management programs, the anti-corruption working group of United Nations Global Compact Principles for Responsible Management Education (PRME) has developed a curriculum framework[6] for a systematic and scientific education of anti-corruption-related issues. The framework comprises of identified set of topics, cutting across the functional core management courses as well as the suggested teaching methodologies. The curriculum broadly aims at developing anti-corruption competencies among students studying at the postbaccalaureate level management and business education. However, implementation of the curriculum requires its alignment with the different education processes and subsystems, and that too without disturbing the spirit of mainstream management education. Anti-corruption integration in management education has a number of challenges in terms of how one should go about teaching anti-corruption and what methods and approaches are required.[7] This becomes quite clear that in teaching the anti-corruption, teaching method "must" include the tools that look into the value-change dimension of the target learners. In view of the required value focus, the PRME Anti-corruption Toolkit[8] also recommends the use of Giving Voice to Values (GVV) approach[9] as a teaching tool for anti-corruption education in management and business education.

The integration of ethical and anti-corruption issues at graduate level academic program should look into the issue of relevant knowledge creation and delivery, as the process affects the overall quality of the program. Quality of the management program is a function of the quality of the input and efficiency of the process.[10] It directly depends on the process quality, which in turn, depends largely on delivery effectiveness. While integrating anti-corruption issues in management program curriculum, it becomes essential to explore the required balance between subject-specific outcome and overall program quality and relevance. Further, the degree and magnitude of teaching–research integration varies according to the specific knowledge-skill requirement of a particular course of study. Given the high degree of variation in target learning groups' perception about ethical issues, which is mainly due to subjectivity in the interpretation of moral dilemmas, the dynamic update of knowledge contents becomes quite a challenging task.

In view of the multidimensional requirements of anti-corruption integration in management education, this chapter looks into the following issues:

(a) What are the practical challenges that trigger the need for value focus in anti-corruption education?

(b) How can the GVV approach be helpful in teaching anti-corruption in management and business programs?

(c) How should the GVV approach be used for accomplishing the desired course learning outcomes?

The conceptual foundations in the chapter are developed by reviewing the relevant literature on related issues. The chapter also draws insights from author's experience in practically implementing GVV in teaching ethics and values in a master level functional management course, as well as in using as a framework for doctoral research concept development on the anti-corruption theme and thus partly utilizing the exploratory case method.[11] The chapter, in a logical and systematic way, establishes a generic model for incorporating GVV based anti-corruption curriculum integration into academic courses at graduate/postgraduate level management programs.

Value Focus in Teaching Anti-Corruption: Practical Issues

The teaching of ethics, sustainability, anti-corruption, and allied issues in management and business education requires a holistic perspective. Business education should be seen as an odyssey toward personal advancement with balanced spiritual and technocratic behavior, as it can lead to responsible and noble management behavior.[12] The teaching of ethical issues in management requires proper synchronization in contents and delivery method. There has been considerable amount of exploration in the content and teaching methodology for searching the right content and right pedagogical tools for effective teaching of business ethics and allied topics. A survey on sustainability issue integration in business education[13] identified that B-school students need to develop skills that focus their attention both inside the company, toward daily operations and core competencies, and outside the company, toward the wider ramifications of business decisions. In addition there are also skills that traverse inside-outside boundaries. However, linking the required skillset to the teaching content and pedagogy brings a challenge in terms of balancing. In a critical evaluation of business ethics teaching in business schools, a study identified 10 challenging areas and four were related to teaching methods.[14]

Anti-corruption in business and management, being an allied area of the business ethics, also presents a set of challenges in design and delivery of the course. The challenges appear due to a number of factors including nature of the course; degree of fit between ethics curriculum and other courses in the program; and behavioral issues in terms of stakeholder value alignments. The issue of value alignment is directly linked with the methodology adopted for the course delivery. Recalling the Vrooms' classical valence expectancy theory of motivation,[15] it is evident that the effective teaching-learning of any new or emerging subject area requires considerable amount of efforts in delivery to strengthen both the valence and expectancy of the learners. This implies the need for an appropriate methodology that aims not only at delivering the content but also focuses on change in values toward perception of the subject issues and its implications in the real organizational situation.

Recent misconduct and highly questionable behavior has fostered considerable distrust, cynicism, and antagonism among the populace toward the leadership of virtually all social institutions.[16] A study shows that students with more exposure to the ethics were influenced in their perceptions of the importance of instrumental values in comparison to those with less exposure. At the same time it was also found that increased emphasis on ethics in textbooks and courses has had a significant impact.[17] Despite the standardization in curriculum and technological advancements, the student's attitude and values toward management issues are found to vary across contexts.[18] However, merely designing the course on ethical issues will not serve the purpose of ethics education unless it is supported by the sound teaching methodology aiming at developing the desired ethical values.

The study on a specially designed sustainability framework for MBA students relates sustainability with basic concepts and assumptions within the ecocentric, ecological modernization, and neoclassical paradigms to organizational practice and behavior.[19] Organizational practice and behavior both are deeply linked with the managers' values and, therefore, anti-corruption education requires developing a desired set of values. This requires a suitable framework for teaching and also a research framework for knowledge delivery and creation.[20]

Students' performance in management program is also linked to interaction between personality type and learning approaches.[21] Therefore, the teaching methods should be flexible to take the students' values to the set of desired values in a gradual and harmonized manner. This is also confirmed by a study indicating that the value orientation of the prospective managers should be an important aspect of their education and training as it is linked to the organizational culture and environment.[22]

The learning outcomes of the management programs mainly focus on developing the managerial and technical capabilities. Even the behavioral components of the program are often found overshadowed with the management skill focus. For example, one may easily experience in the actual classroom settings how justification of corporate social responsibility or ethical practices is established in terms of their contribution to tangible corporate objectives. It does not necessarily mean that the teaching should not be linked to organizational performance but at the same time also triggers a question of "how to set the performance indicators?" The same logic applies to the issue of anti-corruption. Should our focus be on teaching students not to engage in corruption while pursuing the organizational goals or to move a step further and develop the managers who develop the performance indicators that would not contribute to encourage corrupt practices? Here comes the conflict between the capabilities and values. The business schools need to balance the curricula to focus not only on developing skills and capabilities, but also cultivating values, attitudes, and beliefs.[23] The development of required capabilities along with the desired values needs a continuous interface of teaching and research through synchronization of content and pedagogy.

The management program curricula needs continuous alignment and adjustments to address the changing business requirements.[24] The multidisciplinary nature of the management programs makes the dynamics complex, as the need of course or subject-specific changes vary from one to another. Ethical issues in the management program should be integrated with the regular business courses.[25] When it comes to integrating the ethics or more specifically anti-corruption, it adds to challenge in an effective design and delivery of anti-corruption modules, which are aligned to the changing forces in the business environment. Looking at the fast pace of environmental changes and comparing it with the relatively longer course design-delivery lifecycle, one can easily sense the need for some real-time teaching–research methodology, which can bring the desired equilibrium in the process without compromising with the spirit of the course content.

Deciding the degree of localization or standardization is another important area of concern. The challenges from the ever-changing context require a balance between internationalization and localization.[26] Adoption from other contexts could be feasible for management development in the initial stage, but localization is required for ensuring the flexibility and sustainability of the process.[27] Experience shows that this requirement varies according to the nature and orientation of the course, leading to important questions in terms of "how much," "what contents," and of course, "which course." In context of anti-corruption teaching, it technically appears to influence the applied ethics domain and, therefore, requires methodology that can balance both the dimensions. Similarly, when the anti-corruption content is integrated in other functional courses like operations, supply chain marketing, human resource, international business, etc., the major challenge appears in balancing the content and corresponding course objectives. In the different subject areas, the plenty of anti-corruption-related study material can be easily found, but the question remains how to synchronize the learners' individual values with the required knowledge-skill value-set in the subject/knowledge area under focus?

The different reports and guidelines look into the issue of methodology and delivery of the anti-corruption modules and courses. NIZA (2005) manual, which is based on the experiences from the anti-corruption training sessions, suggests that the anti-corruption teaching sessions should be participatory and teaching tools should be context-specific according to demand and needs of the target audience. U4 Guidelines (2009) also confirm this and suggest that training methods on anti-corruption should be

(a) contextualized and enable the participants to develop and implement anti-corruption tools and strategies adapted to the local circumstances;
(b) participatory to engage participants in the learning process as well as encourage them to act and translate the newly acquired knowledge in their day-to-day work;

(c) action-oriented and problem-solving approaches should be used to relate to problems the participants are confronted with and allow them to use the knowledge and skills in their life; and

(d) maintain the level of motivation and engagement of the target audience.

Based on the review of the emerging issues, requirements for effective anti-corruption teaching method in management and business can be summarized as follows:

(a) Value–linkage focus: Should be able to condition the learners' values by harmonizing the desired core managerial values and ethical values.

(b) Holistic approach: While delivering the anti-corruption issues, the method should be able to relate to the existing functional area knowledge and provide the total picture of the corruption causes and solutions.

(c) Participatory: Should encourage learners' involvement in the process of teaching-learning.

(d) Context-specific: Should offer flexibility to customize the contents as per the local demand and need without diluting the fundamental purpose of the course.

(e) Real-time knowledge creation: Should provide opportunity for creating the knowledge contents by synchronizing the teaching and research function during the course delivery.

(f) Internalization: Should facilitate the internalization of the values that would provide foundation for bringing anti-corruption perspective required for managerial decision-making and ethical behavior.

The parameters identified above are based on the subjective interpretation of the existing knowledge and, therefore, are only suggestive in nature. The desirability of these characteristics would depend on many other factors, which can be judged by the course instructors in view of the context, requirements, and positioning of the course.

Giving Voice to Values as Anti-Corruption Education Methodology

Ethics teaching at large is often confronted with balancing the rigor and relevance of the course in management programs. On the one side, the course may focus on the complex philosophical enquiries[28] and thus positioning the course as applied philosophy course. Some students find such approaches intellectually engaging; others find them tedious and irrelevant.[29] On the other hand, those advocating the relevance focus may shift the focus too much on the practical management challenges, thus diluting the ethical spirit of the course. Also the issue of right level of ethical analysis makes the content and pedagogy decision difficult. For example, the average 30-year-old MBA graduate is not likely to decide whether to run that pipeline across the pristine wilderness or whether to close the company's manufacturing plant. One school of thought on GVV believes that instead of only analyzing the situations, ethics teaching should help future managers and leaders figure out what to do next.[30] The same applies in context of anti-corruption education in the management. It can be seen that building the strong ethical foundation is one aspect of the anti-corruption education while tailoring it to the graduate level program requirements needs something more pragmatic, with potential to demonstrate the tangible and real-situation impact of ethical or unethical decisions. This appears to the point where the graduate level anti-corruption teaching requirements seem to meet the purpose with the GVV approach.

GVV was developed at Babson College in collaboration with The Aspen Institute Business and Society Program as incubator and as founding partner along with the Yale School of Management. Drawing on both the actual experience of business practitioners as well as cutting-edge social science and management research, GVV aims to fill a long-standing and critical gap in business education. The GVV curriculum comprises of a set of exercises, questionnaires, short cases, scenarios, readings, teaching plans, and annotated bibliographies. However, it is interesting to note that the methodology provides for development of the context-specific material based on the active participation of the target learning groups. This makes the approach useful, not only in delivering the contents, but also in developing the knowledge-contents suitable to the need of a specific learning environment. This makes it equally applicable for the purpose of exploratory and qualitative research, aimed at behavioral issues.

GVV is an innovative, cross-disciplinary business curriculum and action-oriented pedagogical approach for developing the skills, knowledge, and commitment required to implement values-based leadership.[31] Emphasis upon the importance of finding alignment between an individual's sense of purpose and that of the organization makes the GVV curriculum distinct. Further, it offers (1) the opportunity to construct and practice responses to frequent reasons and rationalizations for not acting on one's values and framework to build commitment by providing opportunities for participants to practice delivering responses and to provide and receive peer feedback and coaching to enhance effectiveness.[32]

The instructors recommend it for its high potential in facilitating co-creation of contents based on active research–teaching interface.[33] Other scholars using this approach in teaching and research also confirm this co-creation aspect of GVV, i.e. strong bi-directional research–teaching linkage.[34] The GVV curriculum has seven foundational concepts, or pillars. The seven pillars are: (1) values, (2) choice, (3) normality, (4) purpose, (5) self-knowledge, self-image, and alignment, (6) voice, and (7) reason and rationalization.[35] These pillars form an action framework for students and practitioners to realize that it is possible to act on their own values in the workplace and to speak up when confronted with ethical dilemmas.[36]

In the previous section, our discussion focused on identifying and developing set of parameters desired in effective anti-corruption education. The present section focuses on analysis of the important characteristics of the GVV as anti-corruption education framework. Table 7.1 summarizes the desired characteristics of any effective anti-corruption education framework and shows how GVV fits as an effective teaching methodology for teaching anti-corruption.

Based on the analysis presented in Table 7.1, it can be seen that GVV offers a systematic and practical way to approach to educate the managers/prospective managers in anti-corruption issues. However, in order to adopt the methodology in the management programs, some important issues need to be addressed, which are presented in the next section.

Table 7.1. Parameters of Effective Anti-Corruption Teaching Method and GVV

Effective teaching methodology parameters	Giving Voice to Values (GVV) characteristics
Value–linkage focus[37,38,39]	• Aims to synchronize the ethical values with the required managerial values. • Focuses on learners' value development in a practical and learner-friendly manner. • Harmonizes the inter-functional and cross-disciplinary managerial values with the ethical perspective in a practical way.
Holistic approach[40]	• Does not restrict the contents and delivery in the subject-specific boundaries. • Facilitates "total picture" development in ethical problem analysis. • Relates the different aspects of managerial behavior with the learners' own ethical perspective.
Participatory[41,42]	• Provides for learner-centric education. • Encourages learners' active participation in problem identification and analysis. • Brings different viewpoints and perspectives in developing the common perspective on the issue under focus.
Context-specific[43,44]	• Offers great scope in designing and delivering the context-specific modules and courses. • Helps in leading the classroom discussion with focus on the analysis that suits the context.
Real-time knowledge creation[45,46,47]	• Provides opportunities for developing scenarios, cases, and other supporting material by utilizing the GVV questionnaires. • Could be used to synchronize the teaching and context-specific research requirements.
Internalization[48,49]	• Helps in internalization of the desired ethical and managerial values in a systematic and practical way. • Transforms the learners' values without any conflict with existing assumptions, values, and perspectives.

Framework for GVV Adoption in Anticorruption Education in Management Programs

Like the other subject disciplines at higher education level, the management education could also be conceptualized across the dimensions of teaching, research, and outreach. However, the nature and orientation of

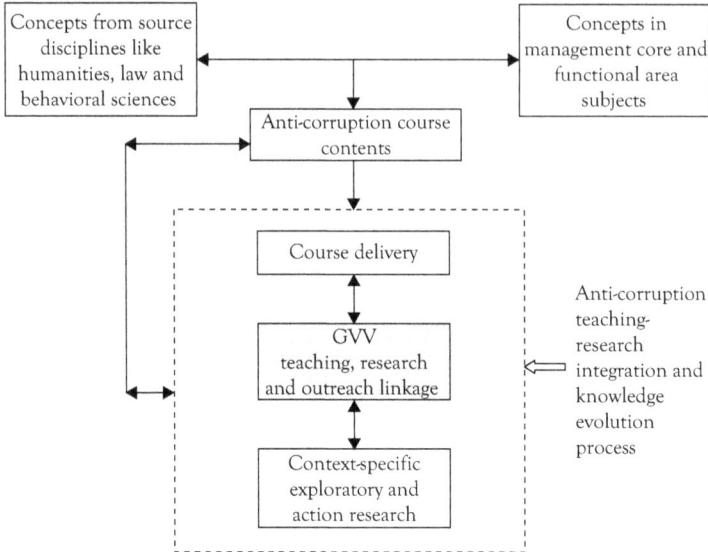

Figure 7.1. Anticorruption teaching–research integration using GVV.

activities across all these three dimensions vary greatly from the other disciplines, as knowledge body is multidisciplinary in nature and draws heavily from the other subject areas.[50] The inclusion of anti-corruption issues in the management presents the challenge in terms of aligning the research, teaching, and other outreach activities requirements. Based on the prior studies,[51] Figure 7.1 presents conceptualization of the GVV's contribution across these dimensions while designing and delivering anti-corruption modules in the management education.

Conventionally, the higher or tertiary level management education has three major dimensions of teaching, research, and outreach, which finds its place in the program design depending on the learning outcome requirements. When we design the content/course for any management or business education program, it becomes important to ensure a proper balance between course learning outcomes and overall program outcomes. This balance is achieved through: the knowledge-skill development requirement, derived from the stakeholder requirements; the teaching–research interface for course and context-specific knowledge evolution; and flexibility in the process adopted for course development and delivery.

As shown in Figure 7.1, the selection and design of the content for anti-corruption issues require a balanced mix of both ethical foundations and management core and functional area issues. By nature, most of the management courses fall in the interdisciplinary category. Further adding the perspectives from the humanities and behavioral science subjects like law, philosophy, psychology, sociology, etc. add to complexity of the course design process. This appears due to the fact that extra-inclination in one direction may disturb the overall purpose of the course, as sometimes reflected in the students' appraisal of the course. At the next level, the issue comes in delivery of the course. Even best-designed courses would fail to accomplish the objectives if not supported with the appropriate teaching methodology.

We have discussed in the previous sections how the GVV methodology can help in addressing the issues related to course delivery and design. Figure 7.1 explains the GVV's possible contribution in content delivery and creation by systematically addressing the teaching–research requirements. Analysis shows that the GVV can effectively help in anti-corruption education by

(a) Delivering the contents in the customized and learner-friendly manner.
(b) Integrating teaching and research by focusing on context-specific knowledge creation.
(c) Offering mechanism for encouraging action-research by involving students in external projects and thus integrating the outreach dimension as well.

It can be observed that the framework offers innovative ways to integrate the wide spectrum of anti-corruption course delivery value chain. The focus on ethical value development without losing the focus of required managerial competencies makes it a valuable methodology for the course delivery. The questionnaires and learners' feedback, particularly in the executive classes, facilitate real-time knowledge content creation and modification in the view of the specific context, where the course is administered. For example, while using the framework in the strategic procurement and supply chain course, we first discussed a set of two GVV cases in the class followed by recording the feedback on GVV question-naires. After analyzing the responses, we then developed a context-specific case by linking a local ethical issue to the students' responses. In the next cycle of the responses, we felt the positive improvements in the students' perception of the issues. At later stage in the course, we asked students to administer the same questionnaire to other colleagues in their respective workplaces and submit the summary of responses, which helped in integrating teaching with the research and action-learning.

Interestingly, some of the GVV tools have also been found useful for developing the research agenda on the anti-corruption-related issues by utilizing the GVV tools in the pilot surveys/focus group interviews. However, this requires some customization according to the need of the research area and participant characteristics. This is particularly useful for the research in subject areas like ethics and anti-corruption, which lacks in recorded context-specific evidences about the behavioral issues and practical challenges.

The discussion shows how GVV framework can be an effective methodology for anti-corruption teaching and research at masters' or postgraduate level. However, in view of the practical challenges, the implementation of the methodology requires some alignments and adjustments before use for content delivery or creation. Some of the important implementation-related issues can be summarized as follows:

(a) The students/target learning group should be prepared well about the GVV methodology before starting the use of the framework. This can be achieved by discussion and use of some supporting tools like practical implication analysis of the ethical/unethical managerial behavior, specific to the context. The focus of this exercise should be mainly to make the participants realize the basic purpose of the course and their possible contribution as a responsible manager. This has been found particularly useful in improving the students' motivation level and engagement during participatory GVV sessions.

(b) Often there are challenges with the executive education participants in terms of their accurate responses. Sometimes, one may find everyone reporting the ideal responses for the particular value-conflict situation. This is quite natural and varies from context to context.

However, with the adequate methodological interventions in teaching and discussion, the problem can be significantly addressed.

(c) The GVV comprises a large number of cases, scenarios, exercises, and supporting teaching material. The selection of specific material would depend on the course requirements, course positioning, target learning group characteristics, and the environmental context. This helps in improving the effectiveness of the delivery in a particular context.

(d) The degree of use of created material should be decided in advance, as with the progress in number of sessions, the instructors can develop a great amount of teaching material. However, it is suggested that the created material use should not be emphasized much initially, as it requires some fine-tuning before use.

(e) Finally, the pre-course and post-course appraisal of the students' value orientation is also suggested to be used as feedback for the future improvements.

The model of GVV adoption in anti-corruption education and suggestions for its implementation arebased on the theoretical conceptualization and experience in using the GVV. The implementation framework discussed above is suggestive in nature and aims to bring the modifications/improvements based on the experience of the scholars and instructors in different contexts. Also, during adaptation, the methodology can be taken as complementary to the other teaching methods/tools on the subject.

Summary

Anti-corruption teaching and research in management programs has presented a great challenge in terms of design and delivery. The lack of available context-specific material further adds to this problem. United Nations Principles for Responsible Management Education developed a comprehensive toolkit for mainstreaming the anti-corruption issues in MBA and other related master's level program in business and management. However, adoption of anti-corruption issue in the management programs required an effective teaching methodology to support the program delivery. The teaching methodology for anti-corruption should conform to the set of desired parameters. Analysis established how Giving

Voice to Values (GVV) approach can be an effective approach in teaching anti-corruption. Looking at the anti-corruption education requirements in the management, an implementation framework has also been suggested to effectively adopt the GVV by integrating it in the teaching and research activities. In view of the challenges in adoption, the implementation of the GVV framework would require some context-specific modification, depending on the course requirements.

Key Terms and Definitions

Anti-corruption education: Refers to inclusion of anticorruption-related teaching, research, and outreach activities in graduate level management degree courses.

B-schools: Are any business and management education provider recognized by law. It includes autonomous institutions, university departments, and institutes.

Course value chain: Refers to the different stages from enrollment to completion of the course including examination and evaluation.

Design and delivery: Refers to the need-based selection of the anticorruption-related contents and delivery methods while integrating anticorruption in management courses.

Giving Voice to Values (GVV): Is a framework, comprising of a set of exercises, questionnaires, short cases, scenarios, readings, teaching plans, and annotated bibliographies, developed for value-focused teaching and research.

GVV Integration: Refers to the application of GVV framework in a particular course for required anti-corruption teaching and research.

Graduate level business and management programs: Refers to any full-time, part-time, or executive business or management related program at master's level.

Managerial corruption: Is defined as corrupt practices and behavior within or outside the organization for private gains using organizational means and resources.

Process quality: Refers to the quality of teaching and research as measured against the intended outcomes of the course.

Teaching and research subsystems: Are interdependent parts of anticorruption education process, allowing creation of the contents and their application in the targeted courses.

Study Questions

1. "Teaching of applied ethics issues like 'anticorruption' in any management program presents a number of challenges related to content and pedagogy. The varying nature of different courses adds to this further." In the view of a given statement, analyze the possible challenges in anticorruption integration in different management courses.

2. Often it is observed that teaching of ethics and values in management education requires careful considerations in terms of balancing academic rigor and relevance. In your opinion, how Giving Voice to Values (GVV) can be used as a tool to integrate anticorruption issues in management teaching and research?

3. What are the key requirements for a pedagogical tool to be effective in teaching of anticorruption issues? How does GVV fit as a pedagogical tool on these requirements? Critically evaluate.

4. What are the important factors that influence choice of method in teaching anticorruption and other similar applied ethics issues? Do these factors vary according to structure and nature of the course? How can GVV help in addressing the required variation across courses while integrating anticorruption issues?

5. What steps would you follow to integrate GVV in teaching and research of anticorruption issues in any management course? What preparations would be required for effective GVV integration?

Additional Reading

Anti-Corruption Training and Education, U4Brief, CHR Michelsen Institute October 2007, No. 13, p. 2 (Retrieved from http://www.cmi.no/publications/file/2762-anti-corruption-training-andeducation.pdf on September 9, 2012).

Anticorruption guidelines ("Toolkit") for MBA curriculum change, Anti-Corruption Working Group, Principles for Responsible Management Education (PRME) initiative, United Nations Global Compact (Retrieved from http://www.unprme.org on August 28, 2012).

Gentile, M. C. (2010a). *Giving Voice to Values: How to speak your mind when you know what's right*, Yale University Press (Available at http://www.givingvoicetovaluesthebook.com/).

GVV (2010b). "*New Approach to Values-Driven Leadership Curriculum*," Giving Voice to Values Curriculum Collection (Available at http://www.aacu.org/meetings/psr11/documents/CS11.pdf).

PART III

Anti-Corruption Teaching Across Curriculum and Beyond

CHAPTER 8

The Cultural Dimensions of Corruption: Integrating National Cultural Differences in the Teaching of Anti-Corruption in Public Service Management Sector

Marco Tavanti

Abstract

Teaching and training for good governance and culturally effective anti-corruption practices require a multilevel approach. Based on numerous empirical and theoretical studies on the causes, nature, and correlations of corruption across countries, this study introduces an integrated approach to teach and train on anti-corruption. Building on institutional theory, principal–agent theory and cultural dimension theory the author suggests a multi-level and multi-cultural anti-corruption model. Through the examination of selected cultural dimensions in relation to corruption, the chapter suggests an integrated model for teaching anti-corruption in the public service management sector.

Keywords

bribery clientelism, collusion, cronyism, corruption, cultural dimensions, nepotism

Introduction

Anti-corruption teaching and training in the public service management sector centers on the understanding and practices of good governance.[1] Hence, the prevention of corruption—the misuse of public office for private gain—begins with the right ethical education of public servants. Integrity, accountability, and transparency are the main subjects explaining good governance to public servants and government administrators.[2] However, in spite of the mounting evidence of empirically measured correlations between cultural values and corruption perceptions, the study of cultural competencies and anti-corruption practices in public service education remains a marginal topic. A growing number of training manuals and textbooks promote anti-corruption practices by focusing on personal integrity coped by new economics of organizations based on financial and institutional mechanisms for accountability and transparency.[3] Indeed, anti-corruption requires cross-sector and multidimensional approaches integrating the shared responsibility of individuals, organizations, and institutions in the public sector, private sector, and the third sector. However, all these efforts and strategies to fight corruption would be ineffective without understanding cultural values and the influence that cultural dimensions have on the perception and practice of corruption.[4]

This chapter attempts to answer three questions on the relation of corruption and culture and on the teaching of anti-corruption practices to public service students:

- *Teaching anti-corruption:* How can we teach anti-corruption with its complex, multicultural and multifaceted nature?
- *International differences:* Why is corruption perceived to be more widespread in some countries than others?
- *Culture and corruption:* What is the influence of national cultures in the perception and practices of corruption?

We do so by exposing the main characteristics of corruption in relation to selected cultural dimensions and based on the author's teaching and training practices on public service global ethics. These questions on corruption and concerns on the relation of this phenomenon to culture and capacity building for good governance are frequent in academic studies along with world development and policy reports. Corruption can no longer be seen as an isolated unethical behavior of individual public servants without considering the effect of insufficient or inadequate rule of law and government control mechanisms. The assumption of this study is that public service students need to understand corruption in relation to systems (institutional analysis) and culture (cultural dimensions). Therefore, the author presents this examination of corruption in its definition, cultural aspects, and practical applications as emerging from effective teaching practices with American and international students. A review of empirical and theoretical studies of corruption across cultures is necessary as our students begin their careers and our societies increasingly become more international and inter-culturally related. Hence, effective teaching of anti-corruption and good governance requires intercultural learning and cultural competency.

Corruption is not just an ethical issue and its consequences go far beyond the criminal actions of an unethical person. Individual actions are linked to institutional actions (or lack of them) allowing, tolerating, and sometimes promoting small- or large-scale corrupt practices. Empirical research on corruption has convincingly shown that poor governance, typically in various forms of corruption, is "a major deterrent to investment and economic growth and has had a disproportionate impact on the poor."[5] Poor governance and corruption perpetuate poverty and inhibit common good economics and foreign investments benefiting the creation of sustainable development projects. We also know that corruption is not the sole responsibility of public officials but also of civil society and business sector. Therefore, effective anti-corruption strategies need to have comprehensive multi-sector integrated approaches. A key element of this is the ethical education of public servants. Master programs in public administration, public service, and international development should include in their curricula both theoretical and practical insights on good governance and anti-corruption. The effectiveness of such educational insights depends on international and intercultural competency. It depends also on the curricula articulation of theoretical understanding and practical applications of the complex phenomena of corruption. Effective good governance and anti-corruption teaching would also require being both culturally intelligent and internationally competent, addressing the interpersonal, inter-organization, inter-institutional and intercultural facets of corruption.

This chapter addresses the importance of teaching anti-corruption to public service students with an integrated approach. First, we need to understand what we mean by corruption and how the typology of corruption differs in the interpretation across cultures, sectors, and national societies. Second, we need to examine the causes of corruption in relation to the cultures of the agent, client, and agency. Third, we will consider some theoretical explanations on the influence that national cultures have in the perception and practice of corruption. Fourth, based on the empirical and seminal studies of national cultural dimensions, we will exemplify how power distance, individualism, collectivism, and other cultural values relate to corruption. Finally, we will propose an integrated model for teaching anti-corruption while fostering sustainable and intercultural good government solutions. We offer this analysis of corruption and cultures in the hope that public service managers, students, and instructors would gain better understanding on how culture impacts the perception and practices of public sector corruption.

Understanding the Nature of Corruption

Corruption has diverse interpretations across diverse cultures. What is perceived as "bad," "unethical," and/or illegal behavior in one culture may be regarded as a normal and expected "good" practice in another cultural context.[6] Diversity of values across cultural diversity is not the only issue in detecting corruption. Often corruption is simply stated as "illegal" or "unethical" but without a proper definition or classification. The teaching of anti-corruption for the public service management sector must begin with the proper understanding of this complex phenomenon. Transparency International defines corruption as "the abuse of entrusted power for private gain."[7] Similarly, the World Bank defines corruption as "the misuse of public office for private gain."[8] Unfortunately, these commonly used definitions of corruption do not reflect the complexity of the phenomenon and, without proper explanations, risk to err on the side of oversimplification. It is therefore fundamental to ask the question of what constitutes corruption in its typology and across national cultures. Even in those societies where corruption has a thorough legal designation, certain actions (e.g., lobbying) may be perceived by other cultures as corruption. This means that seeking a more international understanding of the nature of corruption requires an analysis on typologies of corruption across sectors, public functions, and national cultures.

Corruption is present in every sector, society, and affects everyone. We cannot adequately prevent corruption of the public sector without the co-responsibilities of other sectors and stakeholders. Corruption appears to hurt everyone and every sector that depends on the integrity of people in a position of authority. In government, corruption is manifested when private interests are placed ahead of the public good, steering away scarce resources from poor and disadvantaged people. In the private sector, bribery practices distort markets and create unfair competition. Corruption is even present in the nonprofit sector with corrupt charities, fraudulent reporting, and frequently undisclosed conflict of interests. The concept of corruption itself is quite broad and covers a wide range of phenomena. Some of the most common distinctions in corruption typologies are between grant and petty corruption and between episodic and systemic corruption.[9] Petty corruption covers everyday corruption that takes place at the implementation end of policies, where public officials interact with the public. Petty corruption is bribery in connection with the implementation of existing laws, rules, and regulations. Petty corruption often turns out to be anything but petty. It could be quite prevalent in certain contexts where demanding "speed money" to issue licenses to access to schools, hospitals, or public utilities is the norm. When it tends to affect the daily lives of a very large number of people, especially poor, it creates a "culture of corruption."[10] Corruption perpetuates and prospers in contexts characterized by lack of accountability/transparency and a sustained culture of silence. Transparency in government affairs can also overcome the culture of secrecy within bureaucracies to expose the administrative processes to greater public scrutiny.

Public corruption generally refers to public servant officials accepting, soliciting, or extorting a bribe. However, corruption affects every sector and it may mean different kinds of unethical and/or criminal actions. Corruption of public officials can mean not only financial gain but also nonfinancial advantages as in the cases of nepotism, patronage, theft of state assets, and the diversion of state revenues. There are many other forms of corruption and practices often identified between the lines of crime, unethical behavior, and cultural practices. These include favoritism, perks, money laundering, rent seeking, and state capture as a legal way of legalizing corruption. Although studying the complex typology of corruption could be distracting, the reference to these many faces of corruption are important in understanding the complexity and variations of the phenomenon across sectors, societies, and cultures.

Corruption does not happen as an isolated phenomenon. It is a global challenge interlinked to other international threats to our global societies such as human trafficking, illegal trade, and organized crime. Public corruption impacts human development, international cooperation, and the individuals who are targeted to receive humanitarian assistance or poverty reduction assistance. As Transparency International observes, "one cannot protect democratic freedoms and human rights without addressing corruption. And one cannot end corruption without working towards democratic accountability and respect for human rights."[11]

The Cultural Causes of Corruption

There are many causes of corruption in public service. Most empirical and theoretical studies of corruption identify the historical and cultural traditions of a country along its level of economic development. The governance capacities of political institutions are critical factors.[12] Culture is generally recognized to be an important macro variable that influences the perception and practices of corruption.[13] Far from being a mechanical result, the causal explanation of this complex phenomenon has been described with a simple formula: C=R+D-A meaning that corruption is the result of the level of economic rent (R), defined as something valuable to offer, plus the degree of discretion powers (D), and minus the level of accountability (A).[14] This means that (i) corruption is most likely to occur when valuable assets are at stake, numerous restrictive measures, rules, regulations, and administrative orders are too complex or too restrictive; (ii) Corruption is likely to appear when administrators are granted a large degree of discretionary powers in interpreting the rules;

(iii) Corruption will most likely happen when the above conditions are accompanied by a lack of effective mechanisms to hold administrators accountable.

The principal–agent model is often used to explain how corruption occurs.[15] Within the interactions between the principal (the government) that employs the agent (administrator, public servant) and the client (interest groups), corruption occurs under conditions of incomplete and asymmetric information between the principal and the agent. Because the principal is hiring the agent to pursue the principal's interests, potential moral hazard and conflict of interest often occur. The corrupt exchanges pervade when the agent encourages private gain in the making of public decisions. To be noted is that the principal–agent problem with such asymmetric dissociations is not limited to bureaucratic corruption.[16]

Culture interacts with the principal–agent dynamics as illustrated in Figure 8.1. The principal and the agent may have a shared national culture with a set of values and dimensions. However, their decision-making and performance for the public (client) may be aligned or not depending also on the push–pull influence of inner cultural values. The client's culture may refer to a national culture or other collective identities. Cultural values influence decision-making in public service or corrupt behaviors. These dances of push and pull factors affect individual or corporate

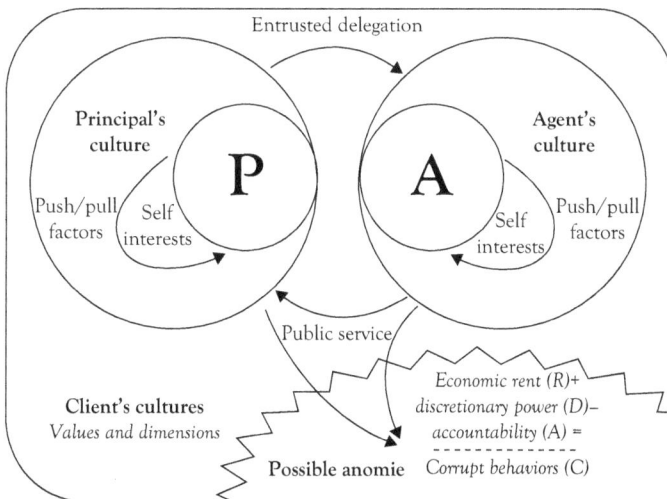

Figure 8.1. Principal–agent model for corruption and culture.

self-interests by legitimizing certain actions and discouraging others. When dissonances in the public service contract occur, conflict of interests and possible anomie emerge at personal, organizational, or institutional levels. When cultural values collide in a context dominated by high level of economic rent, a large degree of discretion power and a low level of accountability, corruption is likely to occur.

In their institutional analysis of the relationship between corruption and cultures, Soma Pillay and Nirmala Dorasamy argue that corruption is a multidimensional phenomenon. Following other studies in political corruption, they propose two fundamental dimensions of corruption: pervasiveness and arbitrariness.[17] They explain pervasiveness as "the degree to which corruption is prevalent in a given country" and arbitrariness as "the inherent degree of ambiguity associated with corrupt transactions in a given nation or state."[18] Their framework of analysis proposes that variations in accountability and discretion can explain variations in the pervasiveness and arbitrariness of corruption in different societies. These dimensions of corruption interrelate with their social and cultural contexts through the institutions and values that shape actions and influence decision-making. Social institutions and national cultures are therefore central to understand the dynamics of corruption.

Cultural Theory and Corruption Practices

Fighting corruption in public officials requires more than a strict policy regarding conflict of interest. Culture matters in the perception and practices of public sector's corruption. We need to consider how diverse cultural values affect expectations and perceptions of behaviors. Numerous studies have shown that the practices and causes of corruption are correlated to cultural values.[19] Although diverse national cultural dimensions have an effect on corruption, the institutionalization processes associated with globalization and location can strive to find a shared set of core values, particularly around integrity, transparency, and accountability. While corruption is a concept emerging from Western culture, any society understands the difference between practices that are acceptable and those that cause outrage. Every culture has a sense of right and wrong and has their own notions of corruption. However, defining what constitutes corruption is to some extent arbitrary and culturally constructed. For example, the giving of gifts is an important ritual in many cultures and the discernment of what may constitute a bribe difficult. Some would consider even tipping a form of bribe.[20]

Building on the various empirical studies demonstrating the influence of culture on corruption, we suggest an integrated model that begins with a value-based notion of culture. This examination of national cultural dimensions is primarily based on Geert Hofstede's cultural dimensions theory.[21] In the latest evolution of his model, Geert Hofstede, with Gert Jan Hofstede and Michael Minkov, endorse six national dimensions as cultural values in relation to:

1. Power as equality versus inequality
2. Collectivism versus individualism
3. Uncertainty avoidance versus tolerance
4. Masculinity versus femininity
5. Temporal orientation versus long-term
6. Indulgence versus restraint

He identified national cultural diversity by measuring the variances of 93 national cultures across these six dimensions.[22] His well-known computer analogy explains culture as "collective programming of the mind that distinguishes the members of one group or category of people from others."[23] Most people in the same culture carry the same values, with a value being defined as "a broad tendency to prefer certain states of affairs over others."[24] Values are therefore of essence to cultures and culturally driven choices. Cultural values are embedded in people's attitudes and beliefs. Although many other studies on the classification of national cultures have emerged, Hofstede's work remains the most widely accepted means of investigating a society's culture.[25]

Robert House's Global Leadership and Organizational Behavior Effectiveness Research Project (GLOBE) largely confirms the influence that cultural dimensions have on individual values and behaviors.[26] The GLOBE study borrowed some and expanded other dimensions from earlier Hofstede's studies examining a total of nine dimensions identified as power distance, uncertainty avoidance, humane orientation, collectivism

I: (institutional), collectivism II: (in-group), assertiveness, gender egalitarianism, future orientation, and performance orientation.[27] The emerged GLOBE's implicit leadership theory is relevant to our discussion on the cultural influences on corruption. According to this theory individuals have implicit theories (beliefs, convictions, and assumptions) about the values, attributes, and behaviors of people in power. Hence, societal cultures legitimize or challenge leader's behaviors based on their implicit cultural assumptions. Such implicit (non-conscious) values and assumptions affect an individual's motives for social influence (achievement, affiliation, and power) and interact with structural factors (structural contingency). Building on GLOBE and Hofstede's models, various empirical studies on the correlation of cultural dimensions with the perception of corruption clearly suggest the need to develop a general theory of the culture perspective of corruption.[28]

The relation and influence of culture to corruption has been studied from a variety of perspectives such as organizational theory, cultural theory, structural-functional theory, and political elasticity theory.[29] While helpful to understand some functionalist (practical) and individualist (moral) aspects of corruption, they do not offer a sufficient explanation of corruption valiance and prevalence due to institutional capacity levels and national cultural dimensions. Empirical and experimental studies on the causes of corruption have identified national cultural variations of values in relation to the values and perceptions of corruption across nations.[30] Culture is one of the macro level variables that influence the perception and practice of corruption across nations. Although it is quite difficult to measure corruption empirically, some scholars have been able to identify variables such as the economic development, legal system, openness to trade, and religious traditions, among others, to have statistical significance in the explanation of variance of corruption across nations, regions, and cultures.[31] "Countries with Protestant traditions, histories of British rule, more developed economies, and (probably) higher imports were less 'corrupt'."[32]

Studies have also shown how corruption is correlated to economic, educational, public culture, organizational, judicial, and political measures.[33] However, a very limited number of studies have been able to identify national and societal cultures as antecedent for corruption. Such a distinction is fundamental, as prescriptions for remedies on corruption may need different solutions and strategies across cultural variations. Any legal, economic, management, and accountability approach to fight corruption would require an attentive consideration of the underlying factors determined by cultural dimensions. Effective intervention in corrupt behaviors, similar to effective teaching and training methods on anticorruption, needs to have a comprehensive and multilayered approach. In other words, cultural dimensions need to be integrated as anteceding factors along macro level factors (economy, politics, legal, education, social systems) and micro level factors (pervasiveness, accountability, arbitrariness, and transparency).

The perspective of these seminal and comprehensive studies on national and societal cultural dimensions emerges from an institutional perspective. Subsequent studies have shown that the government corruption in relation to dynamics across nations is best explained by institutional theory.[34] Therefore, before we examine the selected cultural dimensions in relation to national perception and practices of corruption we need to understand institutional theory. This is a fundamental step also in effective anticorruption teaching and training. Institutional theory is particularly helpful to explain the deeper relation that culture has on corruption. We cannot dismiss the fact that some clear correlations exist between culture and corruption. However, to merely think that certain national cultures are prone to corrupt practices without considering other macro- and micro level factors is a simplistic explanation to a complex phenomenon.

Institutional theory is a helpful approach to explain individual actions, administrative performance, and institutional practices. In relation to corruption, institutional theory clearly resembles Durkheim's sociological theory on "anomie."[35] Although anomie theory does not explain per se the relation and influence of culture in corrupt practices, it does offer a lucid explanation of the weakening of cultural values and societal norms. This phenomenon is often visible in societal rapid changes and it is characterized by deinstitutionalization of the preexisting normative control systems. The tension that societal changes create is often recognized as a duality between traditional normative and modernity expectations. Public service students and international development professionals alike need to be equipped with the capacity to understand corruption from an institutional anomie and cultural change standpoint. An integrated understanding of the nature of corruption requires an analysis of national macro cultural dimensions in relation to other macro- and micro level factors. Although no national culture is exempt from corruption, the variations on the perceptions and practices of corruptions across cultural lines requires a more careful consideration. It requires reviewing the value assumptions in cultures and how they affect institutional progress and institutional anomie.[36]

Cultural Dimensions of Corruption

For the purpose of this examination of the relation of culture and corruption we will concentrate on Hofstede's original model with the four core national cultural dimensions known as power distance, uncertainty avoidance, individualism/collectivism, and masculinity/femininity. Although these dimensions have been expanded from the original studies published in Culture's Consequences (1980), and further elaborated in the GLOBE and subsequent studies, they remain the most widely accepted cultural dimensions. They have been subject of numerous analyses on their correlation with the corruption perception index (CPI) and other measures of corruption.[37]

Power Distance Index (PDI) and Corruption

Power distance is an important cultural dimension in the perceptions and practices of corruption in a particular country. A significant level of power distance in a country implies fewer checks and balances against power abuse and power is associated more with "privilege" than "responsibility." Power distance is defined as "the extent to which the less powerful members of institutions and organizations within a country expect and accept that power is distributed unequally."[38] In relation to public service, PDI measures the degree to which members of a department or country expect and agree that power should be stratified and concentrated at higher levels of governance. The PDI is not an objective difference in power distribution, but the country average in the perception and degree of tolerance of unequal distribution and utilization of power.

In low power distance (low PDI) countries, people expect and accept power relations that are more consultative or democratic and they are related more informally with authority. Subordinates are more likely to challenge authority, demand their rights, and criticize the decision making of those in power. Low PDI societies expect and accept more equal power relations in more consultative and democratic practices. They will be more likely to monitor, critique, and challenge the decision making of institutions and people in power. The 10 third countries with the lowest PDI include Austria, Israel, Denmark, New Zealand, Switzerland (Ge), Ireland, Sweden, Norway, Finland, Great Britain, Germany, Canada, and the United States.[39]

In high power distance (high PDI) countries, people expect and accept power relations that are more autocratic and paternalistic. Subordinates are more likely to accept the power of others simply based on where they status and formal position. They acknowledge and respect the actions and decisions of institutions and people in power simply based on their subordinate position in the hierarchy of an organization or political structure of a country. The top third countries with the highest PDI include Malaysia, Slovakia, Guatemala, Panama, Philippines, Russia, Romania, Serbia, Suriname, Mexico, China, India, Singapore, and other Arabic and West African countries.[40]

Empirical studies testing the correlation between power distance (PDI) and corruption perceptions (CPI) show that high PDI societies result in more corruption cases.[41] As in the famous aphorism "power tends to corrupt and absolute power corrupt absolutely." Large power distance means fewer checks and balances on the use of power and the possibility of more public servants to use their publicly entrusted positions to enrich themselves. High PDI means that corruption situations, which undermine the rights and equality of people, are more tolerated because the country itself tolerates inequality and authoritarianism. Hence, scandals and power abuses occurring in high PDI contexts tend to be covered up and tolerated more than in low PDI contexts. Power and culture also play a role in the in-group and out-group performances. Powerful members in high PDI countries may try to increase the power and influence of their in-group much more than ordinary people in the out-groups. They may do so even through corruption as this is "expected" of them.

In addition, the laws and regulations in high PDI countries may be set as advantageous for powerful people making situations of corruption at easy reach.

The institutions and organizations of high PDI societies are usually characterized by a strong respect for authority and centralized decision-making. Subordinates do not challenge authority and change is achieved only by revolutions often characterized by violence, resistance, and repression. Political leaders in those high PDI societies base their powers on family or friends and citizens and their relations with citizens are often characterized by emotions. Civil servants and elected officials in high PDI countries enjoy a significant degree of autonomy from public pressure resulting in higher level of discretion and arbitrariness. It should be noted that unequal distribution in public services, typical in high PDI countries, are often attributed to expectations and norms in international relation and not necessarily related to hopes for individual financial gains.

Uncertainty Avoidance Index and Corruption

The second dimension, the uncertainty avoidance index (UAI), measures a society's (in)tolerance for uncertainty and ambiguity. Hofstede defines uncertainty avoidance as "the extent to which the members of a culture feel threatened by ambiguous or unknown situations."[42] It reflects the extent to which members of a society attempt to cope with anxiety by minimizing uncertainty, the occurrence of unknown and unusual circumstances. People in cultures with high uncertainty avoidance (high UAI) tend to manage or avoid risks, and proceed with changes with carefully planned strategies. They implement highly structured organizational activities and valuing rules and regulations while inhibiting ambitions and discouraging fast changes. On the contrary, people and cultures with low uncertainty avoidance (low UAI) accept and are more tolerant of change, feel comfortable in unstructured situations, and try to have as few rules as possible.

As high UAI cultures are generally characterized by highly structured and regulated organizational activities they would logically leave little room for corrupt activities. However, if the formal rules do not specifically define "inappropriate behaviors" financial auditors are less likely to challenge the manager. Also, there is a possibility that high UAI (especially when combined with high IND) may urge public servants to the creation of wealth, including illicit wealth creation, as a way to diminish uncertainty and maximize financial security. Countries with low UAI include Denmark, Singapore, Sweden, Hong Kong, Vietnam, China, Ireland, Great Britain, Malaysia, India, Philippines, and the United States.[43] Countries with high UAI include Greece, Portugal, Guatemala, Uruguay, Belgium, Malta, Russia, El Salvador, Poland, Japan, and Serbia.[44]

Some have argued that within those societies where a "large gap is perceived to exist between the degree of uncertainty avoidance desired (*valued*) and the uncertainty avoidance provided by the legal structure on commercial and public sector activities (*practice*)" corruption may be seen as a tool for restoring fairness.[45] Other strategies for reduced uncertainty may include bribery, fraud, and political corruption as a way to establish a favorable and reliable relation with politician or public service administrator.

Individualism vs. Collectivism (IDV) and Corruption

Extreme individualism and extreme collectivism are the opposite poles of a second most important global dimension of national cultures, after power distance. The individualism (IDV) index measures the degree of individualism (independence and freedom) versus collectivism (integration and loyalty). Hofstede defines this dimension as follows: "Individualism pertains to societies in which the ties between individuals are loose: everyone is expected to look after him- or herself and his or her immediate family. Collectivism as its opposite pertains to societies in which people from birth onward are integrated into strong, cohesive, in-groups, which throughout people's lifetime continue to protect them in exchange of unquestioning loyalty."[46] In individualistic societies, the stress is put on personal achievements and individual rights. People are expected to stand up for themselves and their immediate family, and to choose their own affiliations. In contrast, in collectivist societies, individuals act predominantly as members of a life-long and cohesive group or organization with mutual expectations of protection, loyalty, and special treatments for the in-group member of the family, organization or society. The strong cohesion of in-group dynamics goes hand in hand with the exclusion of members of other groups.[47]

Among the various key differences between collectivist and individualist societies is their relation to harmony, respect, and honesty. In collectivist societies and institutions (e.g., family), "harmony should always be maintained and direct confrontations avoided." On the contrary, in individualistic societies "speaking one's mind is a characteristic of an honest person."[48] In the workplaces of collectivist societies employees are members of in-groups that will pursue the in-group's interests, management is management of individuals and in-group customers get special treatments (particularism). In the workplaces of individualist societies employees are "economic persons" who will pursue the employer's interest if it coincides with their self-interests, management is management of individuals and every customer should get the same treatment (universalism).[49]

The GLOBE study builds on Hofstede IDV dimension but specifies it as institutional collectivism and in-group collectivism. Institutional collectivism refers to the degree in which a society, institution, or organization practices encourage and reward collective distribution of resources and collective action (e.g., group rewards rather than individual rewards). In-group collectivism refers to the degree to which individuals express pride, loyalty, and cohesiveness in their organizations and families. "Organizations in which members hold loyalty more to the organization rather than to personal gain would be an example of high in-group collectivism."[50] The GLOBE study contributes to understanding the nature of accountability and how it varies in individualistic and collective societies. Individualistic cultures are more likely to rest accountability on the responsibility of individuals. Hence, clear documentations with lists of signatures and clear job descriptions and reporting would be essential to establishing individual accountability and creating lines of communication. On the other hand, accountability (and therefore blame) in collective cultures would be more likely to rest in groups and rarely traceable to individuals. Hence, written documents and long lists of signatures would rarely be used.[51]

Masculinity vs. Femininity (MAS) and Corruption

This dimension is not about gender but desirability of assertive behavior against the desirability of modest behavior. Because of the obvious gender generalizations implied in this terminology, users of Hofstede's work sometimes prefer to describe this dimension as Quantity of Life vs. Quality of Life.[52] Although most men exemplify the "masculinity" characteristics, the cultural behaviors expressed by this dimension are relative and gender neutral. Hofstede defines this dimension as follows: "A society is called masculine when emotional gender roles are clearly distinct: men are supposed to be assertive, tough, and focused on material success, whereas women are supposed to be more modest, tender and concerned with the quality of life. A society is called feminine when emotional gender roles overlap: both men and women are supposed to be modest, tender, and concerned with the quality of life."[53]

Another confusion in the literature is between masculinity/femininity with individualism/collectivism. These dimensions are related but distinguished as masculinity/femininity are more about a stress on ego and on relationships.[54] From a government and public service standpoint, feminine societies are characterized by welfare systems with a regulated system of assistance to the poor and marginalized sectors of society. Masculine societies on the other hand are better characterized by performance and a general support of the strong. Feminine cultures are characteristic of more permissive societies while masculine cultures are corrective societies. Feminine cultures place more value on relationships and quality of life whereas masculine cultures value competitiveness, assertiveness, materialism, ambition, and power. In feminine workplaces, management is done through intuition and consensus while masculine workplaces are decisive and aggressive. In feminine culture people work in order to live (they value leisure over money) while in masculine cultures people live in order to work (they value money over leisure). Feminine cultures expect rewards based on equality while masculine cultures expect them based on equity.[55]

GLOBE distinguished this dimension into Gender Egalitarianism (the degree to which a collective minimizes gender inequality) and Assertiveness (the degree to which individuals are assertive, confrontational, and aggressive in their relationships with others). GLOBE introduces also other cultural dimensions in relation to Hofstede's MAS dimension: Performance Orientation (the degree to which an organization or society encourages and rewards group members for performance improvement and excellence) and Humane Orientation (the degree to which individuals in organizations or societies encourage and reward individuals for being fair, altruistic, friendly, generous, caring, and kind to others). This last dimension is evidenced by a focus on social responsibility, public service, and an expectation that members work well with others. Along these specifications, other studies have shown how MAS dimension plays a role in mental programming at an ethical crossroad. For example, people in high MAS culture have a "societal expectation" to achieve financial goals in "now or never" and "big and fast" ways. Even in front of unethical or corrupt situations, people who are too hesitant to take the advantage of the "big" opportunity could be seen as cowardly. Therefore, MAS cultures are more likely to overlook ethical transgressions in business transactions, leading to the toleration of unethical behavior and the pervasiveness of corrupt practices.[56]

Culturally Integrated Anti-Corruption Model

Effective anti-corruption teaching in public service should seek an integrated approach to understand the nature, causes, and solutions to corruption. The so-called moralist approach (individual responsibility) is basic but insufficient. A functionalist approach (management responsibility) is also necessary but needs to be integrated with an institutional approach (institutional responsibility) based on system analysis and good governance capacity development. Upholding the rule of law by fostering transparency and accountability in the public sector serves not only as means to counter corruption but also as fundamental conditions of good governance. However, it appears that cultural values with the above-described cultural dimensions have a significant impact on either facilitating or restraining the perception and practice of corruption in public service.

The significance of cultural dimensions on corruption is relevant to plan, implement, and evaluate anti-corruption plans in specific cultural contexts and sectors of society. Cultural dimensions also matter for understanding the causes, consequences and dynamics of corruption. An integrated approach that includes intervening factors like economic level, political capacity, legal and social systems (macrolevel) with transparency, accountability, pervasiveness, and arbitrariness factors (microlevel) needs to be integrated with the moral dimensions (individual, community, organizational, and institutional responsibilities) and cultural dimensions (power

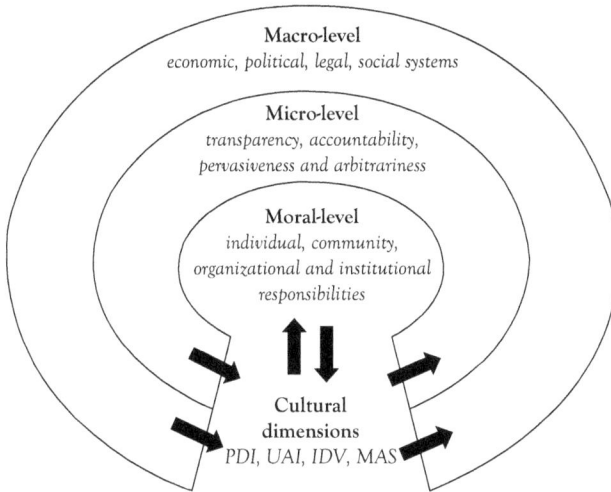

Figure 8.2. Culturally integrated anti-corruption model.

distance, uncertainty avoidance, individualism/collectivism, masculinity/ femininity). Cultural dimensions, although minimized in the institutionalization processes driven by globalization and localization, permeate and influence the moral, micro- and macrolevels. Figure 8.2 represents an integrated model with the interception of culture in the understanding of corruption perception and practices. The arrows represent the influence of culture on the moral, micro- and macrolevels. But they also represent the fact that this is not a mechanic model. Cultural values are practices that evolve in time and in the interaction with systems, institutions, organizations, norms, and different cultural values.[57]

Culture is key to understanding corruption, but not the only explanation. Moral responsibilities, management level issues (micro), and systems (macro) influence the perception, practices, and changes in corruption. Recognizing the intersecting influences that cultural dimensions have on corruption can be predictors of ethical issues within certain national and cultural environments. The inclusion of culture in the study of corruption could lead to developing more appropriate and effective practices and policies to mitigating corruption. Students in public service can develop their cultural intelligence, essential for helping individuals and organizations in dealing with culturally embedded corrupt practices.

Integrated models are common in the study and fight of corruption. The World Bank has been on the forefront of proposing a comprehensive plan to effectively combat corruption. They recognize the importance of engaging all stakeholders (political leaders, champions amongst public servants, civil society, media, academics, the private sector and international organizations) to effectively tackle the causes and consequences of corruption.[58] The Organisation for Economic Co-operation and Development (OECD) also has a comprehensive plan for fighting bribery and corruption. Recognizing that integrity is the cornerstone of good governance and anti-corruption, they articulate mechanisms for promoting, developing, and measuring public service integrity at various levels.[59]

Integrated models are also common in the measurement of worldwide perceptions of corruption. The World Bank, the World Economic Forum, the Economic Intelligence Unit, Gallup International, among others, have been producing numerous survey studies that Transparency International publishes yearly in the Corruption Perception Index (CPI). The annual CPI ranks 183 countries in their perceived levels of public sector corruption on a scale from 10 (very clean) to 0 (highly corrupt). The CPI is just one of the many other tools that measure corruption. However, its simplicity and utility is also due to the integration of several other surveys from independent institutions.[60]

The United Nations Convention Against Corruption (UNCAC), adopted by the General Assembly on October 31, 2003, is another example of integrated aspects of corruption and anti-corruption methods. Extending the 1996 United Nations Convention against Transnational Organized Crime, UNCAC is the first legally binding international anti-corruption instrument comprised of various levels of interventions for prevention, criminalization, international cooperation, and assets recovery.[61] In spite of the long road ahead in technical assistance to effectively link the convention to national and local laws and regulations, this convention will impact anti-corruption only through the effective engagement of sectors and proper understanding of cultural values. Knowledge of these integrated approaches and international conventions is must for anti-corruption educations and training.

Lessons for Teaching Anti-Corruption

Effective anti-corruption education for public servants must integrate appropriate intercultural studies. While respecting the diversity of public service and public administration programs, accreditation agencies like the National Association of Schools of Public Affairs and Administration (NASPAA) should promote and monitor curricula in the teaching of anti-corruption. This should be recognized beyond fiscal responsibility. Public corruption must be examined in the context of cultural competencies, international relations, and local/federal government relations. It must be perceived beyond individual ethical "issues" and articulated within the promotion of good governance practices and institutional capacity development.

The following is a list of recommendations for teaching anti-corruption in public service through a culturally intelligent and multilevel model. As described in this study, effective anti-corruption trainings and educational programs must integrate the study and application of corruption from a systemic, technical, ethical, and intercultural perspective.

1. *Implement anti-corruption across the curricula.* A comprehensive and integrated approach to anti-corruption cannot be covered only in ethical courses. It needs to be articulated across other courses and disciplines starting from institutional systems, and cross-sector analysis. It needs to be integrated with technical, legal, and management elements and it needs to comprehend the cultural dynamics in ethical decision-making and public service administration.

2. *Critically analyze corruption.* Is corruption bad or good? Corruption may be an international unacceptable problem but not for the same reasons that Westerners put forward.[62] The general perception in Western circles is that corruption can just be eliminated with political will. In reality corruption needs to be seen in all of its aspects, including its diverse relations with development. For example, what matters is not just "how much" corruption there is in a country but what corrupt public officials do with the money. While African corruption money generally ends in the pockets of politicians, Asian and East European corrupt state officials tend to reinvest the money in sensible business projects in their countries.[63]

3. *Develop diversity awareness.* To recognize the cultural diversity in the perceptions of corruption practices teaching activities should include real case studies and experiential learning through international projects for capacity building. In culturally diverse classes and trainings with diverse participants, instructors should stimulate learning through assessments on diverse perceptions on corruption. For example, the answers to what appear to be obvious questions may vary greatly in a culturally diverse setting and could spur interesting debate. Using real life case studies in *corruption across cultures* could stimulate a lively debate on ethical decision-making in cross-cultural perspectives.[64]

4. *The 4P approach: Principles, Prevention, Prosecution, Protection.* Anti-corruption curricula may not be the ultimate solution to corruption but it is essential for instilling competent and responsible principles in public servants. As in the Principles for Responsible Management Education (PRME), the anti-corruption principle of the United Nations Global Compact (UNGC) needs to be integrated in training modules and curricula for good governance and responsible business practices. Principles and definitions are important but not enough. They need to be articulated along practical skills, competencies and for preventing corruption, prosecuting criminals, and protecting victims.[65]

Teaching anti-corruption can no longer be an elective in public service education. However, we need to implement effective educational programs that integrate theory with practice, principles with experience, functions with structures, and moral decisions with cultural dimensions.

Conclusions and Applications

Corruption is recognized as one of the world's greatest challenges. But corruption is not just about ethics. It is also about how the government is set up and managed. That is why improving the capacity, accountability, and transparency mechanism of a government is fundamental in fighting corruption. This study has presented an overview of corruption in the context of cultural diversity and the moral, social, organizational, and institutional responsibilities of public servants. We suggested a culturally intelligent and multilayered model for integrating anti-corruption in teaching and training for public servants. Educating socially responsible public servants in a globalizing world would require implementing programs, degrees, curricula, and trainings that integrate ethical decision making with the awareness of structural, technical, and cultural implications of anti-corruption. It would also require seeing public service not in a vacuum of functional administrations but in relation to rights and responsibilities across sectors and culture.

Public service management programs should reconsider the role that culture has in corruption practices and revisit their curricula and learning outcomes. Public servants should be culturally competent. That is, they should be recognizing the assets and limitations made by cultural dimension on corruption's perceptions and practice. Power distance, uncertainty avoidance, individualism/collectivism, and masculinity/femininity are not the only cultural dimensions or factors explaining corruption. However, their influence to ethical decision-making and correlation to perceptions of corruption have been demonstrated by numerous empirical studies and explained in various theoretical works. Universities and training organizations alike should take culture's impact on corruption into serious consideration when designing educational and professional programs.

As government administrations operate more and more in interlocal, interregional, and international dynamics, the need for understanding and dealing effectively with cultural dimensions is no longer an elective in good governance education. Such education should also integrate the contemporary corruption challenges and effective anti-corruption strategies emerging from national agencies, international agencies, and nongovernmental organizations. While the model here presented would require further testing and adaptation into curricula development, it suggests the inevitable interception that culture has in corruption perceptions and practices. It also suggests that teaching anti-corruption in public service education is a must and it should be integrated with adequate moral, micro, macro, and cultural dimensions.

Key Terms and Definitions

Bribery: An offer or receipt of any gift, loan, fee, reward or other advantage to or from any person as an inducement to do something that is dishonest, illegal or a breach of trust, in the conduct of the enterprise's business.[66]

Clientelism: This is an informal form of social organization characterized by patron–client relationships between people of different social and economic status: a "patron" (relatively powerful and wealthy) and his/her "clients" (relatively less powerful and wealthy). The relationship includes a mutual but unequal and often corrupt exchange of favors.[67]

Collectivist culture: Relative to those societies in which people from birth onward are integrated into strong, cohesive, in-groups, which throughout people's lifetime continue to protect them in exchange of unquestioning loyalty.

Collusion: This is a usually secretive act of cooperation or collaboration among two or more parties to mislead or defraud others of their rights.

Cronyism: Favoritism shown in treatment of friends and associates, without regards to their objective qualifications; could be treated as a form of corruption.

Embezzlement: The illegal taking or appropriation of money or property that has been entrusted to a person but is actually owned by another. (In political terms this is called "graft," which is when a political office holder unlawfully uses public funds for personal purposes.)[68]

Episodic corruption: This type of corruption occurs when honest behavior is the norm, corruption the exception, and the dishonest public servant is disciplined when detected.

Extortion: A threatening or inflicting harm to a person, their reputation, or their property in order to unjustly obtain money, actions, services, or other goods from that person (Blackmail is a form of extortion.)[69]

Feminine culture: Relative to those societies when emotional gender roles overlap: both men and women are supposed to be modest, tender, and concerned with the quality of life.

Grand corruption: This type of corruption generally associated with high-level politicians or officials and it involves relatively large bribes from contractors or other corporations.

Individualist culture: Relative to those societies in which the ties between individuals are loose: everyone is expected to look after himself or herself and his or her immediate family.

Kickback: An illegal secret payment made as a return for a favor or service rendered.

Masculine culture: Relative to those societies when emotional gender roles are clearly distinct: men are supposed to be assertive, tough, and focused on material success, whereas women are supposed to be more modest, tender, and concerned with the quality of life.

Nepotism: The practice or inclination to favor a group or person who is a relative when giving promotions, jobs, raises, and other benefits to employees. This is often based on the concept of "familism" that leads some political officials to give privileges and positions of authority to relatives based on relationships regardless of their actual abilities.[70]

Patronage systems: They consist of the granting favors, contracts, or appointments to positions by a local public office holder or candidate for a political office in return for political support. Often patronage is used to gain support and votes in elections or in passing legislation. Patronage systems disregard the formal rules of a local government and use personal instead of formalized channels to gain an advantage.[71]

Petty corruption: This type of corruption often involves lower-level public officials and generally involves smaller amounts but more frequent transactions. This is also known as administrative corruption or retail corruption.

Power distance: A cultural dimension defined as the extent to which the less powerful members of institutions and organizations within a country expect and accept that power is distributed unequally.

Speed money: These are bribes paid to quicken the delivery of services delayed by bureaucratic holdup (red tape) and shortage of resources.

Systemic corruption: Channels of malfeasance extend upwards from the bribe collection points, and systems depend on corruption for their survival.

Uncertainty avoidance: A cultural dimension defined as the extent to which the members of a culture feel threatened by ambiguous or unknown situations.

Study Questions

1. Why are the values of public service instrumental to understand corruption in its general definition?
2. What is institutional theory and how does it help to understand corruption in public service?
3. What are the differences between the culture of corruption, cultures, and corruption and the corruption of cultures?
4. How does the study of cultural dimensions influence and shape the understanding, perception and practice of anti-corruption?
5. Would you be able to give an example of behavior that is considered "corrupt" in one culture and "tolerated" or "culturally accepted" as a norm in another?
6. How does power distance affect the perception and practice of corruption? Give an example from your own culture and one from another culture.
7. How does individualism/collectivism affect the perception and practice of corruption? Give an example from your own culture and one from another culture.
8. How does uncertainly avoidance affect the perception and practice of corruption? Give an example from your own culture and one from another culture.
9. How does masculinity/femininity affect the perception and practice of corruption? Give an example from your own culture and one from another culture.
10. What other cultural dimensions affect the perception and practices of culture? Give an example.

Additional Reading

Callahan, D. (2004). *The cheating culture: Why more americans are doing wrong to get ahead*. Orlando: Harcourt.

Eicher, S. (2009). *Corruption in international business: The challenge of cultural and legal diversity*. Farnham, England: Gower.

Haller, D., & Shore, C. (2005). *Corruption: Anthropological perspectives.* London: Pluto.

Hofstede, G. H., Hofstede, G. J., & Minkov, M. (2010). *Cultures and organizations: Software of the mind: Intercultural cooperation and its importance for survival.* New York: McGraw-Hill.

House, R. J. (2011). *Culture, leadership, and organizations: The GLOBE study of 62 societies.* Thousand Oaks, CA: Sage.

Huntington, S. P., & Harrison, L. E. (2000). *Culture matters: How values shape human progress.* New York: Basic Books.

Smith, D. J. (2007). *A culture of corruption: Everyday deception and popular discontent in nigeria.* Princeton: Princeton University Press.

CHAPTER 9

Understanding and Reducing Business Corruption Through Movies and World Wide Web Videos

Andrew E. Michael

Abstract

This chapter proposes the use of videos on the World Wide Web and movies to teach anti-corruption and develop a foundation for business dignity. It identifies seven movies in which managers, employees, or government officials act in a corrupt way. In these movies, the motive behind corrupt behavior is revealed and the consequences for organizations and their stakeholders made clear. For each movie, thought-provoking questions are raised to encourage reflection on the antecedents and consequences of the corrupt behavior. This chapter also identifies seven videos on the Web in which specific examples of corruption are presented. These videos also include managers and experts who talk about what businesses can do to reduce corruption in developed and developing countries. Three websites dedicated to combating corruption are also presented. Through these audio-visuals and websites the readers will receive messages about what is corruption, why it should be avoided, and what can be done to reduce it. Hopefully, these messages will create awareness about the nature and causes of corruption and also an intrinsic desire to act ethically and in a non-corrupt way in business and in life in general.

Introduction

Corruption is an important ethical and social problem.[1] Corruption in business exists in various forms. For instance, companies offer bribes to win contracts. They misrepresent their profit and loss statements to pay lower taxes or they exaggerate their revenues so that executives can earn bonuses and to increase the company's stock market price. Firms in the financial sector manipulate interest rates; engage in the dubious selling of financial products; and show laxity in the enforcement of money-laundering controls.[2]

It is important, however, to remember that companies are organizations and as such, they are comprised of individuals (even though they are considered as separate legal entities). Thus, to say that companies are tainted by corruption in essence means that certain organizational members engage in unethical and corruptive behavior that detrimentally affect the image of their organizations as well as the rest of society. For instance, when business people offer bribes to influence policy makers and procurement processes, they undermine effective government and reduce fair competition in the markets. This results in policies, decisions and transactions that are suboptimal for society.[3] "According to a 2011 Dow Jones survey, the number of cases where companies faced losses due to unethical or corrupt practices quadrupled from 2009 to 2010."[4] In the end, one may argue that all citizens are negatively affected by corruption in business.[5] One only has to look back at the recent past in the financial sector to see how the mismanagement of certain financial institutions, coupled with regulatory capture, have underlined the recent global financial crisis, leading to the bankruptcy of certain institutions (e.g. Lehman Brothers) and the loss of extremely large sums of financial assets.[6] However, it is not just managers who behave unethically.

Non-managerial employees have also engaged in fraud driven by a desire to have a better life or become rich quickly. The costs resulting from employee theft can be staggering. For instance, in the United States, the United States Department of Commerce estimates that employee theft may cost United States businesses as much as $50 billion annually. Employee theft in the United States is rising and the U.S. Department of Justice reports that nearly one-third of all employees commit some degree of employee theft. Two percent of all business sales are lost to employee theft. Firms often try to recover the losses from employee theft by increasing their prices.[7]

Even in the banking industry, employee theft is common. One would think that the nature of bank employee work and the expected monitoring would deter such fraudulent activities but the media has reported on a number of bank employees in various countries including the United States, United Kingdom, and Australia who have pleaded guilty for embezzling money of various amounts from banks and their customers often only for their own personal use but sometimes for other more corrupt reasons as well.[8] Such unethical behavior reveals the lack of integrity that characterizes certain individuals. It also reflects the inadequate monitoring procedures of certain organizations. The absence of such effective procedures can be devastating.[9] For instance, in 1995, Barings Bank, one of the oldest merchant banks in London, collapsed after one of its employees, Nick Leeson, who worked at the bank's Singapore office, lost £827 million ($1.3 billion) due to speculative investing, primarily in future contracts. More recent examples of the consequences of ineffective monitoring and disclosure procedures can be seen in the cases of the large insurance company, American Insurance Group (AIG), and the Swiss Bank UBS. AIG's derivatives unit in London (although small relative to the firm's total operations) was able, due to lax regulatory oversight, to obscure its accounts and take inordinate risks that would have led to AIG's collapse had it not been for the US government's rescue loan of $85 billion.[10] In the case of the Swiss Bank UBS, its employees colluded amongst themselves and with brokers and traders at other institutions to manipulate interest rates for their own profit.[11]

The results of a recent survey of 500 financial services professionals in the United States and United Kingdom provide additional support to the view that bankers, asset managers, fund managers, and analysts are prone to engage in corrupt behavior, especially if they believe that they are not effectively monitored to follow the rules.[12] Sixteen percent of the respondents admitted that they would illegally engage in trading based on insider information "if they could get away with it." Sadly, less than half stated that they would not use insider information even if they would not get caught. Interestingly, only 25% of these financial services professionals thought that financial watchdogs such as the Securities and Exchange

Commission and other regulators were effective. About a quarter of the respondents stated that they had seen or were aware of wrongdoing in the workplace. Moreover, they believed that to be successful they might have to engage in unethical or illegal conduct. Furthermore, about a third felt "pressure by bonus or compensation plans to violate the law or engage in unethical conduct."[13] However, such behavior, as seen from the afore-mentioned examples, does not affect only those who are corrupt.

When a large firm goes bankrupt as a result of its managers and/or employees' corruptive behavior, the consequences can be dire. Employees and their families suffer due to lost income. Shareholders experience financial losses. Clients may lose their financial investments.[14] Trust in business and markets is weakened.

It is, therefore, important to reduce corruption in business. To this end, it is important to create an environment that does not tolerate cor-ruption. Organizations must improve their transparency and set high standards of integrity. They must establish but also effectively enforce a code of ethics that fosters and maintains an organizational culture that values and believes in integrity. This necessitates, on the one hand, the use of incentives that encourage ethical behavior and, on the other, sanc-tions for corrupt behavior. There is a need for regulations that support effective disclosure. Furthermore, accounting, auditing, and risk-rating standards must be improved.[15] Moreover, managers at all levels must set an example of ethical behavior for their subordinates, suppliers, and clients by practicing what they preach.[16]

The purpose of this chapter is to contribute to our understanding of corruption and develop a foundation for business integrity by using movies and videos on the World Wide Web. The use of videos and movies is often appealing as a means to create interest in learners. It can be an additional pedagogical tool used against corruption. A number of movies show managers, employees, and government officials acting in a corrupt way. In these movies, the motive behind corrupt behavior is revealed and the consequences for organizations and their stakeholders made clear. In most cases, the guilty ones are caught and face the conse-quences of the law. In a slightly different way, there are a number of videos on the Web (e.g. *The Corporations* documentary series) that expose corruption and present clips of managers and experts who talk about how businesses can try to reduce corruption in developed and emerging markets.

This chapter outlines seven movies and seven videos and poses thought-provoking questions in a case-like fashion that allow the reader to ponder on the gains (often short lived) of corrupt behavior whether it is cooking the accounting books to pay less taxes, bribing employees, managers or government officials to win contracts, or violating safety and health laws. These movies and videos convey messages about what is corrupt behavior, why it should be avoided, and what can be done to reduce it.

The movies discussed in this chapter are:

1. *Wall Street*
2. *Wall Street: Money Never Sleeps*
3. *On Deadly Ground*
4. *Erin Brockovich*
5. *Edge of Darkness*
6. *Duplicity*
7. *Inside Job.*

The estimated amount of time required to view the movies and videos has been listed in the chapter along with the amount of time needed for "question contemplation." Ideally, all movies should be watched. However, time constraints may limit the choice to three or four, which should include *Wall Street, On Deadly Ground, Erin Brockovich,* and *Inside Job.* It is recommended that all seven videos outlined in this chapter be watched as they present examples, and discuss important aspects, of corruption. The three websites referred to in this chapter provide a wealth of information on corruption. Particular topics and regions can be chosen according to the reader's interests. It is hoped that the websites, movies, videos, and question contemplation will assist educators in teaching anticorruption in business by contributing to a better appreciation of the antecedents and detrimental outcomes of unethical and corrupt decisions and practices.

Movies

Wall Street

In this 1987 Oliver Stone Picture by 20th Century Fox Film Corporation, one is introduced to a fictional presentation of a dynamic, fast-paced, competitive world of Wall Street in 1985. Buddy Fox (Charlie Sheen) is an aspiring, young broker who wants to make it big time by convincing the successful, experienced investment banker, Gordon Gekko (Michael Douglas), that he "has what it takes" to be worthy of his attention and employment. But what must "one have" to be successful as a stock trader? Through intriguing dialogues, Oliver Stone creates a fictional world that is seemingly not for the faint-hearted and perhaps not for those who are honest. This fictional movie can be a backdrop for viewers to engage in thoughtful reflection of ethics in practice since it suggests that "greed is good" while presenting stock trading as a competitive environment in which the ends justify the means.

Viewing *Wall Street* should allow one to develop an understanding of the pressure and ethical challenges a person is likely to face in high-risk, highly competitive business environments. Additionally, viewers should identify and reflect on how different perspectives of ethics (e.g. Kant, Utilitarianism, Legalism, etc.) would influence the actions and decisions of people who have the opportunity to make substantial monetary gains from unethical behavior.

The duration of this movie is 121 minutes. An additional 30–40 minutes should be allocated for reflection and discussion of the questions below.

Questions for reflection:

- Do you think that one must behave unethically and corruptly to be successful as a stock trader or an investment banker? You may also wish to consider the results of the June 2012 survey of 500 financial services professionals cited in the Introduction to this chapter. You may also wish to conduct a literature search related to this question.
- Do you believe that in life one can make a lot of money only by bending the rules, cutting corners, using inside information? If so, is it worth the risk? More importantly, why should someone not act unethically and corruptly?

- Gekko proclaims that "Greed is good." Do you share this view? How does Gekko justify this belief?
- Is making profit the same thing as greed?
- Why does Bud (Buddy) Fox accept Gekko's challenge to behave illegally? How did Buddy justify and rationalize obtaining information from another company's office? Did Buddy believe that he was actually stealing confidential information at the time he did it?
- How did Bud's friend the lawyer justify and rationalize revealing his client's information, an act which violates the trust responsibility he has to all his clients?
- Would business ethics courses in an MBA program reduce the chances of people doing what Buddy did? If not, what would deter such behavior? Bear in mind that fines and imprisonment for such behavior do exist.
- Do you think that Gekko's feeling of invulnerability affect his decisions and behavior?
- How do his decisions affect his competitors? The lives of other people?
- The use of inside information for trading is illegal. Do you think it should be? Is it realistic to expect that those with inside information will not use it if they think that they will not be caught? If not, why should someone not use inside information if he/she believes that others will?
- In the movie, Gekko's firm buys an airline company that is making losses. Gekko states that he intends to make it profitable. However, soon after the purchase, Gekko changes his mind and decides that it is a better business decision to sell the company's assets to make a quick large profit even though this will result in the loss of 6000 jobs. Was his behavior unethical? Corrupt? Would your answers be different if you knew that this decision was Gekko's true intention from the start?
- Why do you think people continue to work for corrupt bosses? Can an ethical person work for someone like Gekko without behaving unethically themselves?
- Reflect on what happens to Buddy Fox at the end of the movie.

Wall Street: Money Never Sleeps

In this 2010 Oliver Stone fictional film by 20th Century Fox Film Corporation, Gordon Gekko is released from prison. (This may suggest that sooner or later, no matter how good one is at corruption, even the best are taken down by one of their rivals.) In this movie, we are introduced to Gekko's daughter who is, ironically, in love with a young, aspiring stock trader Jacob Moore. The seemingly repentant and wiser Gekko is invited to speak at a university about his new book. In a brief but masterful speech, he summarizes the predicament of the behavior of financial institutions and their decision makers exposing the dangers of speculation and leveraged debt to conclude that they have a bankrupt business model. Ironically, he states that one of the motivating factors behind all of the aforementioned is greed. Although this movie is purely fictional, it can provide food for thoughtful reflection regarding decisions and behaviors with ethical implications. It may also provide insight into the nature of the people who engage in corrupt behavior. Moreover, the last question for reflection below is particularly important with respect to the potential effectiveness of reducing business corruption using various pedagogical tools.

The duration of this movie is 133 minutes. An additional 30–40 minutes should be allocated for reflection and discussion of the questions below.

Questions for reflection:

- What actions, events, and decisions in the movie have ethical implications?
- What do you consider to be the main causes or reasons for the unethical behavior exhibited by some of the movie characters?
- Compare Jacob Moore with Buddy Fox from the first *Wall Street* movie. How are they the same? How are they different? Is Jacob corrupt?
- What is your view on the spreading of the rumor that the oil industry was going to be nationalized by the New Guinean government? Why was this done? Is such behavior ethically acceptable? Why or why not?
- What does Gekko's behavior suggest about people who like money, power, and the good life? Arguably, there is nothing wrong per se in

liking money and the good life. However, if such people are unethical and corrupt, do you think that they can change? If so how?

- What would it take to change such people? If some people cannot or do not want to change, what implications does that have with respect to teaching anti-corruption and reducing corruption in business?

On Deadly Ground

This 1994 movie by Warner Bros Picture is a story about an oil company and the environment. Michael Jennings (Michael Caine) is the CEO of Aegis 1. His goal is to make it the largest rig and oil refinery in the world. The rig and refinery are not yet fully operational. It must be up and running within 13 days otherwise the rights of ownership of the land will return to the local Eskimo residents. Forrest Taft (Steven Seagal) works for Michael Jennings. He is responsible for dealing with explosions and fires at the rig and refinery. Hughe Palmer is one of Mr. Jennings foreman. Hughe believes that Aegis 1 has substandard equipment and more specifically "faulty preventers."

Although fictional, this movie presents the potentially negative effects on the environment arising from the profit-seeking behavior of companies. It also shows the ethical implications of the decisions made by CEOs and top managers in the real business world. A company may be able to increase its profits by engaging in activities that create negative externalities whereby third parties (such as local residents and their animals) are negatively affected by the actions and decision of businesses and their consumers. The ethical implications can become complicated when the products or services of a company that create negative externalities actually help to improve or even save the lives of other people.

The duration of this movie is 97 minutes. An additional 30–40 minutes should be allocated for reflection and discussion of the questions below.

Questions for reflection:

- Due to an explosion at the oil rig certain employees die. Mr. Jennings instructs his public relations officer to "offer standard settlement for the deaths." Is his treatment of the deaths ethical?

- Mr. Jennings is involved in the creation of a television publicity ad to show that his company cares about the earth and the animals. His actual behavior suggests otherwise.
  - Is he a hypocrite?
  - Why is Mr. Jennings willing to actually be in such an advertisement if he really doesn't care about the environment and the animals? Is this ethical?
  - To what extent could this behavior be considered corrupt? Discuss.
- Why was Mr. Jennings willing to authorize the use of substandard equipment at Aegis 1 even though it would jeopardize the lives of workers and create potential environmental hazards? Is his behavior corrupt?
- In one of his public speeches, Mr. Jennings tells the locals that his company meets the acceptable levels of environmental standards. However, a member of the local Tribal Council complains about increased rates of skin cancer, poisons in their local environment that were not there before, women failing to ovulate, and the birth of abnormal babies. Assuming that these problems are true and that Mr. Jenning's company is attaining acceptable environmental standards, is there an ethical issue here? Is this an example of corruption?
- The movie ends with an environmental message about how oil companies are damaging the environment and that they control the lawmakers so that the fines are small enough so that it remains profitable to pollute.
  - Do you think that lawmakers are purposely keeping fines low enough so that oil companies will not be deterred from polluting? (Is this an example of regulatory capture?) If this is true, do you consider this corrupt behavior? If so, what do you think can or should be done to get lawmakers to change their behavior?
  - If this is true but you do not think that it is corrupt behavior what arguments would you use to justify your position?

Erin Brocovich

This 2000 joint production by Columbia Pictures and Universal Studio is based on a true story about a giant utility company, Pacific Gas & Electric (PG & E) and its unethical and illegal treatment of citizens in the town of Hinkley in which one of its branch subsidiaries operated. The utility plants used piston engines that get hot. Water was run through to prevent the temperature from rising too high. The utility company used chromium as a rust inhibitor in the water to prevent corrosion. Then it dumped the excess water into ponds, which it should have lined (but did not) to prevent the chromium from seeping into the groundwater. The problem with this was that the type of chromium that was used in the cooling towers, Hexachrome, was harmful. Moreover, PG & E lied to the residents of Hinkley that chromium was good for them. They even paid for the residents to have a free medical examination carried out by physicians recommended by PG & E.

This is another case whereby a firm's decisions lead to the creation of negative externalities (i.e. external costs). Sadly, the events in this movie are based on a true story. Viewers will realize how difficult it is for law suits to successfully be made against big businesses. The duration of this movie is 126 minutes. An additional 30–40 minutes should be allocated for reflection and discussion of the questions below.

Questions for Reflection:

- How would you evaluate PG & E in terms of social responsibility?
- Can you think of any arguments to justify PG & E's procedures and decisions?
- In what way can these procedures and decisions be seen as corrupt?
- Why did PG & E offer $250,000 to buy the Jensens' home, a price that was more than its market value?
- In an attempt to reach a legal settlement outside court, PG & E made an offer to the law firm representing those who had been negatively affected. In your opinion, was this offer fair? If not, what impression does that create in your mind about the company and its managers?

- The outcome of the case came down to whether PG & E headquarters was aware of its subsidiary's use of Hexachrome in the Hinkley plant. Evidence that PG & E headquarters was aware of its use was found from an unexpected source. Had this evidence not been obtained, how do you think PG & E's behavior and legal approach might have been different? What would have been the ethical implications of this potentially different approach?
- Erin Brockovich was the person who realized that something was not right with the situation in Hinkley. She was also the one who worked hard to collect the evidence for the case against PG & E. Reflect on what would have happened to the people in Hinkley if Erin had not pursued the matter so vigorously. What does this tell you about the importance of managers not acting corruptly but ethically?
- If Erin had not cared so much, would the law firm for which she had worked pursue this case legally? If not, what does this say about its corporate social responsibility?

Edge of Darkness

Edge of Darkness is a 2010 joint production by GK Films, BBC Films, and Icon Productions. The story is about corruption involving a private company, Northmoor that has a contract with the United States Ministry of Defense. Northmoor has a mandate from the United States government to develop a safe energy source based on fusion nuclear technology. Northmoor is also in charge of maintenance of the nation's nuclear stockpile so that it is operational when needed. Emma Craven is a research assistant at Northmoor. She believes that Northmoor is breaking the law by making nuclear weapons for foreign powers. NightFlower is an activist group. Emma has sought assistance from Senator Jim Pine who did not help her. She also sought advice from a lawyer named Sanderman who has organized Senator Pine's election campaign.

Viewers of this fictional movie will realize that corruption fosters more corruption and that individuals may be willing to bend the laws and act unethically in return for their own personal gain, as was the case with the senator and lawyer. The duration of this movie is 112 minutes. An additional 30–40 minutes should be allocated for reflection and discussion of the questions below.

Questions for reflection:

- Identify the various conflicts of interest that exist in this movie. How did these conflicts of interest arise? Could they have been avoided? Did their existence lead to corruption?
- Emma blew the whistle on Northmoor but Senator Jim Pine was not willing to help her. Was the senator protecting national security?
- Did Emma commit a crime by violating security of her workplace?
- Jedburgh ("a friend of the court") has been approached by people in the U.S. government to do whatever it takes to protect national security even if this means killing Emma's father, Boston detective Tom Craven. Comment on Jedburgh's behavior. Has he acted unethically or with integrity? Support your thoughts.
- One may argue that acting with integrity requires that organizational members who become aware that their company is behaving corruptly and engaging in illegal activities should blow the whistle even if this puts in jeopardy their lives and jobs. Do you agree with this view? Discuss.
- Officer Bill Whitehouse was put in charge of investigating a crime. Bill eventually faced a difficult dilemma. Was Bill corrupt? What does this say about how easy or difficult it is to not act corruptly?
- Citing examples of his decisions and tactics in the movie, how would you describe Jack Bennet, Northmoor's CEO?
- Can people like Jack Bennet, Sanderman, and Jim Pine be taught to behave in a non-corrupt way? Discuss.

Duplicity

Duplicity is a 2009 fictional movie about corporate espionage. The events take place between 2003 and 2008. Equikrom and Burkett Randle are two rival companies. The companies' CEOs, Howard Tully of Equikrom and Dick Garsik of Burkett and Randle, are both trying to find ways to outperform each other. Both firms have some sort of espionage or counter intelligence unit. The movie is about a "world of duplicity and theft" in which "the fabric of integrity has been so abused and mangled that it is little more than a memory."

This movie will help viewers to understand that due to fierce competition, managers may feel the pressure to do anything they can to gain a competitive advantage. The important message in this movie is that spying is unethical and that firms need to take measures to improve their monitoring and to better protect private information. The duration of this movie is 120 minutes. An additional 30–40 minutes should be allocated for reflection and discussion of the questions below.

Questions for reflection:

- Do you think that corporate espionage really occurs? If yes, in what ways and to what extent?
- Does corporate espionage occur only in the United States?
- Do you find the behavior and tactics of the two CEOs rational?
- Would you consider their behavior and tactics corrupt?
- If you were one of the CEOs in this movie and you believed that your main competitor was trying to steal your company's secrets, how would you react? What measures would you take to protect yourself? Would you consider these measures to be ethical? If not, why would you engage in unethical behavior?
- Has the fabric of integrity been so abused that it is not realistic anymore to expect anyone, and especially managers, to behave in non-corrupt ways?
- Discuss whether firms can compete without their managers and employees being corrupt?

Inside Job

Inside Job was produced in 2010 and directed by Charles Ferguson. It masterfully exposes the corruption in the U.S. banking industry and how bankers, politicians, regulators, credit rating agencies, and even academics all directly or indirectly contributed to a large or small extent to the financial crisis.

Questions for reflection:[17]

- Do you think that it is acceptable for former bank and financial services CEOs to become employed by the government, or for former government officials to become CEOs? If yes, are there any potential conflicts of interest that might arise?
- What forces led to the deregulation of the financial services market? Do you believe that academic researchers who argued for deregulation were corrupt? Did they act ethically? Justify your answer.
- Why did a number of people inside and outside the financial sector not acknowledge that there was a crisis until Lehman's bankruptcy? Why did risk managers at banks who became aware of the dangers involved with the way their companies were being operated not voice their concerns?
- Some of the banks that received government financial assistance paid out bonuses to their top managers. Were bank managers personally responsible for the crisis? Was it ethical for these banks to use taxpayers' money to pay out bonuses? Was this an example of corruption? What might this decision suggest about the type of people who manage banks and other financial institutions?
- To what extent is there evidence of the regulators and politicians being "captured"?
- Do you believe that academic economists in this movie acted corruptly? Justify your answer.
- A repeated theme in this chapter is the need for more effective regulation and monitoring. Assume that a government strengthens its regulations and demands more compliance from the financial institutions operating in its country. Would such action be acceptable to you if the financial institutions were to decide to move their headquarters and operations to countries with laxer controls? Justify your answer.
- Are consumers in any way to blame for the crisis?

Videos on the World Wide Web

The World Wide Web has a plethora of videos (including documentaries) on the topic of business corruption. The videos identified below are only a small sample and are not presented as necessarily the best ones available. However, they do allow the potential viewer to hear various views from businesspeople, researchers, and other experts about the topic of corruption. These videos are thought-provoking and can be used by educators and trainers to highlight the complexity of the corporate world and its interrelationship with government. By watching these videos viewers will have the opportunity to develop a better understanding of business corruption and how it can be more effectively challenged. Additional videos can be found on INSEAD's website.

The following videos are outlined in this chapter:

1. *Economic Fraud and Corruption*
2. *Corruption Risks Europe's Financial Recovery*
3. *The Corruption Trap*
4. *The Corporation: Case Histories* (5/23)
5. *The Corporation: Unsettling Accounts* (17/23)
6. *Scandals in Business—The Ethics Guy on CNBC's "Surviving the Market"*
7. *Business Anti-Corruption Portal*

Economic Fraud and Corruption (SEC Levitt Economy Bailout)

(Duration: 2 minutes and 25 seconds)

http://www.youtube.com/watch?v=V2JlZm60JC8

In this video clip from EP2 of the BBC documentary "The Trap" (March 2007), Arthur Levitt, Chairman of the United States Securities and Exchange Commission (1993–2001) talks about the widespread fraud and corruption in both the economic and political systems of the United States. According to Mr. Levitt, those who ran many of America's corporations were faking profits on a large scale. Moreover, the giant accounting firms had become corrupt. However, he does believe that well run companies can comply with anti-bribery regulations while still remaining competitive. He argues that to reduce corruption, companies must create and effectively implement and monitor anti-corruption compliance programs.

One of the important arguments to note from this video is that it is possible for a firm to effectively compete without its managers and employees behaving corruptly. In fact, one lesson to be learned here is that sooner or later corrupt practices will be uncovered and such practices ultimately lead to financial hardships for the firms.

Corruption Risks Europe's Financial Recovery

(Duration: 1 minute and 31 seconds)

http://www.youtube.com/watch?v=g4GVqloqneE

According to the anti-corruption watchdog Transparency International (TI), corruption threatens to further weaken Europe's efforts to overcome its debt crisis. In its latest report released to the European Union (EU), TI warned that a lack of political accountability across the EU has led to a rise in populism. The Managing Director of Transparency International Cobus de Swardt believes that there is a need to increase accountability to deal with populism. Due to corruption and accountability, scarce public money risks being wasted.[18]

The Corruption Trap (INSEAD Business School for the World)

(Duration 7 minutes and 20 seconds)

http://www.youtube.com/watch?v=-BO_w0o1ICA

In this INSEAD Knowledge video, Shellie Karabell hosts Craig Smith, professor of ethics and social responsibility. Professor Smith notes that money can be made in emerging markets due to pent up consumer demand, cheap labor, and few and lax regulations. However, "just under the surface lies the murky world of corruption, ready to derail even the most scrupulous businessperson." Professor Smith explains why firms operating internationally may act corruptly. He also describes the types of corruption that may occur.

The Corporation: Case Histories (Part 5 of 23)

(Duration: 22 minutes and 54 seconds)

http://www.youtube.com/watch?v=H3m5lq9FHDo&feature=autoplay
&list=PLFA50FBC214A6CE87&playnext=1

The Corporation is a Canadian documentary made by March Achbar, Jennifer Abbott, and Joel Bakan comprised of 23 parts. Through the use of specific cases, Part 5, *Case Histories* attempts to show how and why the corporation has an incentive to create external costs or negative externalities. Essentially, businesses can have lower costs and greater profits by not taking measures to prevent these resulting external costs. One such externality is the exploitation of employees through the use of sweatshops in developing countries. Other business practices such as the use of artificial hormones can result in adverse health effects such as cancer, birth defects, and other toxic effects. Another externality is the damage to the biosphere or the environmental costs resulting from the way corporations operate; costs that will be passed off to future generations.

The Corporation: Unsettling Accounts (Part 17 of 23)

(Duration: 11 minutes and 28 seconds)

http://www.youtube.com/watch?v=eZkDikRLQrw&feature=BFa&
list=PLFA50FBC214A6CE87

In part 17 of *The Corporation* documentary, journalists Jane Akre and Steve Wilson were fired by the Fox News television station they worked for because they refused to change their investigative report on Posilac, a bovine growth hormone (BGH) made by Monsanto. Their research documented potential health and safety problems of drinking milk treated with the synthetic hormone. Monsanto threatened Fox with legal action. Fox managers were then reluctant to allow the story to be broadcast unless the negative effects of the hormone were played down. Jane Akre and Steve Wilson were unwilling to withhold the truth from the public. An appeals court eventually threw out Akre's whistle blower lawsuit on the basis that falsifying the news was not against the law.

This video exposes the extent to which firms are willing to act corruptly in order to make profits. It shows that even academics, the media, and the Food and Drugs Administration (FDA) can all knowingly or unknowingly be exploited by private firms that will do what they can to pursue their profit objectives.

Scandals in Business—The Ethics Guy on CNBC's "Surviving the Market" (2010)

(Duration: 5 minutes and 24 seconds)

http://www.youtube.com/watch?v=85HgXXjyw2Q&feature=related

Why should businesses care about ethics? Dr. Bruce Weinstein, The Ethics Guy, explains how everyone wins when ethical standards are the foundation of business. In contrast, unethical behavior can detrimentally affect the image of a business regardless of its size. Hence, ethics has to be viewed more seriously in the workplace otherwise customers' trust will diminish. He stresses that what should be guiding our decisions is ethics and not merely the law. He agrees that MBA students are not being taught what is right but rather how not to end up in jail.

Business Anti-Corruption Portal (October 2007)

(Duration: 9 minutes and 51 seconds)

http://www.youtube.com/watch?v=WzDYzsJgAWY

This is an interview by Changemakers.net with Jens Berthelsen, a partner of Global Advice Network (Denmark). Mr. Berthelsen describes the Business Anti-Corruption Portal, a winner of the www.changemakers.net Ending Corruption collaborative online competition. He initially identifies some of the reasons for the existence of corruption and then explains its negative impact. He states that corruption is the biggest killer of business activity in the Third World driving small businesses into the underground economy. More information about this portal is presented in the next section.

World Wide Web Sites

In addition to the movies and videos above, certain organizations have websites particularly dedicated to combating corruption. These websites can be used by educators and trainers as sources of information and cases to promote anti-corruption in business. Some of these are Transparency International (http://www.transparency.org/), the Business Anti-Corruption Portal (http://www.business-anti-corruption.com), and the Center for International Private Enterprise [CIPE] (www.cipe.org).

Transparency International was created in 1993 and is now present in more than 100 countries. Its mission is "to stop corruption and promote transparency, accountability and integrity at all levels and across all sectors of society." Each year it compiles the Corruptions Perceptions Index, which scores countries on how corrupt their public sectors are perceived to be. It prepares a series of Global Corruption Reports and conducts research on a country-by-country basis. Its publications include *Transparency in Corporate Reporting: Assessing the World's Largest Companies; Exporting Corruption? Country Enforcement of the OECD Anti-Bribery Convention—Progress Report 2012;* and *Money, Politics, Power: Corruption Risks in Europe.* It also creates the Bribe Payers Index that ranks the wealthiest nations by their firms' propensity to bribe abroad, and its Global Corruption Barometer is a worldwide public opinion survey on views and experiences of corruption.

The Business Anti-Corruption portal is produced by the Global Advice Network (http://www.globaladvicenet.com/). "The purpose of the Business Anti-Corruption Portal is to provide a comprehensive and practical business tool, and to offer targeted support to small and medium-sized enterprises (SMEs) in order to help them avoid and fight corruption, thereby creating a better business environment."[19] Various links provide guidance about various anti-corruption tools, on how organizations can carry out due diligence and how they can implement an integrity system involving anti-corruption policies, codes of conduct, and general risk assessment procedures.

One of the goals of the Center for International Private Enterprise (CIPE) is to "improve governance through transparency and accountability in the public and private sectors."[20] CIPE utilizes a cross-sector approach involving the cooperation of governments, civil society, and the private sector to tackle the root causes of corruption. To this end, it emphasizes the need to create strong, balanced institutions that reward transparency and honesty and punish bribery and corrupt practices. Its web site includes an Anti-Corruption Manual for SMEs from the Hills Program on Governance.[21] The manual aims to explain what corruption is and why it occurs; in what situations might an SME face corruption; how an SME can conduct business without engaging in corruption; and what can SMEs do to fight corruption. The site also includes an Action Guide on Business without Corruption.

Conclusion

Corruption exists in all countries in both the private and public sectors. It permeates many spheres of society detrimentally affecting people's lives. This chapter has identified various movies, videos on the World Wide Web, and other websites that provide insight into the causes and consequences of business corruption. It is hoped that these resources can be used to foster an anti-corruption mentality and behavior, thus contributing to the efforts of creating a more honest and less corrupt world.

Key Terms with Definitions

Corruption: The immoral, dishonest, or illegitimate abuse of power for personal gain; this definition is applicable to all forms of corruption

Fraud: Criminal deception

Integrity: Behaving consistently according to morally justifiable principles; it should be noted that this definition is only one of many that have been proposed by different researchers

Insider information: Information that is available to organizational members but not yet known by the general public

Negative externalities: External costs experienced by third parties who are not directly involved in the production and/or consumption of a good or service

Underground economy: The hidden economy in which economic transactions are not recorded and made known to the relevant tax authorities; for instance, the selling of goods to buyers without the issuing of receipts is an underground economic activity

Utilitarianism: Ethical theory that upholds the view that an action can be considered as right or ethical if it results in the greatest good or happiness for the greatest number of people

Study Questions

1. Compare and contrast various forms of corruption.
2. Discuss why people behave corruptly.
3. Conduct research to investigate whether corruption is related to a country's culture or level of economic development.
4. Discuss why efforts should be made to reduce corruption.
5. What can employers, managers, and employees do to reduce corruption?
6. Is it realistic to believe that anti-corruption efforts can be successful? Critically examine the effectiveness of various measures proposed to reduce business corruption.
7. Using examples and supported arguments, discuss whether Business Ethics courses offered by universities can actually help to reduce corruption.
8. Conduct a search of the World Wide Web to identify anti-corruption laws that have been enacted in various countries. Discuss the extent to which such laws are effective.
9. On a daily basis, reflect on whether there are any ethical issues that you come across in the news media (e.g. newspapers, business magazine articles, radio, and television) or in films on television or at the cinema.

Additional Reading

Anonymous (Nov/Dec, 2007). Assessing the dimensions of business fraud. *Debt 3, 22*(6), 14–16.

Bayar, G. (Jan/Feb 2011). Causes of corruption: Dynamic panel data analysis of some Post Soviet countries and East Asian countries. *The Journal of Applied Business Research 27*(1), 77–86.

Brito-Bigott, O., Faria, H. J., Rodriguez, J. M., & Sanchez, A. (2008). Corruption and complex business rules. *The Journal of Private Enterprises 24*(1), 1–21.

De Graaf, G. (Spring 2007). Causes of corruption: Towards a contextual theory of corruption. *PAQ*, 39–86.

Kowalczyk-Hoyer, B. (2012). *Transparency in corporate reporting: Assessing the world's largest companies.* http://www.transparency.org

Labaton Sucharow (2012, July). *Wall Street Fleet Street Main Street: Corporate Integrity at a Crossroads*, a US & UK Financial Services Industry Survey. http://www.labaton.com/en/about/press/Labaton-Sucharow-announces-results-of-financial-services-professional-survey.cfm

Lindgreen, A. (2004). Corruption and unethical behavior: Report on a set of Danish guidelines. *Journal of Business Ethics, 51*(1), 31–39.

Pedersen, M. H., & Victorien, W. (Jan/Feb 2006). Business integrity in China. *The China Business Review, 33*(1), 32–36.

Pellegrini, L., & Gerlagh, R. (2008). Causes of corruption: A survey of cross-country analyses and extended results. *Econ Gov 9*, 245–263.

Petrick, J. A., & Quinn, J. F. (2000). The integrity capacity construct and moral progress in business. *Journal of Business Ethics, 23*(1), 3–18.

Siddiquee, N. A. (2010). Combating corruption and managing integrity in Malaysia: A critical overview of recent strategies and initiatives. *Public Organization Review, 10*(2), 153–171.

Swamy, K. (2011). Financial management analysis of money laundering, corruption and unethical business practices: Case studies of India, Nigeria and Russia. *Journal of Financial Management and Analysis, 24*(1), 39–51.

Transparency International (2012). *Putting corruption out of business.* Retrieved September 12, 2012, from http://www.transparency.org

CHAPTER 10

Applying a Religious Lens to Ethical Decision-Making: My Ten Commandments of Character for the Workplace Exercise

J. Goosby Smith and Susan Schick Case

Abstract

People in organizations across the globe are struggling to make ethical decisions and avoid corrupt behavior. In an effort to help people develop a "deeper" understanding of their ethical standards for behavior, we introduce an exercise that requires participants to develop, articulate, and utilize their own *individualized* Ten Commandments of Character drawn from their religious and spiritual teachings, upbringings, and cultures. We draw on Telushkin's book, *The Ten Commandments of Character* but, unlike the book, we do not prescribe particular commandments; rather, we facilitate a process enabling the development of personal ethical codes eliciting individually written Ten Commandments of Character for the Workplace. As a result of the exercise, participants will be able to clearly recognize, succinctly articulate, and act upon the foundations of their ethical decision-making choices, decreasing their tendency to act in dishonest ways.

Keywords

ethical decision-making, religious ethics, work-related ethics, anti-corruption, leadership integrity, moral character, exercise for ethical behavior

Introduction

There is an international crisis in ethical decision-making creating cultures of corruption throughout the globe.[1] Both economic and political interests now drive corruption, whereas it was previously the intellectual territory of moralists and ethicists.[2] Attempts to stem corruption exist everywhere, including Sub-Saharan Africa,[3] Thailand,[4] India,[5] Lithuania,[6] Latin America,[7] China,[8] Australia,[9] the United Kingdom,[10] and the United States.[11] However, many organizations' and countries' efforts to thwart corrupt behavior fail. These failures may stem from the predominantly culture-blind and legalistic focus of most anti-corruption education efforts. After all, big businesses and major world powers try to maximize their trade returns[12] not necessarily develop the character of their employees and citizens.

Current anti-corruption efforts focus on explaining legal requirements rather than connecting to and facilitating the elucidation of individually held ethical standards and tying them to workplace behavior—where much corruption and dishonesty occurs. For example, one national integrity system, described as a "comprehensive method of fighting corruption" comprises eight pillars (public awareness, public anti-corruption strategies, public participation, "watchdog" agencies, the judiciary, the media, the private sector, and international cooperation).[13]

However, none of these pillars address aspects of individual-level character development like being a good person, leading with integrity, practicing honesty, empowering people, sowing seeds of respect, and developing empathy. While explaining existing laws is necessary to stem corrupt behavior, it is insufficient because of desires for competitive advantage, egotism, greed, power, and control. These desires lead individuals to perpetuate grossly corrupt actions like those that led to the collapse of the Lehman Brothers and Enron.

Most ethical transgressions, however, are smaller scale acts of dishonesty such as deception and theft.[14] How individuals behave and where they set boundaries differs based on what they think constitutes dishonest behavior. This depends on their own level of character development, sense of integrity, conscience awareness, and enactment of clear moral standards that they possess.

We tend to think of people as either honest or dishonest. We like to believe that a few bad apples (like Raj Rajaratnam, fallen hedge fund billionaire founder of Galleon group convicted of insider trading; Lance Armstrong, caught in doping scandal in Pro Cycling Tour de France that stripped him of all his wins; James Frey, involved in a scandal exposing his fictionalized account of his best-selling memoir; or Rod Blagojevich, former two-time governor of Illinois, convicted on 18 counts of corruption including trying to sell or trade the U.S. Senate seat vacated by President Obama) are exceptions to most of us who consider ourselves virtuous. If this were true, it would be much easier to remedy societal cheating and dishonesty throughout the globe.

All of us face temptations. It is easy to compromise our ethics for personal gain, to dodge embarrassment, to impress our friends, or to save the time and energy needed to think through tough issues. It is easy to dismiss minor ethical compromises like the manager who misses an appointment but, being embarrassed to tell the truth, says that she was sick; or the salesman who inflates a travel voucher because he feels he is underpaid; or the boss who takes credit for the work of subordinates in order to get promoted. Each of these may seem minor, and be rationalized as not really ethical lapses, but as they become a habit, we lose sight of the principles we are violating. These violations compromise our character. In this chapter, we present an exercise designed to elucidate pillars of character by tying them to individuals' most deeply held beliefs: those derived not only from upbringing and culture, but from their religious and spiritual teachings.

Factors Leading To Honesty and Dishonesty

In a wide variety of experiments, Dan Arieley and colleagues have identified many factors that can lead to people behaving more or less honestly.[15]

Some of the conditions increasing dishonesty include organizational cultures with widespread norms that encourage dishonesty, watching others behave dishonestly, benefitting from dishonesty, previously acting dishonestly, conflicts of interest, and ability to rationalize behavior. Surprisingly, the amount of money to be gained or the probability of being caught had no effect. They also showed that everyone has the capacity to be dishonest, and that almost everyone cheats a little, right up to the point where they lose their sense of integrity.[16] It is this type of small-scale mass cheating, not the high-profile cases, that are most corrosive to society. These include things like white lies, secrets, promises not kept, overbilling, and putting others at risk.

In previous work, we defined integrity as "part of one's character, consisting of discrete virtues, such as behavioral consistency between words and actions and espoused values and enacted values, across time and situations; avoiding hidden agendas and acting morally, transparently, and sincerely from internal values—even in the face of adversity or temptation. Such behavior demonstrates a commitment to principled behavior, standing courageously for religiously-anchored principles, bearing the difficult consequences of convictions and acting ethically and altruistically."[17]

In the experimental research mentioned earlier, reminding people of moral codes, such as the Ten Commandments, had the most significant effect on increasing honesty. A group of 450 participants were split into two groups. They were given a matrix task.[18] Half were told to recall the Ten Commandments; the other half to recall ten books they had read in high school. The group that recalled the books had widespread moderate cheating. The group that recalled the Ten Commandments had none. The experiment was repeated reminding students of their school's honor code, and again with a group of self-declared atheists, asking them to swear on a Bible. In each of these conditions, the same no-cheating results were obtained.

These research implications are important for increasing anti-corruption behavior. Reminders of morality, at the point where people are making decisions, have a large effect on behavior, reigning in the vast majority of people who cheat just a little. This could include fibbing to round up billable hours, claiming higher losses on insurance claims, submitting mileage estimates above what was driven, recommending unnecessary medical treatments, creating unnecessary revenue enhancements with hidden fees and penalties, slowing down check processing to hold money for an extra few days, or charging exorbitant fees for overdraft protection and ATM use. Ethical transgressions tend to fall into three categories: forms of deception[19] including lying[20] and cheating, stealing,[21] and harming another or putting them in harm's way.[22]

These are the smaller and more ubiquitous forms of dishonesty that affect all of us. Cheating is contagious.[23] In studies of thousands of students by the Center for Academic Integrity, over 70% admitted to one or more instances of cheating and over 40% to some form of plagiarism.[24] These incidents involve contagion and acceptance because of felt pressure to perform. In 2006, a Harris interactive survey showed that more than half of office workers pilfered supplies, with 1 in 20 taking home plants, paintings, and furniture.[25]

In order to effectively control corruption, strategies need to transcend the current technocratic approaches.[26] One alternative strategy is to focus education at the individual level so that leaders can more confidently make a morally correct decision when faced with an ethical dilemma. Leadership decision-making has been found to be important in fighting corruption.[27]

Religion as a Source for Ethical Guidance

For many people, the most prominent strains of ethical guidance come from religion. We propose that the sacred texts of the Abrahamic religions can be used to remind us of the values and virtues we draw from them, forming the foundation for our moral character, including integrity. Whether a "believer" or not, we soak up ethical principles from scriptures, parables, and stories from the prophets and other disciples. Even atheists pick these up since they are woven into the social and cultural fabric of society.

Throughout the "Old Testament" there are many narratives of disobedient heroes and heroines who maintain a capacity for independent thought and action. Unlike Richard Dawkins's view in his bestseller, *The God Delusion* (2006), that religious belief discourages questioning by its very nature, the Hebrew Bible is radical in its endorsement of human questioning, seeking, and arguing. It allows for personal conscience, action with courage, and speech with candor.

In developing our own moral compasses, we can look to the major heroes and heroines in the Bible, all depicted as independent minded, disobedient, and even contentious.[28] Abraham, Isaac, and Jacob, Joseph's brothers, Moses and Aaron, Gideon and Samuel, prophets like Elijah and Elisha, and biblical figures such as Esther, Mordechai, Mahlah, and Daniel are all portrayed as confronting authority and breaking laws and demands of kings. For this behavior, all of them are praised. They each initiate their own disobedience without any divine command, each standing entirely on their own authority. Thus the Egyptian midwives Puah and Shiphrah resist Pharaoh's order to murder Israelites boy babies in the Exodus narrative. Similarly, Jochebed and Miriam, Moses's mother and sister, hid him as an infant, knowing they were breaking the law.

Biblical figures provide even more background for moral courage since they also dared to argue with and criticize God. Abraham challenged God over the fate of Sodom: "Will not the judge of all the earth do justice?" Moses repeatedly argues against God's intention to destroy Israel. Similar arguments with God appear in Isaiah, Jeremiah, Ezekiel, Jonah, and Job. Not only do these biblical figures argue with God, but they also disobey. Abel disregards God's instructions to work the soil. Moses disobeys God's command to lead the people of Canaan after the sin of the golden calf. The daughters of Tzelofhad demand Moses alter God's law because it is unjust. Throughout the narratives of the Bible such resistance is endorsed and independent-minded men and women are held in esteem. The Bible explicitly acknowledges this pattern when God gives the name "Israel" to Jacob and his descendants, saying: "Your name will no more be called Jacob, but Israel, for you have contended with God and with men and have prevailed."

Pillars of character are developed when individuals freely determine the kind of person they want to be and how they will live in and engage with the world. Virtues in Jewish ethics include making the world a better place, as well as questioning and challenging what is not understood, just, or ethically wrong. Strict obedience too is not a virtue. The importance of questioning and challenging based on conscience is developed from embedded Jewish religious values. In Christian ethics, virtues include following the example of the life of Jesus who also challenged current views of his time. For example, in Mark 3:1-6 Jesus met with resistance from the Pharisees for healing a man's shriveled hand on the Sabbath. Working on the Sabbath was against the law. In sum, all of these heroes broke laws to bring about a more just society.

Religious and spiritual teachings help followers of those traditions clarify their most deeply held beliefs for acting with integrity and moral responsibility within the workplace, the community and the world. This clarity avoids moral relativity in actions where nothing is absolute and everything is subjective often based on obedience to authority and fear of repercussions. When people have clarity and moral mindfulness of their deeply held values and virtues that form their pillars of character, they are more grounded and consistent in their behavior over time and situations. Being in touch with one's Ten Commandments of Character, drawn from values and virtues illuminated in Judaism, Christianity, and Islam, is one way to discourage small transgressions that can lead to larger ones over time. In his Farewell Sermon, the Prophet Muhammad warned his followers: "Beware of Satan … He has lost all hope that he will be able to lead you astray in big things, so beware of following him in small things."[29]

Within organizations, this connection with deeply held values enables individuals to dialogue across their differences, check and correct assumptions, and find commonalities of vision and purpose. Groups of individuals who are clear about their boundaries for ethical action serve as checks and balances within organizations that can help eliminate many forms of wrongdoing. Such individuals' conscious code of ethical action helps create an ethical culture without unquestioned obedience to authority where you go along with the boss because you are afraid you will lose your job. Of course people will hold different values, but that is true whether you bring religion into the workplace or not. With freedom of religion, rather than a workplace of freedom from religion, people will be more able to draw on their own moral compass and use it for ethical decision-making at work.

We are aware that it is easier to have higher ethical standards in good economic times. We do not expect people to be perfect. Susan Dwyer, an associate professor of philosophy at the University of Maryland said, "I think people have a great deal of difficulty being honest and straightforward." As an Australian, she found Americans coy about saying in both personal and professional relationships, "This is an uncomfortable situation and I don't want to do it."[30] Being in touch with a religiously or spiritually inspired moral compass, including Ten Commandments of Character in the Workplace, will help individuals as they strive to be good and to do the right thing.

Our exercise aims to intervene at the individual level to better equip leaders to make decisive, ethical decisions to stem corruption of any form. We are aware of corporate wrongdoing at the highest levels and the high price whistle-blowers often pay for speaking up. They often suffer economically and emotionally for challenging their employers. Being highly principled, with a strong sense of right and wrong, is a luxury many believe they cannot afford.

Being aware of the difficulty of such high levels of integrity, and the importance of information on wrongdoing, federal regulators in the United States have announced a recent program to make things better for informants who provide fruitful tips about corporate wrongdoing. The U.S. Securities and Exchange Commission now gives a cut of penalties won by regulators to whistle-blowers.[31] Whistle-blowers in recent years have been responsible for getting defective bulletproof vests off the market; revealing how the financial services firm UBS helped thousands of Americans evade taxes with offshore accounts; exposing the improper off-label marketing of drugs, kickbacks to doctors, and violation of Medicaid pricing laws by Pfizer; and disclosing waste and fraud by oilfield services company Halliburton in Iraq. It is not clear that people who commit these massive acts of corruption even think that what they did was wrong. Hank Greenberg, the former CEO of AIG, the insurance giant, which overstated its assets by $2.7 billion, criticized stricter regulations. He said regulators were turning "foot faults" (a tennis reference) into murder.[32]

Ethical Decision-Making Strategies

Individuals use ethical decision-making strategies to resolve a dilemma whose resolution requires them to wrestle with notions of "right and wrong."[33] James and Smith (2007) identify six ethical decision-making strategies that individuals use to determine what is "right": (1) Kant's Categorical Imperative (relies on absolute rules and universal laws of right and wrong that must be followed by everyone, regardless of what the situation seems to urge, no matter the consequences). By this standard, some actions (telling the truth, helping others) are always right, while others (lying, cheating) are always wrong[34]; (2) legalism (bases decisions on societal or organizational laws or policies, with justice and fairness guaranteeing the same basic rights and opportunities to everyone). When these basic requirements are met, the responsibility of a leader is to give consideration to the least advantaged[35]; (3) cultural relativism (using cultural norms to determine what is right, focusing on responsibilities to the larger community and to make decisions that support the common notion of good, not depending on absolute truth); (4) enlightened self-interest (determines the costs and benefits to the decision maker to determine what is right); (5) utilitarianism (weighs the costs and benefits of moral choices, seeking to do the greatest good for the greatest number of people); and (6) light-of-day (weighs costs and benefits according to the opinions of others using the likely opinion of important others to determine what is right).

Altruism, which we include as a seventh decision-making ethical lens, is based on ancient scriptures and traditional wisdom.[36] It argues that love of neighbor is the ultimate ethical standard, putting help for others as primary whatever the personal cost, a type of selflessness. This moral reasoning approach, much like communitarianism, has a lot in common with contemporary virtue ethics.[37] Many of the virtues of people with high moral character like honesty, fairness, compassion, generosity, respect, and empathy reflect an other-centered concern for people.

The Dalai Lama urges his followers to practice an ethic of compassion.[38] Judaism and Christianity have greatly influenced Western thought with their altruistic emphasis important to leaders and society. The command to love God and to love others as we love ourselves is one of the most important obligations within Judeo-Christian ethics. Some version of the Golden Rule is present in Judaism, Christianity, and Islam. Because humans are created in the image of God, we have an obligation to love others, including loving the stranger.

In the parable of the Good Samaritan in the New Testament (Luke 10:25-37) Jesus illustrates what an altruistic act is when asked what must be done to inherit eternal life. Jesus spoke of a man robbed, stripped, beaten, and abandoned on a road half-dead. Both a priest and a Levite saw the suffering man, but passed him by. A Samaritan, as he traveled, saw him, pitied him, ministered to his wounds, put him on his own donkey, and took him to an inn to care for him.

Altruism means performing an action and forgoing the fruits of the action.[39] It is rewarding in itself because it is considered the right thing to do. The righteous gentiles in Germany and other parts of Europe, who risked their lives to help Jewish countrymen and women escape during World War II when Adolph Hitler was engaged in executing his program of cultural genocide, provide another example of altruistic ethical behavior. The non-Jews who helped Jews did what they did based on selflessness, doing good for others, and serving them without expectation of reward. Similarly, Jews played an integral part in the U.S. Civil Rights movement. For example, out of altruism, Michael Schwerner and Andrew Goodman ended up sacrificing their lives to help blacks during this struggle. Hospice volunteers are a modern-day example of the unconditional love portrayed in the story of the Good Samaritan, the rescuing of Jews during the Holocaust, and the sacrifices made during the Civil Rights era in the United States for equal rights for blacks. Hospice volunteers meet the needs of people who are dying, providing compassionate help without expecting anything in return.[40]

The ethic of care is a contemporary altruistic feminist approach developed to counter the more traditional male-oriented approaches to ethics mentioned earlier. Both the categorical imperative and legalism theories emphasize action based on abstract moral principles, impartiality, and treating others fairly. Carol Gilligan (1982), Nel Noddings (2003), and others argued that women have a "different voice" to moral decision-making based on valuing human interdependence and caring for others through their relationships. They put the needs of specific individuals first, thinking of how people are impacted by decisions. Newer research has demonstrated that men as well as women often prefer an ethic of care to one of justice.[41]

The ethic of care has five components: (1) a focus on meeting the needs of those for whom you are responsible; (2) values cultivation of moral emotions like sympathy, sensitivity, empathy, and responsiveness;

(3) specific needs and relationships take priority over universal moral principles like rights and freedoms; (4) barriers between public and private spheres are broken down; and (5) people are viewed as both relational and interdependent, embedded in particular families and cultures, with a need to take responsibility for others, and not leave them alone to exercise their individual rights.[42]

When we compare good to evil, altruistic acts by moral heroes come to mind because they ignore personal risks to confront evil. Jeffrey Wigand is one of the better-known U.S. heroes, who as a daring and important whistle-blower was the industry insider who told the public in court, the *Wall Street Journal*, and on *60 Minutes* that tobacco companies were trying to get people hooked on nicotine. He told of their extensive campaign to conceal from the public their knowledge that cigarette smoking was highly addictive and caused lung cancer. As head of research and development for Brown and Williamson, the third largest tobacco company, he believed that his role when he joined the organization was to reduce the risks of smoking and produce a safer cigarette. His courage and moral outrage brought great risk to his personal life, but also led to stronger government curbs on the behavior of the tobacco industry. This included tobacco companies agreeing to pay billions of dollars to states to offset medical costs they incurred treating smoking-related illnesses. To this day Wigand maintains that he did what any decent human being in his situation would have done. He did what was right, with no regrets, and would do it again.[43]

Religion as a Framework for Anti-Corruption Behavior: The Individualized Imperative

Though the aforementioned ethical decision-making strategies are commonly used and cited, often as conflicting approaches to moral reasoning, they are also combined in a type of ethical pluralism[44] where more than one perspective is used in order to solve an ethical dilemma. An examination of the scriptures of Judaism, Christianity, and Islam indicate that another ethical framework for anti-corruption can be employed using wisdom from these traditions. Since religion shapes many of the deepest values of people across the globe, identifying religiously oriented ethical decision-making strategies bolsters the ability to make sounder ethical decisions, providing a foundation for moral character, courage, and candor. The meaning and memories of religious teachings provide a way to analyze the consequences of one's behavior. Who will be helped by what you do? Who or what will be hurt? What are the benefits and harms that need to be considered? What are both long-term and short-term consequences? Are you acting with moral virtues like honesty, fairness, justice, and courage; emotional virtues like compassion and respect; social virtues like trustworthiness and generosity; and political virtues like service and citizenship? These are the virtues that embody character,[45] with integrity the most cited.[46]

In this chapter, we introduce an exercise to employ an eighth ethical decision-making strategy: Individualized Imperative. While Categorical Imperative involves the individual relying on an abstract universal standard that applies to all, Individualized Imperative involves individually derived standards to which one holds consistently, across situations, no matter the personal cost or temptation.

It is clear that many people do not use religiously derived ethical values in their daily business decisions even though they apply these consistently in their personal lives.[47] In Jackall's in depth, multiorganizational study, *Moral Mazes: The World of Corporate Managers*, he found that a "bureaucratic ethic" guided managers' behavior where right and wrong was decided by those with the most clout within the organization.[48] The exercise we propose is to eliminate this ethical relativism that necessitates separating personal values, including religious ones, from work, in order to conform to those in the corporate hierarchy in order to please. As Case and Smith (in press) have stated, "religion links to our 'conscience', our sense of right and wrong, which is developed through religious role expectations and internalized as our religious self-identity... Attention to our conscience makes ethical issues accessible, while listening to feelings from it guides our behavior."

For many of us, the combination of stories and ethical principles from our religious or spiritual heritage are starting points for behaving with integrity throughout our lives. For example, the story of The Ten Commandments (Exodus 20: 2-17; Qur'an 6:152-155) is inspirational, providing a foundation for many current laws governing business, including truthfulness in transactions. They can serve individuals as a starting place for developing their "Ten Commandments of Character."

One author has written her own guiding personal commandments of character based on her religion's values and virtues for morally responsible behavior. They include commandments such as: "Be a person of integrity with a kind heart who demonstrates respect, pursues kindness, and caring for others"; "Exert myself ethically on behalf of others with care, compassion, and responsibility"; "Always conduct myself in interactions in a trustworthy and transparent way, doing what is right, fair, and just even if it creates personal difficulty"; "The highest form of charity for me is making time for others through dialogue, coaching, mentoring"; "Act with spiritual audacity by questioning and challenging authority when justice is at stake." These Commandments of Character form a prism for determining behavior in her workplace and life (Case, in press). They are a salient part of her internalized character of what it means to be a moral human being and part of her core identity. For this author, integrity is standing for something, demonstrating moral purpose, and acting with virtuous behavior.[49]

Building upon participants' religions, the "My Ten Commandments of Character in the Workplace" exercise provides an individualized and practical litmus test for actions and attitudes about what is the right thing for them to do when confronted with questionable practices and temptations in the workplace. It helps in the drawing of ethical lines to consistently guide actions. It draws on expected moral behavior for acting with integrity that they live by as adherents to that religion. This exercise can bring them into contact with their own moral intuitions and values (which may be hidden) and create new ways to recognize moral issues. It is not an exercise to monitor thought, but rather to use voices from religious teachings to establish ethical ideas as guides for deeper thought about ethical behavior. Religious guidance is full of diffuse, and often contradictory "shalls." This exercise helps participants decide which elements they call their own that answer the question: What does "right" behavior require? When they complete the exercise, they have developed their own concise guidelines and principles for action that take them beyond a mechanical following of rules from scripture.

Unlike Joseph Teluskin's advice for living an honorable, ethical, and honest life, in which he provides specific "Ten Commandments for Character,"[50] we ask participants to develop their own ethical standards and take responsibility for them, figuring them out by listening to their inner voices. These individually derived Ten Commandments then become a self-help guide, assisting each individual in avoiding everyday compromises through a renewed consciousness using clearer thinking and an awareness of how to behave. It is our hope that their code will lead to not only doing the right thing, but a striving to use their Ten Commandments to do the best things they can at work, making ethical choices and living their life with meaning and integrity.

This exercise is specifically designed to help leaders and other individuals of the Abrahamic faiths more explicitly connect their ethical values with their faith, deriving their own religiously inspired code of conduct that stimulates high moral standards and counteracts misconduct. It serves as a decision-making tool offering clear ethical guidance broadly applicable to common and ethically sensitive situations. It is constructed in a form that is easy to understand and apply.

Assessing religious values and virtues leads to moral mindfulness. This is an ethically inspired attitude of endeavoring to do the right thing for the right reason (Case and Smith, 2012).[51] However, this exercise can be used by anyone, ranging from those of different faiths, to atheists and secular humanists. Each of these groups can reflect upon their different religious, spiritual, or humanistic secular teachings and philosophies.

One of the authors completed a version of this exercise based on Judaism, with two students who practiced Islam, a Nigerian Catholic, and a self-proclaimed "anti-theist." All indicated the exercise grounded them in their value systems, understood the religious embeddedness of their values,[52] became more mindful of their inner voice, and clearer about their own behavior in the workplace. They described enhanced understanding of what they would question and what they would or would not do in the workplace as a person of integrity and conscience, committed to their Ten Commandments of Character.

A secondary use of this exercise is to elicit *commonalities* in values amongst participants of diverse religious, spiritual, and secular practices. This assists in creating an unexpected community of shared values that enable organizational dialogue for the common good, rather than individual fear and suppression of voice. Such dialogue could assist in the recognition of moral challenges.

We believe that by helping individuals more clearly articulate their most deeply held standards for acting with impeccable character, we can better empower them to be decisive leaders who can quickly, confidently, and consistently make ethical decisions. The following exercise forms the basis of a new course in a management school on Religion, Business, and Leadership Integrity to be taught by one of the authors, in spring 2013.

The Exercise: My Ten Commandments of Character for the Workplace

Learning Objectives

This exercise has three learning objectives for participants:

- Understanding the role that one's religious and spiritual teachings, upbringing, and culture place upon one's value system
- Identifying from these abstract teachings, concrete, real-life moral principles derived consciously or unconsciously from their religion, upbringing, and culture becoming mindful of their inner voice
- "Committing in advance to ethical principles by which one is willing to live for disciplined choices and ethical guidelines developing a personal ethical code of Ten Commandments of Character for the Workplace.

The first objective is addressed by participants determining the salient religious or spiritual teachings and messages from their family and culture important to their views of what it means to be a good person, acting ethically with integrity.

We then encourage them to bring to the learning community scriptures or sacred writings that form the bases of these teachings. In the case of Jewish, Christian, or Muslim participants, this means bringing a copy of the Torah, Bible, or Qur'an to the session to use as a reference for the exercise, or other forms of traditional wisdom that embolden their behavior around virtues and values.

The second and third objectives are addressed by the "My Ten Commandments" Exercise, which will be described in the next section.

Procedures

The exercise is conducted in five parts: reflection, personal application, initial refinement, workplace application, and further refinement.

Part 1: Reflection

During the reflection portion of the exercise students are asked to reflect upon their sacred teachings to determine a personal Ten Commandments of Character, a personal code clarifying their ethical principles to guide decisions in their work and life, and to help them resist temptations. What are the ten principles your inner voice holds clear? What does your religion tell you about ethical workplace behavior? Who are your top ethical role models from biblical narratives and parables?

The code each person develops should describe the very best version of the "you" that you can be, reflecting a thoughtful ethical self, confident of ethical choices, and imbued with a sense of integrity. Since it is used to remain true to oneself, there is a need for participants to listen to and educate their own inner voice on personal rules for ethical behavior. Each of us has an idea of what is right and what is wrong. We often do not listen well enough to see our compromises for what they are, missing opportunities for self-examination and growth. Since this is their code, it must work for each of them, inspiring them to think when they have choices.

There is a need to resist any temptation to criticize the ethics of others. The main purpose of the reflection portion of the exercise is improvement in ethical actions. The question for each person is "What do you want to continue to embrace and what actions will you discard?" The goal is to help participants clarify their own principles, which if not followed will not only lead to remorse, but also an eroding sense of integrity.

Because of the amount of reflection (and possible consultation) required to do this exercise well, we recommend Part 1 as a written homework assignment to be submitted to you, the facilitator, well in advance of facilitation of the other parts of this exercise.

Prompt

The prompt for the homework assignment follows:

Think about and identify unique temptations in your own lives. When you think about these ethical issues, which ones have left you with a legacy of remorse? Where do you need some clarity about what is right and what is wrong?

1. Based upon your religion or belief system, come up with Ten Commandments that you would want to use to guide your behavior in the workplace. Once you come up with your personal "Ten Commandments," reword them, if necessary, to reflect how you will behave in the workplace.
2. Indicate from where you derive each commandment: religious scriptures, spiritual teachings, biblical stories or parables, or philosophical background. If your commandments are inspired by religious texts such as the Torah, Bible, or Qur'an, cite appropriate passages. What is the message you take from this concerning expected behavior? Be as specific as possible in describing your Ten Commandments for workplace behavior.
3. Then include how you would follow each commandment in the workplace.

Present each value and statement as a commandment (e.g., "Value my time and the time of others.").

Sample Commandment

"I will value my time and the time of others."

"By the (token of) time (through the ages)! Surely Man is in loss, except those who believe and do good, and exhort another to Truth, and exhort one another to patience." (Qur'an, 103:103)

The value of time is paramount in Islam just as it is important in the workplace. This surah explains that one should not misuse the amount of time they are given but instead should use it wisely and consciously. Being lazy or "killing time" is not acceptable as spare time should be used in the betterment of yourself or the help of your neighbor."

When at work I will arrive on time, work consistently to complete tasks, be prepared when I work with others demonstrating respect for their time, and put in a full day's work, staying late when necessary to complete organizational priorities.[53]

Part 2: Personal Application[54]

Ask participants to recall an ethical decision in their lives where they still have remorse. They may not know why, but it remains in their memory.

1. Ask them to identify the category of wrongdoing such as deception, lying, stealing, harming, or other? What were the consequences?
2. Then have them test their Ten Commandments of Character for its usefulness in guiding their actions around this dilemma. How well do their commandments operate in everyday life? Are they practical? Do they mean them?
3. Ask the following questions concerning the universality of the commandments as applied to their ethical scenario:
    - How would you feel if the shoe were on the other foot?
    - Would you think the same way if your behavior were reported on the first page of the *Wall Street Journal, New York Times*, or your hometown newspaper read by your friends?
    - Would this be a behavior you would expect and accept from your children?
    - What if the person on the receiving end were a loved one?
    - What would your mother think?
4. Now check the reciprocity of the Ten Commandments asking:
    - Would you want everyone to follow this?
    - Would you want other people applying the same rule to you?
5. Now check them for their usefulness:
    - Are your Ten Commandments practical?
    - Do you really mean what you wrote?

Part 3: Initial Refining of The Ten Commandments of Character

In this section have participants draw sharper lines for their ethical behavior so that they can ensure compliance with the standards they set. They want to have their code sharpen their own thinking and have it assist in changing their own behavior. It should be quickly accessed and useable without remorse.

Part 4: Workplace Applications

In this section of the exercise, we provide vignettes for students to individually, then in triads,[55] reflect upon and discuss what their Ten Commandments of Character would have them do.

With each vignette, students are asked:

"Using your own Ten Commandments of Character in the Workplace, please describe *in detail* what you would do and say if you found yourself in this vignette. Please note which of your commandments is guiding your behavior. Alternatives should be evaluated against each person's own individual code. If you discover that you have omitted a commandment that would help prescribe your behavior in this situation, by all means, write it down for a homework reflection paper and refer to it on the Vignette sheet."

After initial discussion of the vignette, then apply the following three questions to each:

- What would your ethical role model do? (Compare to the standard of their behavior).
- What would the other shoe test suggest you do? (Test for reciprocity).
- What if everyone did it? (Test for universality).

Vignettes

Depending upon the size of the group, you may first want to do one of the vignettes together as a model for what the triads will do later. Feel free to use our original or adapted vignettes, or Telushkin's vignettes in the *Ten*

Commandments of Character, or vignettes from your own lived (or observed) experience.

Vignette A

Your present company is trying to minimize the impact of a downward trend in sales. In last month's meeting, top management announced that alcoholic beverages were no longer being covered on business trips. This policy was instated to avoid employees claiming alcohol as reimbursable "food" expenses. This week, you and two colleagues are at a training class out of town. Last night, while you and your colleagues were talking and having dinner, you noticed that your coworker ordered two martinis. You also noticed that when your coworker requested a bill for his portion, that he requested the server to re-label his martinis as appetizers, without altering the price.

Vignette B

You are an Information Technology consultant. Instead of working at your company, you work each day at your firm's client, ABC, Inc. One of the managers, Chris, who is the same gender as you, keeps making comments with sexual innuendo to you. Today, while getting coffee, Chris made yet another pass at you … this time physically brushing past you and commenting about how good you smell. ABC is your company's largest client and you know that your long-term contract brings in a lot of revenue. Chris is one of the managers reporting directly to the cost center manager—who is the manager who contracts your services from your firm.

Vignette C

You are a student working to earn your MBA part-time while you work full-time. You are in your final course, Policy, which is graded solely based upon group responses to case studies. You find out that a close friend of yours took the class two years ago. While talking to her, you discover they did three of the same cases you are assigned this semester. If you don't make a "B" or better in this class, your company will not pay your tuition, which is in excess of $900/credit hour.

Vignette D

You are in charge of recruiting a business analyst to work for your firm. You have attended three career fairs this month to gather resumes of qualified candidates. Last week when you spoke with your father, you told him about your travel and the position for which you were recruiting. Today, when you checked your mail, you noticed a resume and cover letter from Cory Smothers, the son of the CEO of your father's company. While Cory has a degree from a top business school, he has no work experience. Many of the candidates from the career fair have had at least two years of experience as business analysts, as well as internships with top corporations.

Vignette E

You are a consultant and know that your bid for phase one on a project at $500,000 will be more than your client wants to spend. You could low-ball the bid to $250,000, knowing that once you began the work the client would have to agree to the extra work and the extra expense since they are already well into the project. You are tempted to understate the cost.

Vignette F

You are currently looking for a job. During the job hunt you accept an offer, promising the company that you would start on a particular date. But knowing that this wasn't exactly what you wanted, and the salary wasn't as good as you think you deserve, you continue to look for other positions. Two days before your start date you get another job offer, breaking your promise to the first company.

Vignette G

You are new to a job. While hanging out with your new colleagues, one of them tells the group a racist joke that has everyone laughing. You are shocked, finding the joke disgusting. Being new to your position, and wanting to fit in and make a good impression, you are tempted to keep quiet, and even consider smiling. Your personal ethics forbids deception. You also are afraid that keeping quiet might give people the impression that you approve of such humor.

Vignette H

A group of your friends live together in an apartment while working part-time and attending school. You see an ad at a local store that will provide a 50-inch screen TV free for 90 days. The condition is that you need to return it in that time period, indicating that you have decided you do not want it. You and your three friends are discussing acting as a tag team. Each would take a 90-day turn, ending up with a whole year of use of a TV you all were unable to afford.

Vignette I

When you were ready to leave a company party celebrating the success of a desired acquisition, you realize you have had too much to drink. It is late. You are expected home. At this time of night there are unlikely to be many people driving on the road. In spite of recognizing that you are impaired, you decide to drive your car home.

Vignette J

Sarah and David are single, mid-twenties professionals who are thinking about their careers after graduating with large loans to pay off. Both have been offered attractive high-paying jobs in growth industries. These positions also offer excellent advancement opportunities and about 50 hours of work a week. Sarah was offered a position in the clothing industry and David in tobacco production. Sarah's firm uses factories in Southeast Asia for manufacturing, exploiting its workers who not only receive low pay, but work in unsanitary and unsafe conditions. David's firm pays its employees well, including pensions and an expensive health care plan. David is concerned that this firm produces a cancer-causing product marketed extensively to teenagers. Each of them likes that these jobs would let them quickly pay off student debts and help them take care of aging parents. Both are troubled by moral compromises they would have to make if they worked for these companies (adapted from Dorf and Newman, 2008).

Part 5: Further Refinement

During this final stage of the exercise, participants are asked to reflect upon their group discussions of the vignettes. The goal of this stage of the exercise is to further clarify and make more specific (if and where necessary) the Ten Commandments of Character in the Workplace that each student developed.

Prompt

Now that you have tested the usefulness of your individualized Ten Commandments with a series of vignettes, take time to refine, modify, and further clarify them to enhance their usefulness in guiding ethical action.

Evidence of Participant Learning

One way to measure participant learning is to compare the list of commandments initially submitted from the homework assignment to the robustness of their revised list of commandments as a foundation for leadership integrity and moral courage to guide ethical decisions in the workplace. Learning is demonstrated through an understanding of the role that one's religious and spiritual teachings, upbringing, and culture place upon one's values. Through personal experience and both reflective observation and reflective writing, it is possible to identify abstract teachings, concrete real-life moral principles derived consciously or unconsciously from their religion, upbringing, and culture, and mindfulness of their inner voice.

In the newly developed course, short reflection writing will be linked to code development. This will include writing of a moment of remorse, ethics in the news, a personal definition of integrity and moral character, ethical and moral touchstones of character, exploration of exceptions, and applying the code to workplace scenarios. The last reflective writing that provides evidence of participant learning involves an assessment of personal learning and reflection on the code development process and outcome as a committed blueprint for moral leadership, acting with integrity, disciplined choices, and ethical guidelines for workplace behavior.

Tips for Implementing the Exercise

Unless you are a theologian holding a doctorate in comparative religious studies, refrain from correcting *any* participant's citations (even those who share your religious, spiritual, or philosophical beliefs), even if you feel an urge to do so. In the classroom, particularly with assignments carrying such ambiguity, participants often seek certainty. Your role is to facilitate *their* process of reflection and discovery. It does not matter if they are "right" according to your standards; it only matters that they converge upon coherent, concise, and executable commandments.

If you are doing this assignment in an academic setting, we recommend excluding theological accuracy from the grading criteria. Instead, we recommend grading based upon coming up with Ten Commandments of Character, clearly expressing one's ideas, and properly citing the bases for one's commandments and their usefulness in guiding their actions. We advise refraining from editing their commandments. However, we encourage asking probing questions when you are not clear as to what participants mean.

Some students will feel uncomfortable with the exercise. They may feel that they are setting themselves up for failure. They may feel pressured to live up to the commandments that they put down on paper. If this is the case, ensure them that very few human beings *always* live up to their standards, but that they should always try. But do emphasize that having no standards is not the alternative to feeling disappointed in oneself.

Facilitator Preparation and Background Information

First and foremost, we strongly recommend that as the facilitator, you do the "My Ten Commandments of Character for the Workplace" exercise yourself before facilitating it. We recommend that you document (including a citation) specific religious, philosophical, or spiritual principles that guide your behavior. This enables you to give participants examples of what you're asking them to do. It also demonstrates to them that you think this exercise is important because *you* have completed it yourself. This will enable you to understand intimately the cyclical reflective process that participants will experience. Finally, doing the exercise gives you the confidence to encourage students who may be struggling with the exercise.

We also recommend that you have materials from the major religions in the classroom while students are doing the applied portion of the exercise. This means, at minimum, having a Torah, Bible, and Qur'an available in the classroom. We also recommend having Telushkin's *Ten Commandments of Character* present as a secular alternative to students who are agnostic or atheist. Character is an issue that transcends religion, spiritual practice, or faith tradition.

Conclusions

We believe that intervening at the individual level is a feasible complement to legalistic, compliance-based approaches to anti-corruption education. By encouraging students of all (or no) religions to simultaneously reflect upon, document, discuss, and refine their ethical behavioral standards through the development of a behavioral code, we believe that we contribute to equipping them to be decisive and ethical leaders in today's ethically challenged workplace. Our work can also be used for dialogue where religion is viewed as a rich resource on which we can broadly build and draw people together around a common good.

Key Terms and Definitions

Abrahamic religions: "Judaism, Christianity, and Islam, listed in chronological order of development, are monotheistic religions developed in the Middle East originating from the same patrilineage of Abraham who lived 4000 Years ago."[56]

Altruism: argues that love of neighbor is the ultimate ethical standard, putting help for others as primary whatever the personal cost, a type of selflessness.

Christian ethics: combines elements of duty and virtue. (See perspectives on Duty.) The Seven Heavenly Virtues are Faith, Hope, Charity, Courage, Justice, Temperance, and Prudence. Jesus taught and exemplified Humbleness, Generosity, Forgiveness, Purity, and Love. To be more virtuous, which brings harmony to one's soul and society, you are to follow the example and inspiration of Jesus.

Corruption: "illicit … behaviors, including bribery, extortion, fraud, nepotism, graft, speed money, pilferage, theft, embezzlement, falsification of records, kickbacks, influence-peddling."[57]

Cultural relativism: using cultural norms to determine what is right, focusing on responsibilities to the larger community and to make decisions that support the common good, not depending on absolute truth.

Deception: "failing to correct an inaccurate impression, feigning ignorance, not telling the whole truth, withholding information, sugarcoating the truth, or overusing tact. Deception is intentionally giving a false impression with or without telling a lie."[58]

Enlightened self-interest: determines the cost and benefits of moral choices, seeking to do the greatest good for the greatest number of people.

Ethics: the principles of right and wrong that people use to guide their behavior.[59]

Ethical decision-making: making decisions about dilemmas with an ethical dimension.[60]

Ethical decision-making approaches: the thought processes and rationales that individuals use to resolve ethical dilemmas.[61]

Ethics of care: contemporary altruistic feminist approach arguing that a different voice to moral decision-making based on caring for others through their relationships rather than the abstract moral principles of a justice (legalistic) approach. Put need of specific individuals first, thinking how individuals are impacted by decisions.

Ethical perspectives: articulate, commit to and defend specific values, principles, and ideals by which to live one's life that ground ethical judgments about who to be and what to do.

Harm: use of or threat to use violence against another person … also includes acts that may lead to physical injury to another … causing risk or harm to others.[62]

Individualized imperative: individually derived standards to which one holds consistently across situations, no matter the personal cost or temptation.

Integrity: part of one's character, consisting of discrete virtues, such as behavioral consistency between words and actions and espoused values and enacted values, across time and situations; avoiding hidden agendas and acting morally, transparently, and sincerely from internal values – even in the face of adversity or temptation.[63]

Jewish ethics: is virtue ethics. Jewish virtues include *tikkun olam*, a Hebrew phrase meaning "repairing the world," contributing to not only making the world a better place, but fairness, honesty, respect, loving your neighbor, being charitable, desiring to learn, questioning what you do not understand, striving for social justice, and ethically responding to others. Virtues are important because they help a person live his or her life in service to others, improving the world, community, and him or herself.

Kant's categorical imperative: involves three principles. First is individual relying on abstract universal standards of right and wrong that must always be followed when acting, regardless of the situation or consequences. Emphasizes behavior based on abstract moral principles of obligation, impartiality, and treating others fairly apart from consequences. Some actions (like telling the truth) are always right while others (cheating) are always wrong. Universality means if an action is right for you, it would be right for everyone to act the same without inconsistency. A second principle includes that each person is of value. To use another person as a means to further one's own ends denies their status as a rational human being. Within this principle is an obligation to devote time to improving oneself and helping other people. The third principle states the importance of freely choosing to adopt and impose specific moral obligations. This forms a guideline for moral awareness of one's own freedom as a human being and the ethical freedom of others.

Kant's ten commandments: sees the Ten Commandments as valid ethical commands. Criticizes that they lay no requirements on having a good moral disposition based on reasoning, but simply are laws to be followed rather than the individual behaving as a moral agent.

Legalism: bases decisions on society's laws or policies, with justice and fairness guaranteeing the same basic rights and opportunities to everyone.

Light-of-day: weighs costs and benefits according to the opinions of others using the likely opinion of important others to determine what is right.

Lying: telling someone something we know not to be true with intention of misleading him/her.[64]

Perspectives on duty: a duty-based perspective of the Ten Commandments says that you are to follow certain rules laid out in the Bible including not only the Ten Commandments but also many other laws stated in the Bible and other religious texts. It is possible to believe the Ten Commandments but understand ethics to be virtue-based. This perspective tells you to not violate the duties set forth in certain religious texts. Follow these rules to either please God who will reward you if you follow them or punish you if you do not. Others follow the rules because they believe they provide a foundation for virtues and a stable society.

Reciprocity: mutual action. In the case of an ethical code the questions to ask are (1) "Would I want other people applying this rule to me?" and (2) "Would you want everyone to follow this?"

Other shoe test: a self-test for rationalization, the process of constructing a justification for a decision which you suspect is flawed, blurring right and wrong, and distorting thinking. It involves the age-old question, "How would you feel if the shoe were on the other foot?" What would the other shoe test suggest you do as a further test for reciprocity as a step in making a quality decision by testing the ethical quality of the alternatives to distinguish between good, bad, better, and best.

Stealing: appropriating the property of others without permission … including outright theft like shoplifting, embezzlement, or swindling … taking or accepting something that is not ours, or acquiring another's property without permission ... downloading copyrighted digital files, profiting from others' inadvertent mistakes, appropriate incidentals ... buying under false pretenses, infringing on other's property, underpaying, overbilling, and borrowing to point of violating another's trust.[65]

Universality: applying to everyone. Ask the questions: (1) "Would you think the same way if your behavior were reported on the first page of a newspaper read by your friends?" (2) Would you accept this behavior from your children?" (3) What would your mother think?"

Usefulness: practical, serves a purpose, beneficial, advantageous. Can be applied in a variety of situations and contexts leading to reasonable effectiveness or successful outcomes.

Utilitarianism: weighing the costs and benefits of moral choices, seeking to do the greatest good for the greatest number of people.

Study Questions

1. After participating in this exercise, do you feel more able to succinctly articulate your personal values? Why or Why not?
2. What role does your religious, spiritual, or philosophical stance play in helping you navigate ethical conflicts?
3. Did this exercise better equip you to dialogue across differences in religious or spiritual stances? If so, how?
4. What, if any, commonalities did you find between your Ten Commandments of Character and those written by others with differing belief systems?
5. What will you do to integrate your Ten Commandments of Character into your daily life?

Additional Reading

Ariely, D. (2012). *The (Honest) truth about dishonesty: How we lie to everyone—especially ourselves.* New York: Harper-Collins.

Bazerman, M., H., & Tenbrunsel, A. E. (2011). *Blind spots: Why we fail to do what's right and what to do about it.* Princeton, NJ and Oxford, UK: Princeton University Press.

Cohen, R. (2012). *Be good: How to navigate the ethics of everything.* San Francisco, CA: Chronicle Books.

Comer, D. R., & Vega, G. (Eds.) (2011). *Moral courage in organizations: Doing the right thing at work.* Armonk, NY and London, England: M.E. Sharpe.

Del Mastro, M. L. (2006). *All the women of the Bible.* Edison, NJ: Castle Books.

Eisler, R. (2007). *The real wealth of nations: Creating a caring economics.* San Francisco, CA: Berrett-Koehler Publishers.

Gardner, H. (2011). *Truth, beauty, and goodness reframed: Educating for the virtues in the twenty-first century.* New York: Basic Books.

James, C. J., & Smith, J. G. (2007). George Williams in Thailand: An exercise in ethical decision-making. *Journal of Management Education, 31*(5), 696–712.

Haidt, J. (2012). *The righteous mind: Why good people are divided by politics and religion.* New York: Pantheon Books.

Hicks, D. (2011). *Dignity: The essential role it plays in resolving conflict.* New Haven, CT and London, UK: Yale University Press.

Kristof, N. D., & WuDunn, S. (2009). *Half the sky: Turning oppression into opportunity for women worldwide.* New York: Alfred Knopf.

Manz, C. C. (2011). *The Leadership Wisdom of Jesus: Practical Lessons for Today.* San Francisco, CA: Berrett-Koehler Publishers.

Manz, C. C., Manz, K. P., Marx, R. D., & Neck, C. P. (2001). *The wisdom of Solomon at work.* San Francisco, CA: Berrett-Koehler Publishers.

Mele, D. (2012). *Management ethics: Placing ethics at the core of good management.* Hampshire, England, UK: Palgrave Macmillan.

Pava, M. (2011). *Jewish ethics in a post-madoff world: A case for optimism.* New York and Hampshire, England: Palgrave Macmillan.

Pava, M. L. (2009). *Jewish ethics as dialogue: Using spiritual language to re-imagine a better world.* New York and Hampshire, England: Palgrave Macmillan.

Schwartz, B., & Sharpe, K. (2010). *Practical wisdom: The right way to do the right thing.* New York: Riverhead Books.

Schulweis, Rabbi H. M. (2008). *Conscience: The duty to obey and the duty to disobey.* Woodstock, VT: Jewish Lights Publishing.

Shiller, R. J. (2012). *Finance and the good society.* Princeton, NJ and Oxford, UK: Princeton University Press.

Wankel, C., & Stachgowicz-Stanusch (2011). *Effectively integrating ethical dimensions into business education.* Charlotte, NC: Information Age Publishing.

Wilkinson, R., & Pickett, K. (2009). *The spirit level: Why greater equality makes societies stronger.* New York: Bloomsbury Press.

Wolfe, L. (2002). *Leadership secrets from the Bible.* New York: MJF Books.

PART IV

Teaching Anti-Corruption Effectively

CHAPTER 11

Testing the Effectiveness of Innovative Teaching Tools to Train Anti-Corruption Students

Ernestina Giudici, Federica Caboni and Roberta Atzori

The partner of the crime of corruption is often our indifference.

Abstract

One of the most frequent topics that occupy the TV news and newspaper pages is certainly corruption. This phenomenon is so prevalent nowadays as well as throughout the history of humanity. Moreover, it is so multifaceted that it is difficult to apply a unique shared definition.

Taking the spread of corruption into consideration, the aims of this work are: to understand what students knowledge is about the damages that corruption can cause; verify if we as teachers are adequately preparing our students to be ethically correct and not corrupt; which form of communication and teaching tools are more able to interact with students to create a durable awareness of how damaging corruption can be.

To have unequivocal answers, we directly involved the students of the Business Communication course at the University of Cagliari (Italy) to become co-producers of teaching tools. The results of the experiment highlight that students respond positively to being directly involved in their learning process, and that their preferred tools are social networks, comics, movies and storytelling. In this chapter some student work will be presented.

Introduction

Corruption is a phenomenon that can be observed throughout the history of humanity. If the previous observation is true, we can question why the phenomenon has drawn more attention from scholars, politicians, managers, and so on only from certain decades?

A possible answer can be found by considering the shift from a closed to an open world.[1] In fact, corrupted actions in a not interconnected world consume their effects inside the area in which they occur; on the contrary, in the actual world in which each area is highly interconnected with each other, also the corrupted actions are more widespread all over the world than in the past.

The above cited is only one of the numerous reasons that put the corruption phenomenon in the headlines and therefore it is not possible not to deal with focus and determination: it is impossible to derogate any longer.

To combat and prevent the corruption phenomenon, the engagement of the most important international organizations has clearly been increasing from the end of the previous century to today.

One of the first international official documents where corruption is clearly named as a serious crime is the Global Compact.[2] More exactly principle 10 (of the 12 that compose the Compact) state: *Business should work against corruption in all its forms, including extortion and bribery.* The Global Compact is a set of rules that are voluntarily subscribed to: on September 2010, 6,000 participating companies from 135 countries, and 2,300 non-business participants had joined.

The United Nations with its United Nations Office on Drugs and Crime (UNODC), referring to corruption states that: "Corruption is a complex social, political and economic phenomenon that affects all countries. Corruption undermines democratic institutions, slows economic development and contributes to governmental instability."

It is on December 14, 2005 that the United Nations Convention against Corruption (UNCAC)[3] entered in force. The UNCAC is the only legally binding universal anti-corruption instrument. This Convention is relevant for many reasons, but first of all because it presents a clear, strong, unequivocal position of intolerance towards corruption and a public declaration to combat this detrimental phenomenon with all the necessary tools. This convention marked a big change: it brought to light a phenomenon that in the past was only whispered.

To invite all the people of the world to discuss, organize actions, report corruption, and so on, December 9 was elected as the International Anti-Corruption Day.

In December 2011, the motto was: *What Can You Do? Act against Corruption!* The site of the event invites people to say a big "No" to this crime and suggests that we "Engage the youth of your country about what ethical behavior is, what corruption is and how to fight it, and to demand their right to education. Ensuring the future generations of citizens are brought up to expect corruption-free countries is one of the best tools to ensure a brighter future."

As a demonstration of the continuing and growing attention to supporting states, organizations and citizens in the fight against corruption, on September 1, 2011, UNODC has launched a web-based anti-corruption portal known as Tools and Resources for Anti-Corruption Knowledge.

Also the European Parliament pushes for European Union (EU)-wide sanctions against corruption.[4] Corruption costs the EU €120 billion per year, almost as much as the EU's annual budget. The economic crisis in many EU countries makes anti-corruption measures all the more urgent.

A question can be posed: why despite the efforts of the abovementioned international institutions, has corruption not decreased significantly? Is it because the efforts are not aimed at the right portion of the population, which is at young people (as the Anti-Corruption Day aim suggests)? And, also if the attention is aimed at young people, are we sure that the most appropriate tools and language are adopted?

To know what students think (as a significant representation of young people) we did an experiment involving students of the Managerial Economics Course (II level), attending the Communication course for the academic year 2011–2012 at the University of Cagliari. The experiment had the aim of understanding what kind of teaching tools are more useful to interact with students, speaking their own language. The expected results were, in this way, suggestions on the most correct tools able to help teachers engage in preventing corruption.

The next point is devoted to discussing the complexity of finding a shared corruption definition with the help of scholar's contributions. The subsequent point—the core of the chapter—is devoted to analyzing the experimented work with students as co-producers. Finally, some comments are presented.

Not an Easy Task: To Find a Shared Corruption Definition

How should we define corruption? To find a definition for corruption universally accepted by scholars is very hard because different forms of corruption exist in society, in several sectors. In a general way corruption can be defined as the use of money or gifts to get certain kinds of benefits and advantages or utilities,[5] or synthetically, corruption can be defined as "a private gain at public expense."[6]

The term corruption may be related to behaviors that are carried out at various levels to obtain a certain goal: institutions, organizations, human beings. As Vargas-Hernandez points out, all forms of corruption are based on the potential conflict between the individual's professional and personal interests and values but to find out the causes of different forms of corruption proves to be a difficult task.[7] To highlight the destructive force that corruption may have, Carvajal[8] defines them as "a social pathology. It has much the same effect on the development of a nation that cancer has on the life of a biological organism."

On the more or less possibility of the diffusion of corruption, culture can play a significant role. As Jing and Graham[9] argue, cultural values significantly affect the level of corruption of a certain country. They found that countries with higher power distance and lower individualism tend to be more corrupt. The previous observation is confirmed also by Hofstede's[10] contribution: he underlines that corruption can have a fertile ground in societies in which people tend to accept authority and dependence and power is not equally distributed and where group membership and cooperation is widespread and people are not expected to look only after themselves and their immediate family.

The capillary diffusion of corruption may appear clear in considering some other definitions: Waldman[11] states that corruption regards public officials who misuse their authority and power to violate legal norms, while Dion[12] observes that the main agent of corruption is not always a public official, but the phenomenon also includes corruption among private agents. Cragg[13] proposes a definition highlighting that corruption is any attempt, whether successful or not, to persuade someone in a position of responsibility to make a decision or recommendation on any grounds other than the intrinsic merits of the case with a view to the advantage or advancement of himself or herself or another person or group to which he or she is linked through personal commitment, obligation, or employment or individual, professional, or group loyalty.

Corruption is often seen as "someone corrupting someone else," while Dion[14] categorizes corruption levels by arguing that corruption does not only concern people, organizations, and institutions, but firstly, it regards the corruption of principles and the corruption of moral behavior inside individuals.

Considering corruption as a result of an acquired role of power, Anechiarico and Jacobs[15] define corruption as abuse of authority for material gain; an alternative definition of corruption is the exchange of wealth for power, where the power is rooted in a public position proposed by Jain.[16] "Bribery is committed when a public servant is offered, promised or granted, in return for an action already carried out or is to be expected."[17]

Two other scholars, Rendtorff and Wankel,[18] give suggestions on the way to go to reduce the corruption emergence and growth. Rendtorff[19] gives attention to the ethical responsibility and points out that without ethical responsibility, political power is doomed to end in corruption. Politicians need a strong integrity not to be tempted by corruption; a person with strong moral principles and who does not accept being bought by money, gifts, or other types of support. Wankel[20] invites us to reflect on the role of corporate culture and writes: "Since a corporate culture is largely a reflection of the shared values of the members of an organization, changing the values of those entering into organizations is one way to spark organizational culture change in the future."

These two last contributions invite us—as teachers—to reflect on how essential our role is in instilling in our students the awareness of anti-corruption. In fact, supporting the Wankel observation, if we are able to form students' awareness of how dangerous corruption is, when they are inserted in an organization may work to create a new organizational climate able to involve all organization members and develop a place with a strong corruption reduction. For this reason, business school and all levels of education play an important role in being part of the solution against corruption by developing moral fiber in their students. By adopting several teaching tools, it is possible to help students to understand the consequences of corruption for society, and in this way to spark anti-corruption behavior.[21]

To involve students in lectures that permit them to understand the negative consequences of corruption practices, it is necessary to use teaching tools close to the perceptions, languages, and the way of thinking of the new generation of students, such as social media (e.g., Facebook, Twitter), comics, cartoons, and other similar interactive tools.

Normally we talk about corruption in political, economic, and public administration sector, but probably these are only sectors in which it is simple to find corruptive practices. Indeed, several forms of corruption such as bribery, collusion, fraud, extortion, abuse of discretion, favoritism, nepotism, and many others, can be found in all sectors of society today,[22] in the private sphere, in the public sphere, in the enterprises sphere and in the sphere of many other societies. And for these reasons it is fundamental to engage people in their first phase of life, such as students, in order to develop a strong awareness of how damaging corruption can be for society as a whole, based on the internalization of principles that are like a protective armor to anti-corruption behaviors. In order that today's students can be honest citizens and managers of tomorrow, it is necessary to speak about corruption in order to explain to them that any unlawful behavior can change to corruptive behavior and it can lead to the destruction and degradation of a community.

According to Pfeffer and Fong,[23] the role of schools in creating a culture of honesty and anti-corruption behaviors is fundamental; in fact, subjects should have a responsibility to provide practitioners with training in the basics of ethics that would ideally lead to an informed workplace and act as a catalyst to stimulate socially and ethically grounded corporate activities and programs.

What Teaching Tools Are Able to Prevent Corruption? Student's Point of View (Co-Producers)

Today's students will be tomorrow's citizens and managers: this observation may appear obvious and trivial, but are we adequately preparing our students to be ethically correct and not corrupt? Do we really know what they think about corruption? Which form of communication and teaching tools are more able to interact with students to create a durable awareness of how damaging corruption can be?

In agreement with Luthar and Karri,[24] the more widespread perceptions of students are not always aware of the connection between ethical business behavior and the success they can achieve for themselves and their businesses. Is this perception correct?

To have unequivocal answers, what could be better than directly involving the students? Therefore, we decided to work together with students during the Communication course (academic year 2011–2012) from March to June, at the University of Cagliari where the authors work. The students' involvement was deemed essential to understanding what students think about corruption, what teaching tools are more able than others to better interact with them, and what kind of communication they choose to speak student-to-student stimulating their sensibility.

The activity/experiment evolved through several steps.

The first one was devoted to creating a common awareness of what corruption is. Students were invited to read several papers[25] to be discussed in class together. In this way it was possible to share different definitions of corruption. Through student discussion, various kinds of corruption that express more or less level of corruption but all with a damaging influence to societal and economic systems were underlined.

An observation that clearly emerged from the student's discussion was that some behaviors, even if they cannot be classified as corruption—*strictu sensu*—should be underlined and closely fought as signs of a potential tendency toward corruption: the example highlighted was cheating during exams.

The students' belief is also supported by the study from McCabe, Butterfield, and Treviño[26] that found that 56% of MBA students admitted to having cheated in class. Also, according to Tang,[27] business students tend to behave unethically. Such unethical behavior becomes problematic when brought into the working environment and business by graduating students.[28]

Students gave attention to the not *strictu sensu* corruption also because they possess the basic knowledge of the system thinking methodology, whose essential concept is the understanding of the existing interdependence among events, even if they seem insignificant at first glance.[29] More exactly, students are aware that "if the reality is not analyzed by adopting the system thinking approach, it is impossible to get a correct perception of the strong and numerous interdependences that exist among events. This also means that the unethical behavior does not appear randomly, but by combination, as system complexity explains."[30]

Once the corruption concept was shared, it was time to analyze some teaching tools to give students the basic knowledge to become "co-producers" in the experiment. Indeed, teachers and students together had the aim of verifying what teaching tools are more suitable to interact with students to help them not to be corruptible in their future life. Tools taken into consideration were narratives, social media, movies, comics, and cartoons. At the end of this analysis, each student chose his or her preferred tool and 20 small groups were trained.

The last step was the presentation of all jobs for which each student had to express his or her evaluation responding to few questions including: Is the object of communication clear? Who directed the communication? Do you think that the tool adopted has been effective?

Here not all the group work was analyzed (even if all of a really high standard!) but only a few with attention paid to taking several categories of teaching tools into account, and among those the tools that students estimated to be more effective.

The Student's Perception of Corruption

A useful starting point is the contribution of the group[31] that inserted a questionnaire on Facebook receiving 400 answers in 48 hours (a total of 645 in a couple of days). The interest in this work is dual: First, the survey clearly highlights that 75% of students are convinced that the corruption phenomenon is spread inside society nowadays; second, that mass media does not give adequate attention to corruption (38%), while others

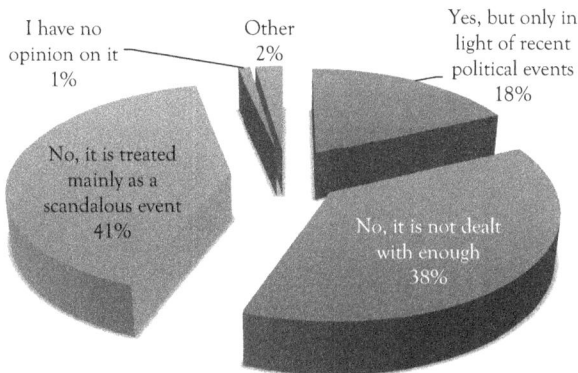

Figure 11.1. Do you think that the phenomenon of corruption has the right emphasis in the media?
Source: The data were collected by the students: Francesco Caria, Casula Patrizia, Deidda Lisa, Illary Mei, Emanuela Pilloni.

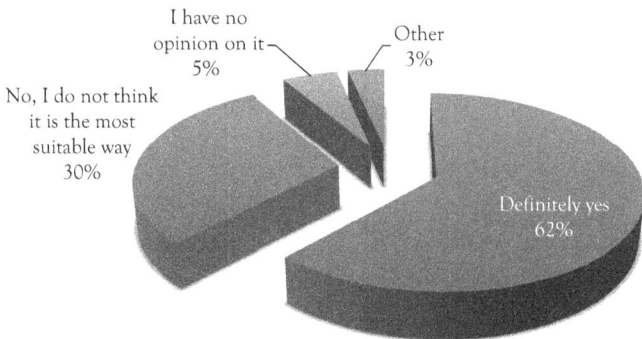

Figure 11.2. Do you believe that actively participating in discussions in social media is easier to bring out the importance of the corruption phenomenon?
Source: The data were collected by the students: Francesco Caria, Casula Patrizia, Deidda Lisa, Illary Mei, Emanuela Pilloni.

observed (41%) that the topic is treated only as a scandalous event (Figure 11.1).

The data that commands the most attention is that 62% of students expressed trust in the role of social networks in addressing the problem of corruption (Figure 11.2): this means that it is the tool that students consider the more familiar and the more adaptable as a vehicle for their communications. Another result has some interest: to the question "Do you think that the active participation of citizens can contribute to the fight against corruption?" 86% of students said "Yes."

The survey also highlighted that students consider politics the most corrupted category (77%, while the economic system 10% and the health system 7%). To communicate with effectiveness, these results students chose to project a few minutes of one of Totò's movies (The Honorable, 1963): the scene refers to a discussion between three members of the Italian Parliament who are organizing corruptive activities. Students chose this scene because corruption is ridiculed but it is useful as a starting point to compare the point of view of the past with the present. In fact, as the percentages highlighted above confirm, the political system is the most corrupted in people's perception: unfortunately, with no changes from the past to present.

Small Bribes, Big Damages

Other groups chose to take into consideration actions that can appear not so dangerous or close to corruption, but only at first glance.

The first group taken into consideration[32] chose to communicate how dangerous it can be to download music, movies, etc. illegally. Some might observe that even if illegal downloading can be considered a crime, it cannot be strictly included in the corruption concept. Students decided to include downloads because if it is true that particularly young people do this for their own use (illegal action that may open the door to future corruptive behavior), it is not exactly the same as the behavior of those organizations that download music, movies, etc. to sell it, obviously with the compliance of another party.

As Rendtorff[33] noted, both the person who uses bribery and the one who accepts it are responsible. Corruption is in fact a double relation between the two parts: it is possible to bribe someone only if this person accepts bribery; at the same time, in order to be accepted, somebody must offer the bribe.

The work of this group is a combination between social media and narratives. Of interest are the three steps of the path chosen to get in touch with young people, to attract their attention and to keep it.

The first step was devoted to creating a page on Facebook by inserting phrases creating curiosity and inviting subject to answer to the questionnaire. The inviting phrase was: *"Download and file sharing: tell us your opinion! … and continue to follow us."* The second part of the phrase is the most important because it means that a "community" is beginning its life: people who choose to participate are accepting to be involved in discussions on corruption. Close to this phrase there was the link to the questionnaire with another inviting phrase to fill it out (Enter the Facebook page http://wwwfacebook.com/downloadlegale and fill out the questionnaire. Thanks!).

The second step was devoted to the analysis of the survey results: 329 people responded in a couple of days. As expected, 92% of respondents regularly download from the Internet in their spare time. The podium of the most downloaded is: first music, second movies and TV series, and third software. To the question "In your opinion is it correct to download illegally?" 52% answered "no" and 48% answered "yes." The main reasons for the "no" is "It is incorrect to the authors," and for the "yes" is "Legally downloading is too expensive" and "It is the easiest way I know."

The third step focused on the inclusion on the community page created in the first step: (a) the survey results and (b) a specific created story.

The phrase inserted to introduce the survey results, and also to invite who responded to the survey to continue to contribute toward discussion on the corruption is: *"Are you sure that there is nothing as an alternative to illegal downloads? … continue to follow us!"* Moreover, students created and inserted a story on the Facebook page (Marco's story) with the aim of highlighting how detrimental downloading illegally can be when considering the loss of jobs this could create. The story tells of a young man who is proud to download files illegally and does not understand why he should not do so, until he discovers that the father of one of his friends has been fired: he worked in a music store.

Table 11.1. Small Bribes, Big Dramas
Source: This comics has been created by students Silvia Atzu, Andrea Marcello, Marco Mereu and Claudio Andrea Saiu.

Close to this work, is that of another group[34] who chose comics as a tool to communicate how damaging corruption can be: obviously the situation is presented in a paradoxical and extreme way to cause a strong impact. The created comic, not randomly entitled Kevin Butterfly, is composed of 11 panels (Table 11.1) the sequence shows: a situation of a young college student who has clearly entered into an agreement with a colleague to copy during exams; the day of graduation with honors; the hiring as financial manager; his incompetence that emerges; the firm closing due to bankruptcy; all the workers bushing to survive. The last panel shows two sentences: Theories or sad reality? Small bribes, big dramas.

It is by reading the last panel that suggestions on the meaning of the name of the character emerges: in fact, the famous Lorenz butterfly effect inspired it: *"Can the beating of a butterfly's wings in Brazil set off a tornado in Texas?*" No matter how big the bribe is, because the effect is always harmful.

In the students' opinion (because each piece of work, as noted, was presented and evaluated by all the students attending the communication course) this comic was estimated one of the most effective ways to help young people understand the way in which behavior, not clearly considered as a bribe, can have harmful effects: just like the butterfly effect.

The work of this group is relevant from another point of view: sometimes we, as teachers, are not entirely conscious of the impact that concepts that we transmit to our students have, and above all, the methodologies that we use to teach. A clear example is the butterfly effect: it is a topic certainly not central to the first university level (that means minimum three years before the considered project), but it is a topic that is always discussed with the active involvement of students invited to recognize examples of the butterfly effect in the reality that surrounds us. It is a way to learn the role that "weak signals" are widespread, and it is common that students do not forget topics experienced firsthand, as the work presented in few lines above shows.

The Strength of Values

Two other groups chose to prepare both a short movie presentation: one regarding the AGESCI (Italian catholic scouts association),[35] and the other a sports association named Amsicora.[36] The common message is: if strong principles are given to young people, they will be incorruptible forever.

To better understand the message that comes from the Agesci movement with reference to acts to prevent corruption, it is important to underline that from the first moment that a child decides (or their parents) to be part of the movement, he/she begins to learn the essential values of scoutism, that is the values of the scouts' identity. The result is the creation, day by day, of a strong identification and the sharing of values that would render any unethical, illegal, corrupted behaviors impossible.

In their work the students particularly focused their attention on the senior partners' role: those who are engaged not only in transmitting ethical concepts but bearing witness with their lives. One phrase can be considered significant: *Agesci teaches a child the right way to grow up.*

More exactly, having as a reference values like cooperation, mutual respect, altruism, group life, loyalty, active citizenship, faith, the Agesci is engaged on the frontline to prevent corruption … to live the world a little better than how we found. *Once a scout, always a scout!*[37] The movie was developed inserting adequate music, with the correct time of each sequence, with an accurate choice of colors and a really strong effectiveness of sentence choices.

Amsicora is a sport organization born in Cagliari (Sardinia, Italy) in 1897. This date highlights the long life of this organization that has never become a big sporting organization as it steadfastly practiced the philosophy of honesty and correct behavior, which each of its CEO and all the associated sporting staff followed year after year .

The CEO of this organization, in the past and today, refused to accept sponsors seeking to declare an amount greater than that really paid to support various sports. In this way Amsicora often gets into economic trouble, but its determination not to succumb to corruption remains unchanged. It is usual in corruptive behavior that gifts are the tools adopted to insert corruption in a way that may appear not so unethical and not so damaging to all the people involved. It is not easy to refuse money that can help solve urgent problems for an ideal that considers sports activities capable of creating a future generation, which is not affected by the terrible cancer of corruption.

The movie presented begins with an interview of the sporting manager: only a few minutes with short and clear phrases that highlight the society's philosophy. Close to this interview images regarding different groups of young people or children that are engaged in several sporting activities are presented: the *leitmotif* is the happiness and joy that shines from their faces, also if the green carpet is far from being perfect.

The Influence of a Lack of Culture

The last work is a video regarding a missionary experience in Brazil. Students[38] decided to present some images, one after the other with a quick rhythm, with the aim of immediately capturing the attention of the people to whom the communication is addressed. Once captured, it is possible to transmit the desired message: the lack of education creates a breeding ground for corruption. The challenge of those missionaries is to help the new generation to be educated and in this way understand what behaviors are common in the field of corruption.

The missionary interviewed highlights that "justice is lagging behind and the egoism of powerful people gives the idea that they are able to win any battle." And the interviewee continues by saying: "In this situation, also giving some help is difficult, it is necessary that people are conscious of their rights. In these areas people are without identity, they do not exist. The corruption is the soul of the place and people think that this is the correct behavior: it was the behavior of their parents, their grandparents, and so on. The problem is that they do not know their rights: they do not know that they should have what they want independently of this corrupted system. Our goal is to create awareness of the real situation; it is not necessary to sell their vote in order to have water at home. Water should be considered a basic human right. Our major problem is that we have a lot of obstacles because the powerful people do not agree that people acquire awareness of their rights. But willpower is stronger than any obstacle and surely we should be the winner!"

Discussion and Conclusions

The presented works (but the same message came from those not presented), on the one hand, confirmed that students relished being involved, and, on the other hand, that the best way they prefer to communicate with each other is connected with visual[39] and social network tools.

This is a big suggestion for each teacher, and it is a stimulus to modify (if necessary) the adopted teaching methodology and tools if they are far from the student's language and their way of learning.

Nowadays students are digital natives and teachers have the task of learning this way of interacting: on the contrary, the transmitter (teacher) and the receiver (students) are unable to communicate due to the noise caused by the different ways of learning that require the adoption of teaching tools such as comics, short films, storytelling, and, above all, social networks.

The results that emerge from the student's involvement are clear: in order to help them to be honest men and women, who don't accept corruption and who are ethically correct, it is necessary that the teacher speaks their language. Moreover, it is clear that students need to have an active role in their learning activity and that they prefer ironic communication, adopting metaphors, and dealing with serious subjects with joy.

Their evaluation of comics, social network, storytelling, and videos as the most effective objects is irrefutable: it is the time that teachers accept the challenge of adopting these and other innovative teaching tools.

Key Terms with Definitions

Anti-corruption: Any behavior in contrast to corruption activities, also when not well rendered.

Innovative teaching tools: Tools such as films, storytelling, photos, social media, which when adopted in teaching activities can help teachers in their essential role to instill the awareness of anti-corruption or, in general, the principles of ethical behavior into their students.

Effective teacher: A teacher who is able to communicate with students clearly. They should be in possession of the skills enabling them to use teaching tools close to the perceptions, languages and way of thinking of the new generation of students.

Study Questions

- What lessons from this chapter can be applied to your life?
- In this chapter some new interesting tools are proposed. Do you think that they can help teachers to better interact with their students?
- Scholars have shown different opinions as to the utility of social media tools as innovative teaching tools. What is your opinion, also in light of the content of this chapter?
- Corruption is a more widely spread phenomenon than people can imagine: do you agree that it can be possible to reduce it by involving students in discussions on this topic?

- What is your opinion on the expression: "Small bribes, big damages."
- Storytelling can be considered a good tool to help people to reflect on corruption damages. Do you know an interesting story to confirm or refute the above statement?
- Can you suggest any examples of associations (sports, social, religious, etc.) that work to transmit the values that can protect young people and prevent them from corruptive behavior?

Additional Reading

Cornelius, N., Wallace, J., & Tassabehji, R. (2007). An analysis of corporate social responsibility, corporate identity and ethics teaching in business schools. *Journal of Business Ethics 76*, 117–135.

Falkenberg, L., & Woiceshyn, J. (2007). Enhancing business ethics: using cases to teach moral reasoning. *Journal of Business Ethics 79*, 213–217.

Svensson, J. (2005). Eight questions about corruption. *The Journal of Economic Perspectives 19*(3), 19–42.

Notes

Introduction

1. Scherer and Palazzo (2011); Hansen (2011).
2. Vaara and Faÿ (2012), p. 1023.

Chapter 1

1. Stachowicz-Stanusch (2011a).
2. Pless, Maak and Stahl (2010).
3. Forray and Leigh (2010).
4. Hawawini (2005); Ivory et al. (2006); Lorange (2005); Mintzberg (2004); Mintzberg and Gosling (2002); Pfeffer and Fong (2004); Starkey, Hatchuel & Tempest (2004).
5. Sims & Felton (2006).
6. Stachowicz-Stanusch, A. (2012).
7. Moon and Shen (2010); Crane and Matten (2004); Nicholson and DeMoss (2009); Swanson and Fisher (2008).
8. Mitroff (2004).
9. Mitroff (2004), p. 185.
10. Ghoshal (2005).
11. Neubaum, Pagell, Drexler, McKee-Ryan and Larson (2009).
12. Brown and Treviño (2006); Puffer and McCarthy (2008).
13. The PRME were developed between October 2006 and July 2007 by an international task force of 60 deans, university presidents and official representatives of leading business schools and academic institutions, as well as scholars, who commit to the idea of responsible management education. The idea was officially introduced by the Global Compact Office at the Global Forum "Business as an Agent of World Benefit" at Case Western Reserve University in October 2006. The PRME was launched under the patronage of UN-Secretary General Ban Ki-moon in July 2007.
14. The PRME initiative is in significant part the result of the efforts led by the UN, AACSB International, EFMD, the Aspen Institute's Business and Society Program, EABIS, GMAC, GRLI, Net Impact, and other institutions. These organizations have conducted some of the major learning and

educational initiatives on responsible management worldwide. The PRME project consolidates, frames, and gives new momentum to this joint initiative, framing it entirely by internationally accepted values such as those portrayed in the United Nations' Global Compact on Human Rights, Labour, Environment and Anti-corruption.

15. Reichel and Rudnicka (2008).
16. http://www.unprme.org/the-6-principles/index.php.
17. Kell (2005).
18. Rasche (2010).
19. Rasche (2010).
20. E.g. Wankel (2010); Walker and Arnold (2003).
21. Roberts and Roach (2009).
22. Escudero (2011), p. 211.
23. Solitander, Fougère, Sobczak and Herlin (2012).
24. Blasco (2012).
25. Viswanathan (2012).
26. Blasco (2012).
27. Solitander et al. (2012).
28. Maloni, Smith and Napshin (2012).
29. Forray and Leigh (2010).
30. Source: http://www.unprme.org/sharing-information-on-progress/.
31. The limitation criterion for inclusion of a particular country to the European continent was based on : http://www.unglobalcompact.org/NetworksAroundTheWorld/find_a_network.html.
32. Stachowicz-Stanusch A. (2011b).
33. Viswanathan, M. (2012).
34. Stachowicz-Stanusch (2011b).
35. Forray and Leigh (2010).

Chapter 2

1. The authors are grateful to Professors Mary Gentile, C. M. Ramesh, C. Gopinath and Sheila Webber for their comments and suggestions.
2. Transparency International (2012).
3. Paul (1997).
4. Davis and Ruhe (2003).
5. Hammer (2007).
6. In a recent survey by the World Bank, 42% of firms paid bribes averaging 1.5% of sales. Aterido et al. (2009), p. 12; Davis and Ruhe (2003).
7. Davis and Ruhe (2003); Otunsanya (2011).

8. The US Government's Foreign Corrupt Practices Act implemented in 1977 but increasingly being enforced on US companies. http://www.justice .gov/criminal/fraud/fcpa/docs/lay-persons-guide.pdf
9. Heeks (2011).
10. Heeks (2001).
11. Wharton (2007).
12. Wharton (2007).
13. Transparency International (2011).
14. Transparency International (2011).
15. Central Vigilance Commission (2010).
16. Quoted in Pavarala and Malik (2010).
17. Anand and Joshi (2005).
18. At an exchange rate of approximately 54:1.
19. Quoted in Pavarala and Malik (2010).
20. Wharton (2007).
21. Chene (2008).
22. Recent research suggests that Indians are individualistic on the competitiveness dimension but more collectivist in terms of preference for group work and the dominance of group goals over individual goals. See for instance Ramamoorhty, Kulkarni, Gupta, and Flood (2007).
23. Davis and Ruhe (2003).
24. Hofstede (1980).
25. Wharton (2007).
26. Christie, Kwon, Stoeberl and Baumhart (2003).
27. Hofstede (1997).
28. Christie, Kwon, Stoeberl, P. A. and Baumhart (2003).
29. Ramamoorhty, Kulkarni, Gupta and Flood (2007).
30. See for instance, Carrol and Gannon (1997) and Cheung and Chan (2008).
31. Carrol and Gannon (1997) and Cheung and Chan (2008).
32. Giacalone (2007).
33. Giacalone (2007).
34. For instance, the recent student movement in Thailand with the UNDP (2012).
35. The first author is grateful to Prof Nisigandha Bhuyan for sharing this data from her teaching experiences.
36. Gentile (2009).
37. Values, such as honesty or justice, are seen as reflecting the inherent worth or goodness of a thing or idea that is experienced deeply and internally.
38. The questions and approach are adapted from Gentile (2010).
39. Gentile (2010), p. 2.
40. Gentile (2009), p. 36.
41. Gentile (2009), p. 179.

42. Hofstede (n.d.).
43. Mellahi et al. (2010), p. 363.
44. Fisher et al. (1981), pp. 40–56.
45. Gentile (2009) p. 183.
46. Singh et al. (2011), p. 59.3.
47. Gentile (2009), p. 168.
48. The lead faculty member driving the workshop was Dr. Mary Gentile, who is the proponent of the Giving Voice to Values framework.
49. The students were enrolled at the University of the first author.
50. Elements of this code could include values such as fairness, secrecy, and confidentiality. For a greater description of the role of civil servants, see Wright (1973).
51. The questions were derived from the GVV framework.
52. The values illustrated were in line with universal values mentioned in literature that also had contextual relevance.
53. In the second workshop, a case describing an entrepreneur's ethical dilemma was discussed.
54. Drawn from the GVV framework described above.
55. Jaussi (2007).
56. Hofstede (n.d.).
57. As defined by Balogun (2003) quoted in Agbiboa (2012).
58. Margolis and Molinsky (2006).
59. Hofstede (n.d.).
60. Hofstede (n.d.).
61. http://psych.nyu.edu/trope/Trope%20et%20al.,%202007%20-%20JCP.pdf.
62. http://www.aca.org/research/pdf/ResearchNotes_Feb2011.pdf.

Chapter 3

1. Brown and Cloke (2011).
2. O'Connor and Fischer (2011).
3. Wilkinson, R and Pickett, K. (2009).
4. L. L. Lau, C. (2009).
5. L. L. Lau, C. (2009).
6. Scholtens, B. and Dam, L. (2007).
7. Ardichvili et al. (2011).
8. Barbosa, L. (1992).
9. Barbosa, L. (1995).
10. Ardichvili et al. (2011).
11. Brazil Takes Off (2009).
12. Brazil Takes Off (2009).

13. Vizeu, F. (2011).

14. Griesse, M. A. (2007).

15. Hochstetler, K. (2003)

16. Griesse, M. A. (2007).

17. Griesse, M. A. (2007).

18. Griesse, M. A. (2007).

19. Griesse, (2007).

20. Griesse, (2007).

21. Griesse, (2007).

22. Ardichvili et al. (2011).

23. Ardichvili et al. (2011).

24. Vizeu, F. (2011).

25. Amado and Brasil, (1991).

26. Duarte, F. (2006).

27. Barbosa, L. (1992).

28. Barbosa, L. (1995).

29. Duarte, F. (2006).

30. Duarte, F. (2006).

31. Pinheiro (2000).

32. Amado and Brasil (1991).

33. Duarte, F. (2006).

34. Stevens, M. L., Armstrong Elizabeth, A. and Arum, R. (2008).

35. Stevens, M. L., Armstrong Elizabeth, A. and Arum, R. (2008).

36. Stevens, M. L., Armstrong Elizabeth, A. and Arum, R. (2008).

37. Eicher, T., Gracia-Penalosa, C. and van Ypersele, T. (2009).

38. Schwartzman, S. (1998).

39. Renato and Consultores, (2005).

40. McCowan, T. (2004).

41. McCowan, T. (2004).

42. Renato Consultores (2004)

43. Renato, P., Consultores, S., Integrada and Tendencias, C. (2005).

44. McCowan, T. (2004).

45. McCowan, T. (2004).

46. McCowan, T. (2004).

47. Renato, P., Consultores, S., Integrada and Tendencias, C. (2005).

48. Paulo Renato de Souza Consultores, (200 5).

49. McCowan, T. (2004).

50. McCowan, T. (2004).

51. McCowan, T. (2004).

52. McCowan, T. (2004).

53. Marens, R. (2011).

54. Hochstetler, K. (2003).
55. Lau (2009).
56. Antonacopoulou, E. P. (2010).

Chapter 4

1. All twenty-two Arab League Members are considered. Non-Arab MENA countries such as Turkey and Israel are excluded.
2. Launched in 1995, a new index was developed by Transparency International which measured the perceived level of corruption in the aggregate in most countries throughout the world. The TI Corruption Perception Index (CPI) was groundbreaking for corruption research and policy in many ways. First, it was a free and widely available tool that quickly gained legitimacy and comprehensive geographical coverage. This index provided new measures of analysis possible for economists working on regression models in the empirical study of corruption. This landmark index enabled further strides to be made in analyzing the causes and consequences of corruption.
3. Olken (2007).
4. One in four pays bribes worldwide: study. Agence France Presse. December 8, 2010. Accessed from http://www.google.com/hostednews/afp/article /ALeqM5gODlbjVM5IQW9JNx5Iz6kWQUh8mQ?docId=CNG. ed754de0e678c862bc18161c29a672e9.a61
5. Looney (2005).
6. Transparency International. Corruption Perception Index Report (2011). Accessed from http://cpi.transparency.org/cpi2011/in_detail/
7. Jenkins et al. (2011).
8. Jenkins et al. (2011)
9. Jenkins et al. (2011)
10. Hafez (2009), p. 462.
11. Rose-Ackerman (1978, 1999).
12. Shleifer and Vishny (1993).
13. Glynn, Kobrin and Naim (1997).
14. Makdisi (2011).
15. Makdisi (2011), p. 9.
16. Williams and Beare (1999); Rivera-Batiz (2001).
17. Sachs (2005).
18. Rose-Ackerman (1978, 1997); Shleifer and Vishny (1993); Salem (2003).
19. Looney (2005).
20. Makhoul and Harrison (2004).
21. Salem (2003).
22. Hafez (2009).

23. Rose-Ackerman, S. (1997).
24. World Economic Forum. Partnering Against Corruption Initiative. http://www
    .weforum.org/issues/partnering-against-corruption-initiative, accessed May 22,
    2012.
25. Mauro (1995); Knack and Keefer (1995); Mo (2001); Pellegrini and Gerlagh
    (2004), Rivera-Batiz (2001); Shleifer and Vishny (1993); Zarrouk (2003).
26. Kaufmann, Kraay and Zoido-Lobation (2009); Neeman, Paserman, and
    Simhon (2008); Welsch (2004)
27. Rock and Bonnett (2004).
28. Mauro (1997).
29. Hellman and Kaufmann (2002).
30. Welford, Chan and Man (2007).
31. Von Weltzien Høivik (2004).
32. Gordon and Lacy (2011).
33. Swanson (2005) p. 54.
34. Jamali and Abdallah (2011).
35. Jamali and Abdallah (2011).
36. Principle 10: Businesses should work against corruption
    in all its forms, including extortion and bribery.
37. Schools were selected using Eduniversal school rankings 2011 data.
    Top ranking schools for each country were selected.
38. Swanson (2005); Hartman (2004); Giacalone and Wargo (2009).
39. McCabe and Trevino (1995); Wood, Longenecker;
    McKinney and Moore (1988).
40. Jamali and Abadallah (2011).
41. Sanyal (2000); Thorne LeClair, 2000; Sims, 2002;
    Solberg and Strong, (1995).
42. Hemmasi and Graf (2002); Sanyal (2000).
43. Makhoul and Harrison (2004)
44. Burke and Logsdon (2006); Falck and Heblich (2007);
    Porter and Kramer (2011).
45. Population Estimates CIA World Factbook 2011. https://www.cia.gov
    /library/publications/the-world-factbook/
46. GDP Figures from CIA World Factbook. https://www.cia.gov/library
    /publications/the-world-factbook/
47. HDI of most Arab States have not been adjusted for inequality. A part of the
    HDI project started in 2010, there is not yet data on most Arab States; therefore,
    Polity IV scores have been used to show the level of freedom and democracy
    (which can help indicate levels of equality) within given MENA states.
48. GDP Per Capita for Palestine taken for 2009 from United Nations data. http://
    data.un.org/CountryProfile.aspx?crName=Occupied%20Palestinian%20Territory

49. The Polity IV score of Somalia represents a gap in a period of governance called interregnum.
50. Does not include population of South Sudan.

Chapter 5

1. Tata (2005).
2. Rendtorff, J. (2009).
3. Glanz, J. (2007).
4. Prinsloo, P., Beukes, C. and De Jongh, D. (2006).
5. Miller, W. F. and Becker, D. A. (2011).
6. Amare, N. and Manning, A. (2009).
7. Sullivan, D. W. (2010).
8. Gempesaw II, C. (2009).
9. Poff, D. (2010).
10. Ritter, B. (2006).
11. Okumus, F. and Wong, K. F. (2007).
12. Seipel, M. O., Johnson, J. D. and Walton, E. (2011).
13. Bampton, R. and Maclagan, P. (2005).
14. Horn, L. and Kennedy, M. (2008).
15. Kazeroony (2010b).
16. Kazeroony (2010c).
17. Kazeroony (2009a).
18. Cameron, K. (2006).
19. Madison, R. L. and Schmidt, J. J. (2006).
20. Brink, A. (2009).
21. Osiemo, L. (2012).
22. Elias, R. (2006).
23. Shareef, R. (2010).
24. Amlie, T. T. (2010).
25. Smith, M. L., Smith, K. T. and Mulig, E. V. (2005).
26. Canarutto, G., Smith, K. T. and Smith, L. (2010).
27. Özdemir, A. and Sarikaya, M. (2009).
28. Harris, H. (2008).
29. Yeh, R., M., L. J., Moreo, P. J., R, B. and Perry, K. M. (2005).
30. Christensen, L., Peirce, E., Hartman, L., Hoffman, W. W. and Carrier, J. (2007).
31. Flannery, B. L. and Pragman, C. H. (2008).
32. Berry, G. R. and Workman, L. (2007).
33. Harris, H. (2008).

34. Anderson, R. E., Dixon, A. L., Jones, E., Johnston, M. W., LaForge, R. W., Marshall, G. W. and Tanner Jr., J. F. (2005).
35. Sedaghat, A. M., Mintz, S. M. and Wright, G. M. (2011).
36. Shareef, R. (2008).
37. Van Hise, J. and Massey, D. W. (2010).
38. Valenzuela-Manalo, M. (2011).
39. Wilhelm, W. J. (2010).
40. Cant, G. and Kulik, B. W. (2009).
41. Templin, C. R. and Christensen, D. (2009).
42. Simola, S. (2010).
43. Rice, J. A. (2007).
44. Heuer, M. (2010).
45. Goby, V. and Nickerson, C. (2012).
46. Tata, J. (2005).
47. Glanz, J. (2007).
48. Rendtorff, J. (2009).
49. Kok-Yee, N., Van Dyne, L. and Soon, A. (2009).
50. Raelin, J. A. (2007).
51. Kashyap, R., Mir, R. and Iyer, E. (2006).
52. Samuelson, J. (2006).
53. Moberg, D. J. (2006).
54. H. Kazeroony, (August 3, 2012).

Chapter 6

1. Bass and Bass (2008), p. 238.
2. Bass and Bass (2008).
3. Aquilera and Vadera (2008), p. 431.
4. Waples and Antes (2011), p. 16.
5. Bass and Bass (2008), p. 238.
6. Bass and Bass (2008).
7. Aquilera and Vadera (2008), p. 431.
8. Waples and Antes (2011), p. 16.
9. Khurana (2002); Morris, Brotheridge and Urbanski (2005).
10. Aquilera and Vadera (2008); Ashforth and Anand (2003).
11. Anand, Ashforth and Joshi (2004).
12. Padilla, Hogan and Kaiser (2007).
13. Evers (1992).
14. Rogers (1969), p. 104.
15. Evers (1992), p. 32.

16. Confessore and Park (2004); Ng and Confessore (2010).
17. Brockett and Hiemstra (1991); Candy (1991); Long (1990).
18. Ponton and Carr (1999).
19. Vaill (1996).
20. Bandura (2002), p. 101.
21. Bandura (2008).
22. Rottschaefer (1997).
23. Festinger (1957).
24. Bandura (2008).
25. Bandura (1986); Bandura (1990a); Bandura (1990b); Bandura (1999); Bandura, Caprara and Zsolnai (2000); Hinrichs, Lei Wang, Hinrichs, and Romero (2012); Moore, Detert, Trevino, Baker, and Mayer (2012).
26. Bandura et al. (2000).
27. Bandura (1991).
28. Paciello, Fida, Tramontano, Lupinetti and Caprara (2008).
29. Bazerman and Tenbrunsel (2011).
30. Moore (2008).
31. Barsky (2011).
32. Anand et al. (2004), p. 11.
33. Bandura (2008).
34. Houser (2004).
35. Heywood (1906).
36. Hariman (2003a), p. viii.
37. Crowe (2010).
38. Aquinas (1973/1272).
39. Mensing (1929/2006), p. 31.
40. Aquinas (2005).
41. Aquinas (2005), p. 1.
42. Mintzberg (2011).
43. Hariman (2003b), p. 5.
44. Cessario (2002).
45. Bass and Bass (2008), p. 221.
46. Cessario (2002); Tropman (2008).
47. Bass and Bass (2008), p. 221.
48. Mensing (1929/2006).
49. Duska (1998), p. xiv.
50. Mendonca and Kanungo (2007), p. 89.
51. Daft and Lane (2008); Zauderer (1992).
52. Baron (2010), p. 89.
53. Mendonca and Kanungo (2007), p. 89.
54. Mensing (1929/2006).

55. Havard (2007), p. 108.
56. Pope (2011), p. 11.
57. Mendonca and Kanungo (2007), p. 89.
58. May, Hodges, Chan and Avolio (2003).
59. Mendona and Kanungo (2007), p. 89.
60. Bass and Bass (2008), p. 21.
61. Cessario (2002).
62. Titus (2006), p. 151.
63. Titus (2006), pp. 289–290.
64. Titus (2006).
65. Tillich (1952), p. 36.
66. Tillich (1952), p. 37.
67. Mattison (2008).
68. Aquinas (1922).
69. Newman (1913).
70. Mattison (2008), p 186.
71. Mattison (2008).
72. Duska (1998).
73. Mensing, 1929/2006).
74. Mensing (1929/2006), p. 41.
75. Pieper (1966).
76. Mendonca and Kanungo (2007), p. 89.
77. Baron (2010), p. 115.
78. Bass and Bass (2008), p. 221.
79. Cooper (1987), p. 71.
80. Bandura (1997).
81. Kopp and Wyer (1994).
82. Peterson and Seligman (2004).

Chapter 7

1. Enron (2000).
2. ACTE (2007).
3. NLNP (2009).
4. Otusanya, O. J. (2011).
5. Argandona, A. (2006).
6. ACTK (2012).
7. ACTE (2007).
8. ACTK (2012).
9. Gentile, M. C. (2010a).
10. Neelankavil, J. P., (1994).

11. Yin, R. K. (2009).
12. Anninos, L. N. and Chytiris, L. (2011).
13. WEC (2011).
14. Rond, M. D. (1996).
15. Vroom, V. H. (1964).
16. Allen, W. R., Bacdayan, P., Kowalski, K. B. and Roy, M. H. (2005).
17. Allen, W. R., Bacdayan, P., Kowalski, K. B. and Roy, M. H. (2005).
18. Peppas, S. C. and Yu, T. T. (2007).
19. Stubbs, W. and Cocklin, C., (2008).
20. Tripathi, S. (2012).
21. Taher, A. M. M., Chen, J. and Yao, W. (2011).
22. Strautmanis, J. (2008).
23. Datar, S. M., Garvin, D. A. and Cullen, P. G. (2011).
24. Baruch, Y. and Leeming, A. (1996).
25. Snoeyenbos, M.H. (1992).
26. Chen, X. and Yang, B. (2010).
27. Chen, X. and Yang, B. (2010).
28. GVV (2010).
29. Gentile, M. C. (2010 a).
30. Gentile, M. C. (2010 a).
31. ECCH (2013).
32. Gentile, M.C. (2007).
33. Coco, D (2010).
34. Cote, J., Goodstein, J. and Latham, C. K. (2011).
35. Gentile, M. C. (2010 b).
36. Gonzalez-Padron, T. L., Ferrell, O. C., Ferrell, L. and Smith, I. A. (2011).
37. Gentile, M. C. (2007).
38. Strautmanis, J. (2008).
39. Tripathi, S. (2012).
40. Anninos, L. N. and Chytiris, L. (2011).
41. U4 Guidelines (2009).
42. Gentile, M.C. (2010a).
43. U4 Guidelines (2009).
44. Chen, X. and Yang, B. (2010).
45. Baruch, Y. and Leeming, A. (1996).
46. Gentile, M. C. (2010b).
47. Tripathi, S. (2012).
48. Gentile, M. C. (2010a).
49. Anninos, L. N. and Chytiris, L. (2011).
50. Tripathi, S. (2012).
51. Tripathi, S. (2012).

Chapter 8

1. Munshi and Abraham (2004).
2. Doig (2006).
3. Cox (2009) and also Gichure (2006).
4. Arellano-Gault and Lepore (2011).
5. Campos and Pradhan (2007), p. xi.
6. Spector (2012).
7. Transparency International Official Website http://www.transparency.org
8. The World Bank, *Helping Countries Combat Corruption: The Role of the World Bank, Poverty Reduction and Economic Management Network*, September 1997. See pages 19–20 on definitions of corruption.
9. McMillan (2006).
10. Campos and Pradhan (2007).
11. Transparency International Strategy (2015), p. 7.
12. Treisman (1999).
13. Pillay and Dorasamy (2010).
14. Mathematically speaking, we can say C varies directly with R and D, and inversely with A. See Kiltgaard, Robert, "International cooperation against corruption," IMF/World Bank, *Finance and Development, 35*(1) (1998): 3. As cited in U. Myint, "Corruption: Causes, Consequences and Remedies," *Asia-Pacific Development Journal*, 7(2), (2000), 33–58.
15. Groenendijk (1997).
16. Groenendijk (1997) proposes a principal–agent model of corruption in relation to neoliberal systems.
17. Pillay and Dorasamy (2010) borrow the two dimensional approach of corruption from Rodriguez P., Uhlenbruck K. and Eden L. (2005). Government corruption and the entry strategies of multi- nationals. *Academy of Management Review 30*(2), 383–396.
18. Pillay and Dorasamy (2010), pp. 367–368.
19. Harrison and Huntington (2000); Seleim and Bontis (2009); Heidenheimer and Johnston, (1989b).
20. For further examples and explanations see Hofstede (2001), p. 141.
21. For an interactive overview of the national cultural dimensions see http://geert-hofstede.com; For an overview of the works and contributions on cultural dimensions by Geert Hofstede (now followed by his son Gert Jan) see their academic website at http://www.geerthofstede.nl/
22. Geert Hofstede's original work, *Culture's Consequences*, was originally published in 1980 and included only four dimensions. Later the Value Survey Modules got expanded with the Chinese Value Survey (published in the first edition of *Cultures and Organizations*) and the World Value Survey,

integrated in the third edition. See Hofstede, Hofstede, and Minkov (2010); Hofstede (2001).

23. Hofstede, Hofstede, and Minkov (2010) p. 6.
24. Hofstede, 2001, p. 18.
25. One of the most significant contribution has been from Israeli psychologist Schwartz (1994).
26. House and GLOBE (2004).
27. Hofstede et al. (2010).
28. Seleim and Bontis (2009).
29. Pillay and Dorasamy (2010).
30. Alatas, Cameron, Chaudhuri, Erkal and Gangadharan, n.d.; Seleim and Bontis (2009).
31. Treisman (1999).
32. Treisman (1999), p. 1.
33. Sampford (2006).
34. Rodriquez, Uhlenbruck, and Eden (2005).
35. Agnew and Kaufman (2010); Trent (2008).
36. Harrison and Huntington (2000), Ch. 9.
37. For a detailed overview of various measures of corruption see Hawken, A., and Munck, G. L. (2007). "Measuring corruption: A critical assessment and a proposal." *Technical background paper commissioned for the Asia Pacific Human Development Report on Corruption.* Colombo: UNDP Regional Centre.
38. Hofstede et al. (2010), p. 61.
39. For a complete list of PDI values for 76 countries by regions see Hofstede, Hofstede, and Minkov (2010), pp. 57–59.
40. Hofstede et al. (2010), p. 59.
41. Hofstede (2001), p. 113.
42. Hofstede et al. (2010) p. 191.
43. Hofstede et al. (2010) p. 194.
44. Hofstede et al. (2010) p. 192.
45. Mark Mallinger, Rossy and Singel (2005).
46. Hofstede et al. (2010), p. 92.
47. The World Value Survey interprets these dynamics as exclusionism (v. universalism that treats people as individuals disregarding their group affiliation).
48. Hofstede et al. (2010), p. 113.
49. Hofstede et al. (2010), p. 124.
50. House and GLOBE (2004), p. 461.
51. House and GLOBE (2004), p. 458.
52. The GLOBE study too prefers identifying this cultural dimension in different, less ambiguous, terms.
53. Hofstede et al. (2010), p. 140.

54. Hofstede et al. (2010), p. 146.
55. For more distinctions between feminine and masculine culture see Hofstede, Hofstede, and Minkov (2010), p. 170.
56. Pillay and Dorasamy (2010) p. 373.
57. Hofstede, in his first chapter of *Organizations and Cultures* explains well this evolution of values in relation to culture, time, family, school, and work.
58. For more information on their integrated model see http://www.worldbank.org/anticorruption
59. Read more on the OECD integrated strategy on anti-corruption at www.oecd.org/corruption
60. Transparency International's PDI rely on data from the African Development Bank, the Asian Development Bank, the Bertelsmann Foundation, the Economist Intelligence Unit, Freedom House, Global Insight, International Institute for Management Development, Political and Economic Risk Consultancy, the World Economic Forum, and the World Bank.
61. Read more on UNCAC at http://www.unodc.org/unodc/en/treaties/CAC/
62. Minkov and Hofstede (2011).
63. Minkov and Hofstede (2011), p. 58.
64. Transparency International's Corruption Fighters Toolkits: http://www.transparency.org/whatwedo/tools
65. The PRME Working Group on Anti-Corruption in Curriculum Change http://www.unprme.org/working-groups. See also the resources on anti-corruption available in the UNGC website http://www.unglobalcompact.org/AboutTheGC/tools_resources
66. For more information see Transparency International's Business Principles for Countering Bribery.
67. UNDP, *Tacking Corruption, Transforming Lives* (New York: Macmillan 2008).
68. For a useful list of policies and procedures to fight embezzlement see McMillan (2006).
69. The OECD Guidelines for Multinational Enterprises defines extortion as "a solicitation of bribes accompanied by threats that endanger the personal integrity or the life of the private actors involved."
70. Larmour and Wolanin (2001).
71. Heidenheimer and Johnston (1989a).

Chapter 9

1. Bayar, G. (2011).
2. Anonymous (2007, Nov/Dec); Transparency International (2012a); U.S. Senate Homeland Security and Governmental Affairs Committee.

3. Swamy, K. (2011).

4. Transparency International 2011 Annual Report.

5. Transparency International (2012b).

6. Anonymous (2012, October); Davidson (2012); Kaufmann (2009); Kroft (2012); The Economist (2008).

7. http://www.criminal-law-lawyer-source.com/terms/employee-theft.html http://www.ehow.com/

8. http://minnesota.cbslocal.com/2012/08/07/former-marshall-bank-employee-admits-theft/ http://www.darkgovernment.com/news/bank-employee-steals-2-million-dollars-from-customers/ http://www.huffingtonpost.com/2012/07/17/rachael-claire-martin-barclays-money-plastic-surgery_n_1680112.html http://www.nj.com/gloucester-county/index.ssf/2012/06/authorities_willingboro_bank_t.html http://www.oxfordmail.co.uk/news/headlines/9490084.Bank_clerk_stole_for_Barbados_trip

9. http://www.bankinfosecurity.com/insider-fraud-what-to-monitor-a-5425

10. Kaufmann (2009).

11. Matthews (2012, Dec. 20),

12. The survey "*Wall Street Fleet Street Main Street: Corporate Integrity at a Crossroads*" was conducted in June 2012 by market researcher Populus on behalf of law firm Labaton Sucharow.

13. Labaton Sucharow (2012).

14. Carroll (2003); Kroft (2012).

15. Kaufmann (2009).

16. Huffington Post (2012).

17. Inman and Kingsley (2011).

18. Euronews (2012).

19. http://www.business-anti-corruption.com/about/about-this-portal/

20. http://www.cipe.org/about

21. http://www.rvrcvstarr.aim.edu/hills.asp

Chapter 10

1. Gosine (2011); McDonald and Robinson 2009.

2. De Maria (2010).

3. Demas (2011); De Maria (2010).

4. Mutebi (2008).

5. Tabish and Jah (2012).

6. Doig (2006).

7. Husted (2002).

8. Cole, Elliott and Zhang (2009).

9. Bowman and Gilligan (2007).
10. Roberts (2011); Kenyon (2009).
11. Goel and Nelson, 2011; Apergis, Dincer and Payne (2012).
12. Hoogvelt (1997); Marquette (2003).
13. Doig (2006), p. 275.
14. Howard and Korver (2008).
15. Arieley (2012).
16. Arieley (2012), p. C1.
17. Case and Smith, to appear.
18. The basic matrix task involved a sheet of paper containing a series of 20 different matrices with participants told to find in each of the matrices two numbers that add up to 10. They have five minutes to solve as many of the matrices as possible. They get paid based on how many they solve correctly. Most solved four in five minutes. To induce cheating, they introduced a "shredder" condition where subjects counted their correct answers on their own then put their work sheets through a back room shredder. Then they told the experimenter how many matrices they correctly solved and got paid accordingly. In this condition participants claimed to have solved an average of six in five minutes, two more than in the control condition. This overall increase did not come from a few people who claimed to solve a lot more matrices, but from lots of people who cheated just a little.
19. The English language has a whole vocabulary illustrating the practice of deception. Words and phrases used include bluff, beguile, gloss over, downplay, puff up, leave in the dark, hoodwink, whitewash, sweet-talk, exaggerate, string along, take for a ride, propagandize, and snow (Howard and Kover, 2008, p. 17).
20. Lying is so central in the lives of people who speak English that there are a huge number of words used to describe it. We fib, embroider, doctor, duke, fend, dress up, cover up, overstate, understate, misinform, misguide, stretch the truth, varnish, inflate, embellish, garnish, warp, spin, gild the lily, fake, con, perjure, dissemble, distort, and tell boldfaced lies (Howard and Korver, 2008, p. 13).
21. Words in English for stealing include mooching, filching, pinching, snitching, encroaching, copping, hustling, scrounging, sneaking, cribbing, and lifting.
22. Howard and Korver, 2008.
23. Arieley, 2012.
24. Howard and Korver (2008).
25. Howard and Korver (2008).
26. Mutebi (2008).
27. Johnson (2012); Tabish and Jah (2012); Ashforth and Anand (2003).
28. Hazony (2012).

29. For the Prophet Muhammad's Last sermon, see http://www.usc.edu/dept/ MSA/fundamentals/prophet/last sermon.html.
30. Tugend (2012), p. B5.
31. The price whistle-blowers pay for divulging their secrets, *New York Times*, September 22, 2012, B1, 5.
32. Smith (2005).
33. James and Smith (2007).
34. For Kant, ethics that are pure are based on a principle of "good will," meaning to act out of a sense of moral obligation or duty because it is morally the right thing to do with no fear of punishment for disobedience and no hope for reward for obeying. The good will is good without qualification, full of specific commandments like "keep promises" and always under any circumstances "tell the truth." These ideas make Kantian conscience much like the strict Lutheran he was (Kuntz, 2003, p. 169). Kant was greatly influenced by organized religion, seeking to create a moral religion in tune with human beings living and interacting with one another in society.
35. Johnson (2012).
36. Case and Smith, in press.
37. Bright, Alzola, Stansbury and Stavros (2011).
38. Lama (2011).
39. Gosine (2011).
40. Johnson (2012).
41. Johnson (2012).
42. Held (2006).
43. Wigand's dramatic life story was portrayed in the highly regarded 1999 film, *The Insider*, with Russell Crowe portraying Wigand.
44. Johnson (2012).
45. Case and Smith, in press.
46. Cox, La Caze and Levine (2011).
47. Kim, Fisher and McCalman (2009).
48. Jackall (1988), (2010), p. 6.
49. Case (2012).
50. Teluskin (2003).
51. Karl Weick and his associates developed the concept of mindfulness as a concept for organization attention and ability to deal with complexity, ambiguity, and high risk (Weick, K. E., Obstfeld, D. and Suttcliffe, K. M., 1999).
52. In the case of the anti-theist, there was expressed surprise at the Judeo-Christian Influence on all his values.
53. Sample commandment, Islamic female student (Spring 2012).
54. The personal application portion of this exercise utilizes the ideas of universality, reciprocity, and usefulness from Howard and Korver (2008).

55. Based on group size and time available, the group could be up to four people.
56. Case and Smith (2012), p. 41.
57. Mutebi (2008).
58. Howard and Korver (2008), p. 17.
59. Daft and Marcic, 2001; Messick and Bazerman, 1996.
60. James and Smith (2007).
61. James and Smith (2007).
62. Howard and Korver (2008), p. 23.
63. Case and Smith, in press.
64. Howard and Korver (2008), p. 13.
65. Howard and Korver (2008), p. 21.

Chapter 11

1. Popper (1985).
2. Global Compact (2000, July).
3. United Nations Convention against Corruption.
4. European Union, Plenary session, Justice and Home Affairs, August 15, 2011.
5. Rendtorff (2010), chap. 6.
6. Budima (2006), p. 410.
7. Vargas-Hernandez (2010), chap. 8.
8. Carvajal (1999).
9. Jing and Graham (2008).
10. Hofstede (1991).
11. Waldman (1974).
12. Dion (2010).
13. Cragg (1998).
14. Dion (2010).
15. Anechiarico and Jacobs (1996).
16. Jain (2001).
17. Vargas, Hernàndez (2010), p. 133.
18. Rendtorff (2010); Wankel (2010).
19. Rendtorff (2010).
20. Wankel (2010).
21. Wankel (2010), chap. 2.
22. Vargas-Hernandez (2010).
23. Pfeffer and Fong (2004).
24. Luthar and Karri (2005).
25. At least—but not limited to—Chapters 1, 2, 4, 6, 7, 8, 11, 16, 18, 20 of the book *Organizational Immunity to Corruption*, Agata Stachowicz-Stanusch (2010).

26. Mc Cabe, Butterfield and Treviño (2006).
27. Tang (2008).
28. Shin and Harman (2009).
29. Bertalanffy (1951).
30. Giudici, Varriale, Floris and Dessì (2011), chap 7.
31. Students in the group: Francesco Caria, Patrizia Casula, Lisa Deidda, Illary Mei, and Emanulea Pilloni.
32. Students in the group: Michele Cherenti, Laura Coda, Stefania Farris, Roberta Serra, and Marta Zanda.
33. Rendtorff (2010).
34. Students in the group: Silvia Atzu, Andrea Marcello, Marco Mereu, and Claudio Andrea Saiu.
35. Students in the group: Marta Cruccas, and Ester Napolitano.
36. Students in the group: Lorenzo Asuni, Federica Farris, Simone Moccia and Livia Ruiu.
37. This is the motto created by the founder of Scouting Robert Baden Powell.
38. Students in the group: Maria Antonietta Addari, Nicola Cossu, Francesca Curci, Eva Musa and Paola Porcu.
39. Proserpio and Gioia (2007).

References

ACBSP (2011, June). http://www.acbsp.org/p/cm/ld/fid=12/ASBSP By Laws. Retrieved July 15, 2012, from http://www.acbsp.org/p/cm/ld/fid=12

ACTE (2007). *Anti-Corruption Training and Education.* U4Brief, CHR Michelsen Institute October 2007, No. 13, p.2 (Retrieved from http://www.cmi.no/publications/file/2762-anti-corruption-training-and education.pdf on 09/09/2012).

ACTK (2012). *Anti-corruption guidelines ('Toolkit') for MBA curriculum change.* Anti-Corruption Working Group, Principles for Responsible Management Education (PRME) initiative, United Nations Global Compact (Retrieved from http://www.unprme.org on 28/08/2012).

Agbiboa, D. (2012). Between corruption and development: the political economy of state robbery in Nigeria. *Journal of Business Ethics, 108*(3), 325–345. Doi: 10.1007/s10551-011-1093-5.

Agnew, R., & Kaufman, J. M. (2010). *Anomie, strain and subcultural theories of crime.* Farnham: Ashgate.

Airs, T. (2012, January 25). Bank Clerk stole for Barbados trip. *Oxford Mail.* Retrieved January 31, 2013 from http://www.oxfordmail.co.uk/news/headlines/9490084.Bank_clerk_stole_for_Barbados_trip/

Alatas, V., Cameron, L. A., Chaudhuri, A., Erkal, N., & Gangadharan, L. (n.d.). Gender, Culture, and Corruption: Insights from an Experimental Analysis. *SSRN eLibrary.* Retrieved from http://papers.ssrn.com/sol3/papers.cfm?abstract_id=1088811&http://scholar.google.com/scholar?as_ylo=2008&q=-corruption+and+culture&hl=en&as_sdt=0,14

Alcadipani, R., & Crubelatte J. (2007). The Notion of Brazilian Organizational Culture: Questionable Generalizations and Vague Concepts. *Critical Perspectives on International Business*, *3*(2), 150–169.

Allen, W. R., Bacdayan, P., Kowalski, K. B., & Roy, M. H. (2005). Examining the impact of ethics training on business student values, *Education + Training, 47*(3), 170–182.

Amado, G., & Vinagre, H. B. (1991). Organizational behaviors and cultural context: the Brazilian "jeitinho." *International Studies of Management and Organization*, *21*(3), 38–61.

Amare, N., & Manning, A. (2009). Writing for the robot: how employer search tools have influenced resume rhetoric and ethics. *Business Communication Quarterly, 72*(1), 35–60.

Amlie, T. T. (2010). Do as we say, not as we do: teaching ethics in the modern college classroom. *American Journal of Business Education, 3*(12), 95–103.

Anand, V., Ashforth, B. E., & Joshi, M. (2004). Business as usual: The acceptance and perpetuation of corruptions in organizations. *Academy of Management Executive, 19*(4), 9–23.

Anand, V., Ashforth, B. E., & Joshi, M. (2005). Business as usual: The acceptance and perpetuation of corruption in organizations. *Academy of Management Executive, 19*(4), 9–23. doi:10.5465/AME.2005.19417904.

Anderson, R. E., Dixon, A. L., Jones, E., Johnston, M. W., LaForge, R. W., Marshall, G. W., & Tanner Jr., J. F. (2005). The scholarship of teaching in sales education. *Marketing Education Review, 15*(2), 1–10.

Anechiarico, F., & Jacobs, J. B. (1996). *The Pursuit of Absolute Integrity: How Corruption Control Makes Government Ineffective.* Chicago, University of Chicago Press.

Anninos, L. N., & Chytiris, L. (2011). Searching for excellence in business education. *Journal of Management Development, 30*(9), 882 –892.

Anonymous (2007, Nov/Dec). Assessing the dimensions of business fraud. *Debt 3, 22*(6), 14–16.

Anonymous (2012, October). Greed, reckless behaviour and the financial crisis: a timeline. Retrieved January 30, 2013 from http://www.transparency.org/news/feature/greed_reckless_behaviour_and_the_financial_crisis_a_timeline

Antonacopoulou, E. P. (2010). Making the business school more "critical": Reflexive critique based on phronesis as a foundation for impact. *British Journal of Management, 21*, 6–25.

Apergis, N., Dincer, O. C., & Payne, J. E. (2012). Live free or bribe: On the casual dynamics between economic freedom and corruption in U.S. states. *European Journal of Political Economy, 28*(2), 215–226.

Aquilera, R. V., & Vadera, A. K. (2008). The dark side of authority: Antecedents, mechanisms, and outcomes of organizational corruption. *Journal of Business Ethics, 77*(4), 431–449.

Aquinas, T. (1922). *The "summa Theologica" of St. Thomas Aquinas.* New York: Benziger Brothers.

Aquinas, T. (1973/1272). *Summa theologiae: Volume 36, Prudence* (Trans., Thomas Gilby, O. P.). Cambridge, UK: Cambridge University Press.

Aquinas, T. (2005). *The cardinal virtues: Prudence, justice, fortitude, and temperance* (Trans., R. J. Regan). Indianapolis, IN: Hackett Publishing Company.

Ardichvili, A., Jondle, D., Kowske, B., Cornachione, E., Li. J., & Thakadipuram T. (2012). Ethical cultures in large business organizations in Brazil, Russia, India, and China. *Journal of Business Ethics 105*(4), 415-428.

Arellano-Gault, D., & Lepore, W. (January 01, 2011). Transparency reforms in the public sector: beyond the new economics of organization. *Organization Studies, 32*(8), 1029–1050.

Argandona, A. (2006). The United Nations Convention Against Corruption and its Impact on International Companies, Working Paper WP No 656, IESE Business School, October, 2006 (Retrieved from http://www.iese.edu/research/pdfs/DI-0656-E.pdf on 18/01/2013)

Ariely, D. (2012, May 26–27). Why we lie. *The Wall Street Journal*, pp. C1–2.

Ashforth, B. E., & Anand, V. (2003). The normalization of corruption in organizations. *Research in Organizational Behavior, 25*, 1–52.

Aterido, R., Mary H.-W., & Carmen P. (2009). *Big constraints to small firms' growth: Business environment and employment growth across firms.* (Policy Research Working Paper 5032). The World Bank.

Bampton, R., & Maclagan, P. (2005). Why teach ethics to accounting students? A response to the sceptics. *Business Ethics: A European Review, 14*(3), 290–300. doi:10.1111/j.1467-8608.2005.00410.x

Bandura, A. (1986). *Social foundations of thought and action: A social cognitive theory.* Englewood Cliffs, NJ: Prentice-Hall.

Bandura, A. (1990a). Mechanisms of moral disengagement. In W. Reich (Ed.), *origins of terrorism: Psychologies, ideologies, states of mind* (pp. 161–191). New York: Cambridge University Press.

Bandura, A. (1990b). Selective activation and disengagement of moral control. *Journal of Social Issues, 46*(1), 27–46.

Bandura, A. (1991). Social cognitive theory of moral thought and action. In W. M. Kurtines and J. L. Gewirtz (Eds.), *Handbook of moral behavior and development: Theory, research, and application* (Vol. 1, pp. 71–129). Hillsdale, NJ: Erlbaum.

Bandura, A. (1997). *Self-efficacy: The exercise of control.* New York: Freeman.

Bandura, A. (1999). Moral disengagement in the perpetration of inhumanities. *Personality and Social Psychology Review, 3*(3), 193–209.

Bandura, A. (2002). Selective moral disengagement in the exercise of moral agency. *Journal of Moral Education, 31*(2), 101–119.

Bandura, A. (2008). Reconstrual of "Free Will" from the agentic perspective of social cognitive theory. In J. Baer, J. C. Kaufman, and R. F. Baumeister (Eds.), *Are we free? Psychology and free will* (pp. 86–127). New York: Oxford University Press.

Bandura, A., Caprara, G. V., & Zsolnai, L. (2000). Corporate transgressions through moral disengagement. *Journal of Human Values, 6*(1), 57–64.

Bank Employee Steals 2 Million Dollars from Customers (2012). Retrieved September 12, 2012 from Dark Government http://www.darkgovernment.com/news/bank-employee-steals-2-million-dollars-from-customers/

Banker Sentenced for $17.7 million fraud (2010). Retrieved September 12, 2012 from http://www.verify.co.nz/news-theftnz.php#theftnz20100318#ixzz26NQbsSGc

Barbosa, L. (1992). *O Jeitinho Brasileiro: A Arte de Ser Mais Igual que os Outros.* Rio de Janeiro: Editora Campos.

Barbosa, L. (1995). The Brazilian jeitinho: An exercise in national identity. In D. Hess & R. DaMatta (Eds.), *The Brazilian puzzle: Culture on the borderlands of the western world*, pp. 35–48. New York : Columbia University Press.

Baron, T. (2010). *The art of servant leadership: Designing your organization for the sake of others.* Tucson, AZ: Wheatmark.

Barsky, A. (2011). Investigating the effects of moral engagement and participation of unethical work behavior. *Journal of Business Ethics, 104*(1), 59–75.

Baruch, Y., & Leeming, A. (1996). Programming the MBA programme—the quest for curriculum, *Journal of Management Development, 15*(7), 27–36

Bass, B. M., & Bass, R. (2008). *The bass handbook of leadership: Theory, research, and managerial applications.* New York: Free Press.

Bayar, G. (2011). Causes of corruption: Dynamic panel data analysis of some post soviet countries and East Asian countries. *The Journal of Applied Business Research, 27*(1), 77–86.

Bazerman, M. H., & Tenbrunsel, A. E. (2011). *Blind spots: Why we fail to do what's right and what to do about it.* Princeton, NJ: Princeton University Press.

Berry, G. R., & Workman, L. (2007). Broadening student societal awareness through service learning and civic engagement. *Marketing Education Review, 17*(3), 21–32.

Bertalanffy, L. V. (1968). *General system theory: Foundations, development, applications* (14th revised ed.). New York: Braziller.

Bindley, K. (2012, July 17). Rachael Claire Martin, Barclays bank clerk, stole money for plastic surgery. *The Huffington Post.* Retrieved January 31, 2013 from http://www.huffingtonpost.com/2012/07/17/rachael-claire-martin-barclays-money-plastic-surgery_n_1680112.html

Blasco, M. (2012). Aligning the hidden curriculum of management education With PRME. An inquiry-based framework. *Journal of Management Education 36*(3), 364–388.

Bowman, D., & Gilligan, G. (2007). Public awareness of corruption in Australia. *Journal of Financial Crime, 14*(4), 438–452.

Boyatzis, R. E., & McKee, A. (2005). *Resonant leadership: Renewing yourself and connecting with others through mindfulness, hope, and compassion.* Boston, MA: Harvard Business Publishing.

Brazil Takes Off (2009). *The Economist, Nov. 14th, 2009,* Retrieved from: http://www.economist.com/node/14845197.

Bright, D. S., Alzola, M., Stansbury, J., & Stavros, J. M. (2011). Virtue ethics in positive organizational scholarship: An integrative perspective. *Canadian Journal of Administrative Sciences*, published online in Wiley Online Library (wileyonlinelibrary.com). DOI: 10.1002/CJAS.199

Brink, A. (2009). Hirschman's rhetoric of reaction: U.S. and German insights in business ethics. *Journal of Business Ethics, 89*(1), 109–122. doi:10.1007/s10551-008-9988-5

Brockett, R. G., & Hiemstra, R. (1991). *Self-direction in adult learning: Perspectives on theory, research, and practice.* New York: Routledge.

Brown, E., & Cloke, J. (2011). Critical perspectives on corruption: an overview. *Critical Perspectives on International Business, 7*(2), 116–124.

Brown, M. E., & Treviño, L. K. (2006). Ethical leadership: A review and future directions. *The Leadership Quarterly 17*, 595–616.

Buchholz, R., & Rosenthal, S. (2008). The unholy alliance of business and science. *Journal of Business Ethics, 78*(1/2), 199–206. doi:10.1007/s10551-006-9329-5

Budima, G. (2006). Can corruption and economic crime be controlled in developing economies, and if so, is the cost worth it? *Journal of Financial Crime 13*(4), 408–419.

Burke, L., & Logsdon, J. E. (1996). How corporate responsibility pays off. *Journal of Long Range Planning, 29*(4), 495–502.

Cameron, K. (2006). Good or not bad: standards and ethics in managing change. *Academy of Management Learning & Education, 5*(3), 317–323. doi:10.5465/AMLE.2006.22697020

Campos, J. E., & Pradhan, S. (2007). *The many faces of corruption: Tracking vulnerabilities at the sector level.* New York: World Bank Publications.

Canarutto, G., Smith, K. T., & Smith, L. (2010). Impact of an ethics presentation used in the USA and adapted for Italy. *Accounting Education, 19*(3), 309–322. doi:10.1080/09639280802532109

Candy, P. C. (1991). *Self-direction for lifelong learning.* San Francisco, CA: Jossey-Bass.

Cant, G., & Kulik, B. W. (2009). More than lip service: the development and implementation plan of an ethics decision-making framework for an integrated undergraduate business curriculum. *Journal of Academic Ethics, 7*(4), 231–254. doi:10.1007/s10805-010-9104-1

Carrol, S. J., & Gannon, M. J. (1997). *Ethical dimensions of international business.* (Sage, Thousand Oaks).

Carroll, A. B. (2003). Business ethics in the current environment of fraud and corruption. *Vital Speeches of the Day, 69*(17), 529–533.

Carvajal, R. (1999). Large-scale corruption: definition, causes, and cures. *Systemic Practice and Action Research 12*(4), 335–353.

Case, S. S., & Smith, J. G. (2012). Contemporary application of traditional wisdom: Using the Torah, Bible and Qur'an in ethics education. In C. Wankel and A. Stachowicz-Stanusch (Eds.), *Handbook of research on teaching ethics in business and management education* (pp. 42–67). Hershey, PA: IGI Global.

Case, S. S., & Smith, J. G. (2012). The Genesis of integrity: Values and virtues illuminated in Judaism, Christianity, and Islam for workplace behavior. In W. Amann & A. Stachowicz-Stanusch (Eds.), *Integrity in organizations—building the foundations for humanistic management.* Houndsmills, Hampshire, England: Palgrave Macmillan.

Case, S. S. (2012). Judaism: Impact on research/career journey. *Religious traditions. Spirituality, and the researcher's journey.* Boston, MA: Academy of Management, August 3.

Case, S. S. (to appear). *Guiding lights for morally responsible behavior in organizations: Revisiting the Sacred Texts of Judaism, Christianity, and Islam.* Accepted March 1, 2012 for The Henry Kaufman Forum on Religious Traditions and Business Behavior, Center for Financial Policy, Ross Business School, University of Maryland, College Park, MD.

Central Vigilance Commission. (2010). Annual *Report: 1.1.2010 to 31.12.2010.* Retrieved from http://www.cvc.nic.in/ar2010_01092011.pdf

Cessario, R. (2002). *The virtues, or the examined life.* New York: Continuum.

Chen, X., & Yang, B. (2010). Copying from others or developing locally?: Successes and challenges of MBA education in China (1990–2010). *Journal of Chinese Human Resource Management, 1*(2), 128–145

Chene, M. (2008) *Impact of strengthening citizen demand for anti-corruption reform* (CMI U4expert Answer). Transparency International.

Cheung, H., & Chan, A. H. (2008). Corruption across countries: Impacts from education and cultural dimensions. *Social Science Journal, 45*(2), 223–239.

Christensen, L., Peirce, E., Hartman, L., Hoffman, W. W., & Carrier, J. (2007). Ethics, CSR, and sustainability education in the financial times top 50 global business schools: baseline data and future research directions. *Journal of Business Ethics, 73*(4), 347–368. doi:10.1007/s10551-006-9211-5

Christie, P. M. J., Kwon, I. G., Stoeberl, P. A., & Baumhart, R. (2003). A cross-cultural comparison of ethical attitudes of business managers: India, Korea and the United States. *Journal of Business Ethics, 46,* 263–287.

Coco, D (2010). A Strategy for Speaking Up, *Babson Magazine,* Fall 2010.

Cole, M. A., Elliott, R. J., & Zhang, J. (2009). *Growth, foreign direct investment and the environment: Evidence from Chinese cities.* Discussion Papers 09-15, Department of Economics, University of Birmingham.

Confessore, G. J., & Park, E. (2004). Factor validation of the Learner Autonomy Profile, 3.0 and extraction of the short form. *International Journal of Self-directed Learning, 1*(1), 39–58.

Cooper, E. J. (1987). *What are the cardinal virtues?* Herefordshire, England: Fowler Wright Books, Ltd.

Cote, J., Goodstein, J., & Latham, C. K. (2011). Giving Voice to Values: a framework to bridge teaching and research efforts. *Journal of Business Ethics Education, 8*(1), 370–375

Cox, D., La Caze, M., & Levine M. (2011). Integrity. In E. N. Zaltaq (Ed.), *The Stanford Encyclopedia of Philosophy (Winter 2011 edition)*. Retrieved February 22, 2012 from http://plato.stanford.edu/archives/win2011/entries/integrity/

Cox, R. W. (2009). *Ethics and integrity in public administration: Concepts and cases.* Armonk, NY: M.E. Sharpe.

Cragg, A. W. (1998). Business, globalization, and the logic and ethic of corruption. *International Journal 53*(4), 643–661.

Crane, A., & Matten, D. (2004). Questioning the domain of business ethics education. *Journal of Business Ethics 54*, 357–369.

Crawford, M., & Lauritz, H.-M. (1998). Brazilian Higher Education: Characteristics and Challenge. *LCSHD Paper Series.*

Crowe, F. E. (2010). *Lonergan and the level of our time.* Toronto, Canada: University of Toronto.

Daft, R. & Marcic, D. (2001). *Understanding management* (3rd ed.). Mason, OH: Thompson.

Daft, R. L., & Lane, P. G. (2008). *The leadership experience.* Mason, OH: Thompson Higher Education.

Datar, S. M., Garvin, D. A., & Cullen, P. G. (2011). Rethinking the MBA: business education at a crossroads. *Journal of Management Development, 30*(5), 451–462.

Davidson, A. (2012, Sept. 11). We heard you were dead. *The New York Times.* Retrieved January 30, 2013 from http://www.nytimes.com/2012/09/16/magazine/lehman-brothers-we-heard-you-were-dead.html?pagewanted=all&_r=0

Davis, J. H., & Ruhe, J. A. (2003) Perceptions of country corruption: Antecedents and outcomes. *Journal of Business Ethics, 43*, 275–288.

Dawkins, R. (2006). *The God delusion.* Boston, MA: Houghton Mifflin.

De Maria, W. (2010). The failure of the *African* anti-corruption effort: Lessons for managers. *International Journal of Management, 27*(1), 117–122.

Demas, R. R. (2011). Moment of truth: Development in Sub-Saharan Africa and critical alterations needed in application of the Foreign Corrupt Practices Act and other anti-corruption initiatives. *American University International Law Review, 26*(2), 315–369.

Detert, J. R., & Edmondson, A. C. (2011). Implicit voice theories: taken-for granted rules of self-censorship at work. *Academy of Management Journal, 54*(3), 461–488.

Dion, M. (2010). What is corruption corrupting? A philosophical point of view. *Journal of money laundering control 13*(1), 45–54.

Doig, A. (2006). Good government and sustainable anti-corruption strategies: A role for independent anti-corruption agencies? *Public Administration and Development, 15*(2), 151–165. doi:10.1002/pad.4230150206

Doig, A. (2006). Not as easy as it sounds? Delivering the national integrity system approach in practice—the case study of the national anti-corruption programme in Lituania. *Public Administration Quarterly, 30*(3), 273–313.

Dorf, E. N., & Newman, L. E. (Eds.) (2008). *Money: Jewish choices, Jewish voices, Volume 2*. Philadelphia, PA: Jewish Publication Society.

Duarte, F. (2006). *Exploring the interpersonal transaction of the Brazilian Jeitinho in bureaucratic contexts*. London: Sage.

Duska, R. F. (1998). Introduction: Clarence Walton and the moral manager. In C. C. Walton & R. F. Duska (Eds.), *Education, Leadership, and Business Ethics: Essays on the Work of Clarence Walton* (pp. xi–xviii). Norwell, MA: Kluwer Academic Publishers.

ECCH (2013). *The case for Giving Voice to Values*. European case clearing house collection on GVV (Retrieved from http://www.ecch.com/educators/casemethod/resources/features/gvv on 01/02/2013).

Eicher, T., Gracia-Penalosa, C., & van Ypersele, T.(2009). Education, corruption, and the distribution of income. *Journal of Economic Growth, 14*(3), 205–231.

Elias, R. (2006). The impact of professional commitment and anticipatory socialization on accounting students' ethical orientation. *Journal of Business Ethics, 68*(1), 83–90. doi:10.1007/s10551-006-9041-5

Employee theft (2012). Retrieved September 12, 2012, from Criminal Law Lawyer. Source: http://www.criminal-law-lawyer-source.com/terms/employee-theft.html

Enron (2000). *Enron's "Code of Ethics,"* July 2000 (Retrieved from http://www.thesmokinggun.com/file/enrons-code-ethics?page=2 on 02/09/2012)

Escudero, M. (2011). PRME and Four Theses in the Future of Management Education. In: Morsing, M., & A. S. Rovira (Eds.), *Business schools and their contribution to the society* (pp. 201–212). Thousand Oaks, CA: Sage.

Euronews (June 6, 2012). *Corruption Risks Europe's Financial Recovery*. Retrieved August 29, 2012, from http://www.euronews.com/ and http://www.youtube.com/watch?v=g4GVqloqneE

European Commission for Education and Training, http://ec.europa.eu/education/lifelonglearn ing-policy/doc28_en.htm, Retrieved July 20, 2011.

Evans, F. J., & Marcal, L. E. (2005). Educating for ethics: business deans' perspectives. *Business & Society Review, 110*(3), 233–248. doi:10.1111/j.0045-3609.2005.00014.x

Evans, J. M., Treviño, L. K., & Weaver, G. R. (2006). Who's in the ethics driver's seat? Factors influencing ethics in the MBA curriculum. *Academy of Management Learning and Education, 5*(3), 278–293. doi:10.5465/AMLE.2006.22697017

Evers, C. W. (1992). Ethics and ethical theory in educative leadership: A pragmatic and holistic approach. In P. A. Duignan & R. J. S. Macpherson (Eds.), *Educative leadership: A practical theory for new administrators and managers* (pp. 21–43). Bristol, PA: The Falmer Press.

Falck, O., & Heblich, S. (2007). Corporate social responsibility: doing well by doing good. *Business Horizons, 50*, 247–254.

Festinger, L. (1957). *A theory of cognitive dissonance.* Stanford, CA: Stanford University Press.

Fisher, R., Ury, W., & Patton, B. (1981, 1991, 2011). *Getting to Yes: Negotiating Agreement Without Giving In.* London: Penguin.

Flannery, B. L., & Pragman, C. H. (2008). Working towards empirically-based continuous improvements in service learning. *Journal of Business Ethics, 80*(3), 465–479.

Fleming, A., Pearson, T. A., & Riley Jr., R. A. (2008). West Virginia University: Forensic Accounting and Fraud Investigation (FAFI). *Issues in Accounting Education, 23*(4), 573–580.

Ford, J., Harding, N., & Learmonth, M. (2010). Who is it that would make business schools more critical? critical reflections on critical management studies. *British Academy of Management 21*, (Supp.1), 71–81.

Former Marshall bank employee admits theft (August 7, 2012). Retrieved September 12, 2012 from http://minnesota.cbslocal.com/2012/08/07/former-marshall-bank-employee-admits-theft/

Forray, J. M., & Leigh, J. (2010). Special Issue: Principles of Responsible Management Education (PRME). *Journal of Management Education 34*(5), 775–776.

Fraenkel, C. (2011). *Does Brazil Still Need a Revolution?* Dissent, Winter 2011. *58*(1), 27-32.

Gempesaw II, C. (2009). Do business schools have a role in the current financial crisis? *Decision Sciences Journal of Innovative Education, 7*(2), 333–337. doi:10.1111/j.1540-4609.2009.00234.x

Gentile, M. C. (2009). *Giving Voice to Values: How to speak your mind when you know what's right.* New Haven and London: Yale University Press.

Gentile, M. C. (2010b). *New approach to values-driven leadership curriculum. Resource document.* Babson College (Cited in Gonzalez-Padron, T. L., Ferrell, O. C., Ferrell, L., & Smith, I.A. (2011). A Critique of Giving Voice to Values Approach to Business Ethics Education, *J Academics Ethics* (2012) *10*, 251–269 (Retrieved from http://danielsethics.mgt.unm.edu/pdf/voicetovalues2.pdf on 03/02/2013)

Gentile, M. C. (2010). *Reasons and rationalizations: An Exercise.* Retrieved August 30, 2011 from www.GivingVoicetoValues.org

Gentile, M. C. (2012). Values-driven leadership development: Where we have been and where we could go. *Organization Management Journal. 9*(3), 188–196.

Gentile, M. C. (2007). *Giving Voice to Values, shaping tomorrow's business leaders: Principles and practices for a model business ethics program* Business Roundtable, Institute for Corporate Ethics, p. 10 (Retrieved from http://www.corporate -ethics.org/pdf/mbep.pdf on March 2, 2013)

Gentile, M. C. (2010a). *Giving Voice to Values: How to speak your mind when you know what's right* Yale University Press (Available at http://www.givingvoice-tovaluesthebook.com/).

Ghoshal, S. (2005). Bad management theories are destroying good management practices. *Academy of Management Learning & Education 4*(1), 75–91.

Giacalone, R. A. (2007). Taking the red pill to disempower unethical students: Creating ethical sentinels in Business Schools. *Academy of Management Learning & Education, 6*(4), 534–542.

Giacalone, R., & Wargo, D. (2009). The roots of the global financial crisis are in our business schools. *Journal of Business Ethics Education 6*, 147–168.

Gichure, C. (January 1, 2006). Teaching business ethics in Africa: What ethical orientation? The case of East and Central Africa. *Journal of Business Ethics, 63*(1), 39–52.

Gilligan, C. (1982). *In a different voice: Psychological theory and women's development.* Cambridge, MA: Harvard University Press.

Giudici, E., Varriale, L., Floris, M., & Dessì, S. (2011). Teaching business students to be passionate about ethical sustainable development. In Stachowicz-Stanusch, A. and Wankel, C. (Eds.) *Effectively integrating ethical dimensions into business Education* (pp. 135–158). Charlotte, NC: Information Age Publishing.

Glanz, J. (2007). On vulnerability and transformative leadership: an imperative for leaders of supervision. *International Journal of Leadership in Education, 10*(2), 115–135. doi:10.1080/13603120601097462

Glynn, P., Kobrin, S. J., & Naim, M. (1997). The globalization of corruption. In Elliott, K. A. (Eds.), *Corruption and the global Economy* (pp. 7–27). Washington, DC: Institute for International Economics.

Goby, V., & Nickerson, C. (2012). Introducing ethics and corporate social responsibility at undergraduate level in the United Arab Emirates: An experiential exercise on website communication. *Journal of Business Ethics, 107*(2), 103–109. doi:10.1007/s10551-011-1025-4

Goel, R., & Nelson, M. (2011). Government fragmentation versus fiscal decentralization and corruption. *Public Choice, 148*(3), 471–490.

Gonzalez-Padron, T. L., Ferrell, O. C., Ferrell, L., & Smith, I. A. (2011). "A critique of giving voice to values approach to business ethics education," *Journal of Academic Ethics, 10*, 251–269 (Retrieved from http://danielsethics.mgt. unm.edu/pdf/voicetovalues2.pdf on March 2, 2013)

Gordon, N., & Lacy, P. (2011). *Towards a new Era of sustainability in the banking industry.* UN Global Compact-Accenture CEO Study.

Gosine, M. (2011). *Leadership in the new millennium: Avoiding the culture of corruption.* Boston, MA: Pearson.

Green, J. (2012, June 26). Willingboro bank teller stole $100,000 from account of an accused thief. *Gloucester County Times.*

Griesse, M. A. (2007). The geographic, political and economic context for corporate social responsibility in Brazil. *Journal of Business Ethics 73*(1), 21–37.

Groenendijk, N. (1997). A principal–agent model of corruption. *Crime, Law and Social Change, 27*(3), 207–229. doi:10.1023/A:1008267601329

GVV (2010). "New Approach to Values-Driven Leadership Curriculum," Giving Voice to Values Curriculum Collection, (Retrieved from http://www.aacu.org/meetings/psr11/documents/CS11.pdf on 21/01/2013)

Hafez, Z. (2009): The culture of rent, factionalism, and corruption: a political economy of rent in the Arab world, *Contemporary Arab Affairs, 2*(3), 458–480.

Hammer, J., et al. (2007). Understanding government failure in Public Health Services. *Economic and Political Weekly, 42*(40), 4049–4057.

Hansen, H. K. (2011). Managing corruption risk. *Review of International Political Economy, 18*(2), 251–275.

Hariman, R. (2003a). *Prudence: Classical virtue, postmodern practice.* University Park, PA: The Pennsylvania State University Press.

Hariman, R. (2003b). Theory without modernity. In R. Hariman (Ed.), *Prudence: classical virtue, postmodern practice* (pp. 1–32). University Park, PA: The Pennsylvania State University Press.

Harris, H. (2008). Promoting ethical reflection in the teaching of business ethics. *Business Ethics: A European Review, 17*(4), 379–390. doi:10.1111/j.1467-8608.2008.00541.x

Harrison, L. E., & Huntington, S. P. (2000). *Culture matters: How values shape human progress.* Basic Books.

Hartman, L., & Hartman, E. (2004). How to teach ethics: assumptions and arguments. *Journal of Business Ethics Education 1*(2), 165–212.

Havard, A. (2007). *Virtuous leadership: An agenda for personal excellence.* New York: Scepter.

Hawawini, G. (2005). The future of business schools. *Journal of Management Development 24*(1), 770–783.

Hazony, Y. (2012). *The philosophy of Hebrew scripture*, Cambridge, UK: Cambridge University Press.

Heeks, R. (2011). *Understanding success and failure of anti-corruption initiatives.* (CMI U4Brief, 2, 1–4). Anti-Corruption Resource Centre, University of Manchester.

Heidenheimer, A. J., & Johnston, M. (1989a). *Political corruption: A handbook.* Transaction Publishers.

Heidenheimer, A. J., & Johnston, M. (1989b). *Political corruption: A handbook.* Transaction Publishers.

Held, V. (2006). The ethics of care. In D. Copp (Ed.), *The Oxford handbook of ethical theory* (pp. 537–566). Oxford, UK: Oxford University Press.

Hellman & Kaufmann (2002). The Inequality of Influence. World Bank Working Paper Series.

Hemmasi, M., & Graf, L. A. (1992). Managerial skills acquisition: a case for using business policy simulations. *Simulation & Gaming, 23*, 298–310.

Heuer, M. (2010). Foundations and capstone; core values and hot topics; ethics-LX; skytech; and the green business laboratory: simulations for sustainability education. *Academy of Management Learning & Education, 9*(3), 556–561. doi:10.5465/AMLE.2010.53791837

Heywood, W. (1906). *The little flowers of the glorious messer St. Francis and his Friars.* London: Methuen & Co.

Hinrichs, K. T., Lei Wang, A., Hinrichs, T., & Romero, E. J. (2012). Moral disengagement through displacement of responsibility: The role of leadership beliefs. *Journal of Applied Social Psychology, 42*(1), 62–80.

Hirschman, A. O. (1970). *Exit, voice, and loyalty: Responses to decline in firms, organizations, and states* (Vol. 25). Cambridge, MA: Harvard University Press.

Hochstetler, K. (2003). Civil Society in Lula's Brazil. *Centre for Brazilian studies*, University of Oxford, *Working Paper 57.*

Hofstede, G. (1980). *Culture's consequences: International differences in work-related values.* Beverly Hills, CA: Sage.

Hofstede, G. (1991). *Culture and organizations: Software of the mind.* New York: McGraw-Hill.

Hofstede, G. (1997). *Culture and organizations: Software of the mind. International cooperation and its importance for survival.* New York: McGraw-Hill.

Hofstede, G. H. (2001). *Culture's consequences: Comparing values, behaviors, institutions, and organizations across nations.* Thousand Oaks, CA: Sage Publications.

Hofstede, G. H., Hofstede, G. J., & Minkov, M. (2010). *Cultures and organizations: software of the mind: Intercultural cooperation and its importance for survival.* New York: McGraw-Hill.

Hofstede, G. n.d. National Cultures/Countries. Retrieved from http://geert-hofstede.com/india.html

Homeland Security and Governmental Affairs Committee (July 16, 2012). HSBC exposed US financial system to money laundering, drug, terrorist financing risks. *US Senate Homeland Security and Governmental Affairs Committee Report*, Washington, DC.

Hoogvelt, A. (1997). *Globalisation and the post-colonial world*, London: Macmillan.

Horn, L., & Kennedy, M. (2008). Collaboration in business schools: a foundation for community success. *Journal of Academic Ethics, 6*(1), 7–15. doi:10.1007/s10805-007-9050-8

House, R. J., & Global Leadership and Organizational Behavior Effectiveness Research Program (GLOBE). (2004). *Culture, leadership, and organizations?: The GLOBE study of 62 societies.* Thousand Oaks, CA: Sage.

Houser, R. E. (2004). *The cardinal virtues: Aquinas, Albert, and Philip the chancellor.* Toronto: Pontifical Institute of Mediaeval Studies.

Howard, R. A., & Korver, C. D. (2008). *Ethics for the real world.* Boston, MA: Harvard Business Press. http://www.labaton.com/en/about/press/Labaton-Sucharow-announces-results-of-financial-services-professional-survey.cfm

Huffington Post (2012, April 26). Practicing what you preach: A lesson for Walmart's bosses. Retrieved September 12, 2012 from http://www.huffingtonpost.com/cobus-de-swardt/walmart-bribery-mexico_b_1455596.html?view=screen

Husted, B. W. (2002). Culture and international anti-corruption agreements in Latin America. *Journal of Business Ethics, 37*(4), 413–422.

Inman, P., & Kingsley, P. (2011, February 17). Inside Job: how bankers caused the financial crisis. *The Guardian.* Retrieved from http://www.guardian.co.uk/film/2011/feb/17/inside-job-financial-crisis-bankers-verdicts

Islam, G., & Zyphur, M. J. (2006). *Critical industrial psychology: What is it and where is it?*, Psychology in Society, Vol. 34, pp. 17–30.

Ivory, C., Miskell, P., Shipton, H., White, A., Moeslein, K., & Neely, A. (2006). *UK business schools: Historical contexts and future scenarios.* London: Advanced Institute of Management.

Jackall, R. (1988, 2010). *Moral mazes: The world of corporate nanagers.* Oxford: Oxford University Press.

Jain, A. K. (2001). Controlling power and politics. In A. K. Jain (Ed.), *The Political Economy of Corruption* (pp. 3–10). London: Routledge, Taylor & Francis.

Jamali, D., & Abdallah, H. (2011). Mainstreaming CSR at the core of the Business Curriculum. In Wankel, C., & Stachowicz, A. (Eds.), *Handbook of Research on Teaching Ethics in Business/Management Education* Hershey PA: IGI Global.

James, C. J., & Smith, J. G. (2007). George Williams in Thailand: An exercise in ethical decision-making. *Journal of Management Education, 31*(5), 696–712.

Jaussi, K. S. (2007). Attitudinal commitment: A three-dimensional construct. *Journal of Occupational & Organizational Psychology, 80*(1), 51–61.

Jenkins, C., Meyer, K., Costello, M., & Ali, H. (2011). International Rentierism in the Middle East and North Africa, 1971–2008. *International Area Studies Review 14*(3), 3–31.

Jing, R., & Graham J. L. (2008). Values versus regulations: how culture plays its role. *Journal of Business Ethics 80*(4), 791–806.

Johnson, C. E. (2012). *Meeting the ethical challenges of leadership: Casting Light or Shadow*, 4th ed. Los Angeles, CA: Sage.

Kashyap, R., Mir, R., & Iyer, E. (2006). Toward a responsive pedagogy: linking social responsibility to firm performance issues in the classroom. *Academy of Management Learning & Education*, *5*(3), 366–376. doi:10.5465/AMLE.2006.22697025

Kaufmann, D. (2009, January 1). Corruption and the global financial crisis. *Forbes.com*. Retrieved August 25, 2012 from http://www.forbes.com/2009/01/27/corruption-financial-crisis-business-corruption09_0127corruption.html

Kaufmann, D., Kraay, A., & Mastruzzi, M. (2009). Governance Matters VIII: Aggregate and Individual Governance Indicators 1996–2008. Policy Research Working Paper 4978. World Bank.

Kazeroony, H. (2010). Intersection of regulations, faculty development, and social media: limitations of social media in for-profit online classes. In C. Wankel (Ed.), *Cutting-edge social media approaches to business education: teaching with LinkedIn, Facebook, Twitter, second life, and blogs*. Scottsdale, AZ: Information Age Publishing Inc.

Kazeroony, H. H. (2009). Responding to the learners' skill acquisition needs. *Global Management Journal, 1*(1), 37–44.

Kazeroony, H. H. (2010). Changing higher learning institutions to make positive social impact for global business. *May 2010 Innovation In Management-Global Partnership Conference Proceedings*, Poznan, Poland.

Kell, G. (2005). The Global Compact: selected experiences and reflections. *Journal of Business Ethics 59*, 69–79.

Khurana, R. (2002). *Searching for a corporate savior: The irrational quest for Charismatic CEOs*. Princeton, NJ: Princeton University Press.

Kim, D., Fisher, D., & McCalman, D. (2009). Modernism, Christianity, and business ethics: A worldview perspective. *Journal of Business Ethics, 90*(1), 115–121.

Kitten, T. (2013, January 16). Insider fraud: what to monitor. Retrieved on January 18, 2013 from http://www.bankinfosecurity.com/insider-fraud-what-to-monitor-a-5425

Knack, S., & Keefer, P. (1995). Institutions and economic performance: cross-country tests using alternative institutional measures. *Economics & Politics, 7*, 207–227.

Kok-Yee, N., Van Dyne, L., & Soon, A. (2009). From experience to experiential learning: cultural intelligence as a learning capability for global leader development. *Academy of Management Learning & Education, 8*(4), 511–526. doi:10.5465/AMLE.2009.47785470

Kopp, C. B., & Wyer, N. (1994). Self-regulation in normal and atypical development. In D. Cicchietti & S. L. Toth (Eds.), *Disorders and dysfunctions of the self* (pp. 31–56). Rochester, NY: University of Rochester Press.

Kroft, S. (2012, Aug. 19). The case against Lehman Brothers. *CBS News.* Retrieved February 1, 2013 from http://www.cbsnews.com/8301-18560 _162-57491089/the-case-against-lehman-brothers/

Kuntz, P. G. (2004). *The ten commandments in history: Mosaic paradigms for a well Ordered Society.* Grand Rapids, MI: Wm B. Erdmans Publishing Company.

L. L. Lau, C. (20010). A step forward: ethics education matters. *Journal of Business Ethics. 92*(4), 565–584.

Lama, His Holiness the Dalai (2011). *Beyond religion: Ethics for a whole world.* Boston, MA: Houghton Mifflin Harcourt.

Larmour, P., & Wolanin, N. (2001). *Corruption and anti-corruption.* Asia Pacific Press.

Learmonth, M. (2007). Critical management education in action: personal tales of management unlearning. *Academy of Management Learning and Education 6*(1), 109–113.

Long, H. B. (1990). Psychological control in self-directed learning. *International Journal of Lifelong Education, 9*(4), 331–338.

Looney, R. (2005). Profiles of corruption in the Middle East. *Journal of South Asian and Middle Eastern Studies. 28*(4), 1–20.

Lorange, P. (2005). Strategy means choice: also for today's business school. *Journal of Management Development 24*(9), 783–791.

Luthar, H. K., & Karri, R. (2005). Exposure to ethics education and the perception of linkage between organizational ethical behavior and business outcome. *Journal of Business Ethics 61*, 353–368.

Madison, R. L., & Schmidt, J. J. (2006). Survey of time devoted to ethics in accountancy programs in North American colleges and universities. *Issues in Accounting Education, 21*(2), 99–109.

Makdisi, S. (2011). *Introductory remarks: On the persistence of Arab authoritarianism and prospects for democratization.* Institute of Financial Economics (AUB), The Arab Uprisings—What Happened, What's Next? Working Paper Series-Special, Issue, No. 1, 2012. (http://www.aub.edu.lb/fas/ife/pages/index.aspx)

Makhoul, J., & Harrison, L. (2004). Intercessory wasta and village development in Lebanon. *Arab Studies Quarterly, 26*(3), 25–41.

Maloni, M. J., Smith, S. D., & Napshin, S. (2012). A methodology for building faculty support for the united nations principles for responsible management education. *Journal of Management Education 36*(3), 312–336.

Marens, R. (2011). Speaking platitudes to power: observing american business ethics in an age of declining hegemony. *Journal of Business Ethics, 94*(2), 239–253.

Margolis, J., & Molinsky, A. (2006). Three practical challenges of moral leadership. In Deborah L. Rhodes (Ed.), *Moral leadership: The theory and practice of power, judgment, and policy.* San Francisco, CA: Jossey-Bass.

Mark Mallinger, Rossy, G., & Singel, D. (2005). Corruption across borders: what are the challenges for the global manager? *Graziadio Business Review, 8*(2). Retrieved from http://gbr.pepperdine.edu/2010/08/corruption-across-borders/#_edn11

Marquette, H. (2003). *Corruption, politics and development.* London: Palgrave.

Matthews, C. (2012, Dec. 20). LIBOR scandal: Yep, it's as bad as we thought. *Times Business & Money.* Retrieved February 1, 2013 from http://business.time.com/2012/12/20/libor-scandal-yep-its-as-bad-as-we-thought/

Mattison, W. C. (2008). *Introducing moral theology: True happiness and the virtues.* Grand Rapids, MI: Brazos Press.

Mauro, P. (1995). Corruption and growth. *The Quarterly Journal of Economics.* (3), 681–712.

Mauro, P. (1997). The effects of corruption on growth, investment and government expenditure: a cross-country analysis. In Elliott, K. A. (Eds.), *Corruption and the global economy.* Washington, DC: Institute for International Economics.

May, D. R., Hodges, T. D., Chan, A. Y. L., & Avolio, B. J. (2003). Developing the moral component of authentic leadership. *Organizational Dynamics, 32*(3), 247–260.

McCabe, D., & Trevino, L. K. (1995). Cheating among business students: a challenge for business leaders and educators. *Journal of Management Education. 19*(2), 205–218.

McCabe, D. L., Butterfield, K. D., & Treviño, L. K. (2006). Academic dishonesty in graduate business programs: Prevalence, causes, and proposed actions. *Academy of Management Learning and Education 5*, 294–305.

McCowan, T. (2004). The growth of private higher education in brazil: implications for equity and quality. *Journal of Education Policy, 19*(4), 453–472.

McDonald, L., & Robinson, P. (2009). *A colossal failure of common sense: The inside story of Lehman brothers.* New York: Crown Publishing.

McMillan, E. J. (2006). *Policies and procedures to prevent fraud and embezzlement: Guidance, internal controls, and investigation.* New York: Wiley.

Mele, D., Debeljuh, P., & Arruda M. C. (2006). Corporate ethical policies in large corporations in Argentina, Brazil, and Spain. *Journal of Business Ethics, 63*, 21–38.

Mellahi, K., Budhwar, P. S., & Li, B. (2010). A study of the relationship between voice, exit, loyalty and neglect and commitment in India. *Human Relations, 63*, 349.

Mendonca, M., & Kanungo, R. N. (2007). *Ethical leadership.* New York: Open University Press.

Mensing, C. (1929/2006). *An activity analysis of the four cardinal virtues: Suggested by the writing of St.* Thomas. Published dissertation, Catholic University of America, Washington, D.C.: Kessinger Publishing.

Messick, D. M., & Bazerman, M. H. (1996). Ethical leadership and the psychology of decision making. *Sloan Management Review*, 37, 9–22.

Michalos A. C. (1997). Issues for business ethics in the nineties and beyond. *Journal of Business Ethics, 16*(3), 219-230.

Miller, W. F., & Becker, D. A. (2011). Ethics in the accounting curriculum: what is really being covered? *American Journal of Business Education, 4*(10), 1–9.

Minkov, M., & Hofstede, G. H. (2011). *Cultural Differences in a Globalizing World.* Bingley, UK: Emerald.

Mintzberg, H., & Gosling, J. (2002). Educating managers beyond borders. *Academy of Management Learning and Education 1*(1), 64–76.

Mintzberg, H. (2004). *Managers not MBAs: A hard Look at the soft practice of managing and management development.* London: Pearson Education.

Mintzberg, H. (2011). *Managing.* San Francisco, CA: Berrett-Koehler Publishers, Inc.

Mitroff, I. I. (2004). An open letter to the deans and faculties of American business schools. *Journal of Business Ethics 54*, 185–189.

Mo, P. H. (2001). Corruption and economic growth. *Journal of Economic Development, 29*(1), 66–79.

Moberg, D. J. (2006). Best intentions, worst results: grounding ethics students in the realities of organizational context. *Academy of Management Learning & Education, 5*(3), 307–316. doi:10.5465/AMLE.2006.22697019

Moon, J., & Shen, X. (2010). CSR in China research: salience, focus and nature. *Journal of Business Ethics 94*(4), 613–629.

Moore, C. (2008). Moral disengagement processes or organizational corruption. *Journal of Business Ethics, 80*(1), 129–239.

Moore, C., Detert, J. R., Trevino, L. K., Baker, V. L., & Mayer, D. M. (2012). Why employees do bad things: Moral disengagement and unethical organizational behavior. *Personnel Psychology, 65*(1), 1–48.

Morris, J. A., Brotheridge, C. M., & Urbanski, J. C. (2005). Bringing humility to leadership: Antecedents and consequences of leader humility. *Human Relations, 58*(1), 1323–1350.

Munshi, S., & Abraham, B. P. (2004). *Good governance, democratic societies and globalisation.* New Delhi: SAGE.

Mutebi, A. M. (2008). Explaining the failure of Thailand's anti-corruption regime. *Development and Change, 39*(1), 147–171.

Natale, S., & Sora, S. (2010). Exceeding our grasp: curricular change and the challenge to the assumptive world. *Journal of Business Ethics, 92*(1), 79–85. doi:10.1007/s10551-009-0141-x

Neelankavil, J.P., (1994). Corporate America's quest for an ideal MBA, *Journal of Management Development, 13*(5), 38–52

Neeman, Z., Diniele Paserman, M., & Simhon, A. (2008). Corruption and openness. *Journal of Economic Analysis & Policy, 8*(1), 2013.

Neubaum, D. O., Pagell, M., Drexler, J. A. Jr, McKee-Ryan, F. M., & Larson, E. (2009). Business education and its relationship to student personal moral philosophies and attitudes toward profits: an empirical response to critics. *Academy of Management Learning and Education, 8*(1), 9–24.

Newman, J. H. (1913). *Sermon notes of John Henry Cardinal Newman, 1849–1878.* New York: Longsman.

Ng, S. F., & Confessore, G. J. (2010). The relationship of multiple learning styles to levels of learner autonomy. *International Journal of Self-directed Learning, 7*(1), 1–13.

Nicholson, C. Y., & DeMoss, M. (2009). Teaching ethics and social responsibility: an evaluation of undergraduate business education at the discipline level. *Journal of Education for Business, 84*(4), 213–218.

NIZA (2005). *Train the trainer manual, civic education and community mobilization,* Netherlands Institute for Southern Africa (NIZA), p. 6 (Retrieved from http://www.hrea.org/erc/Library/display_doc.php?url=http%3A%2F%2Fwww.hrea.org%2Ferc%2FLibrary%2Fcivcom05.pdf&external=N on 14/09/2012)

NLNP (2009). New Leaders New Perspectives, A Survey of MBA Student Opinions on the Relationship Between Business and Social/Environmental Issues, Net Impact and The Aspen Institute, March 2009 (Retrievable from http://netimpact.org on 12/01/2013)

Noddings, N. (2003). *Caring: A feminine approach to ethics and moral education.* Berkeley, CA: University of California Press.

O'Connor, S., & Fischer R. (2012). Predicting societal corruption across time: values, wealth, or institutions? *Journal of Cross-Cultural Psychology, 4*(4), 644-659.

Okumus, F., & Wong, K. F. (2007). A content analysis of strategic management syllabi in tourism and hospitality schools. *Journal of Teaching In Travel & Tourism, 7*(1), 77–97.

Olken, B. (2007). Monitoring corruption: evidence from a field experiment in Indonesia. *Journal of Political Economy, 115*(2), 200–249.

One in four pays bribes worldwide: study (2010). *Agence France Presse.* December 8, 2010. Accessed on June 9, 2012. http://www.google.com/hostednews/afp/article/ALeqM5gODlbjVM5IQW9JNx5Iz6kWQUh8mQ?docId=CNG. ed754de0e678c862bc18161c29a672e9.a61

Osiemo, L. (2012). Developing responsible leaders: The university at the service of the person. *Journal of Business Ethics, 108*(2), 131–143. doi:10.1007/s10551-011-1087-3

Otusanya, O. (2011). Corruption as an obstacle to development in developing countries: a review of literature. *Journal of Money Laundering Control, 14*(4), 387–422. doi:10.1108/1368520111173857

Otusanya, O. J. (2011). Corruption as an obstacle to development in developing countries: a review of literature, *Journal of Money Laundering Control, 14*(4), 387–422.

Özdemir, A., & Sarikaya, M. (2009). An analysis of the curricula of business administration departments in Turkish universities with the perspective of civil society awareness. *Journal of Education for Business, 84*(5), 313–317.

Paciello, M., Fida, R. Tramontano, C., Lupinetti, C., & Caprara, G. V. (2008). Stability and change of moral disengagement and its impact on aggression and violence in late adolescence. *Child Development, 79*(5), 1288–1309.

Padilla, A., Hogan, R., & Kaiser, R. B. (2007). The toxic triangle: Destructive leaders, susceptible followers, and conducive environments. *Leadership Quarterly, 18*(3), 176–194.

Paul, S. (1997). Corruption: who will bell the cat? *Economic and Political Weekly, 32*(23), 1350–1355.

Paulo Renato Souza Consultores (2005). Sector study for education in Brazil. *JBIC Sector Study Series 2004-No. 2.*

Pavarala, V., & Malik, K. K. (2010). *Religions, ethics and attitudes towards corruption: A study of perspectives in India.* Working paper 53-2010, University of Hyderabad, Hyderabad, Andhra Pradesh.

Pellegrini, L., & Gerlagh, R. (2004). Corruption's effect on growth and its transmission channels. *Kyklos, 57*(3), 429–456.

Peppas, S. C., & Yu, T. T. (2007). A cross-cultural assessment of attitudes of business students toward business ethics: A comparison of China and the USA, *Chinese Management Studies, 1*(4), 243–256

Peterson, C., & Seligman, M. E. P. (2004). *Character strengths and virtues: A handbook and classification.* New York: Oxford University Press.

Pfeffer, J., & Fong, C. T. (2004). The business school "business": Some lessons from the US experience. *Journal of Management Studies 41*(8), 1501–1520.

Pfeffer, J., & Fong, C. T. (2004). The business school business: some lessons from the US experience. *Journal of Management Studies 41*(8), 1501–1520.

Pieper, J. (1966). *The four cardinal virtues: Prudence, justice, fortitude, temperance.* Notre Dame, IN: Notre Dame University Press.

Pillay, S., & Dorasamy, N. (2010). Linking cultural dimensions with the nature of corruption: An institutional theory perspective. *International Journal of Cross Cultural Management, 10*(3), 363–378.

Pinheiro, P. S. (2000). Democratic governance, violence, and the (un)rule of law. *Daedalus, 129*(2), 119–142.

Pless, N., Maak, T., & Stahl, G. (2010). *Developing Responsible Global Leader Through Integrated Service Learning—Program Ulysses at PWC.* Paper presented on Academy of Management, Montreal 2010.

Poff, D. (2010). Ethical leadership and global citizenship: considerations for a just and sustainable future. *Journal of Business Ethics*, 939–914. doi:10.1007/s10551-010-0623-x

Ponton, M. K., & Carr, P. B. (1999). A quasi-linear behavioral model and an application to self-directed learning. Hampton, VA: *NASA Langley Research Center*, Technical Memorandum 209094, pp. 1–16.

Pope, S. J. (2011). Virtue ethics in Thomas Aquinas. In C. E. Curran and L. A. Fullan (Eds.), *Virtue* (pp. 3–20). Mahwah, NJ: Paulist Press.

Popper, K. R., & Lorenz, K. (1985). *Die Zukunft ist offen. Das Altenberger Gespräch Mit den Texten des Wiener Popper-Symposiums.* Munich, R. Piper GmbH and Co. KG.

Porter, M., & Kramer, M. (2011). The big idea: creating shared value. *Harvard Business Review*, 62–77.

Prinsloo, P., Beukes, C., & De Jongh, D. (2006). Corporate citizenship education for responsible business leaders. *Development Southern Africa, 23*(2), 197–211. doi:10.1080/03768350600707868

Proserpio, L., & Gioia, D. A. (2007). Teaching the virtual generation. *Academy of Management Learning and Education, 6*(1), 69–80.

Puffer, S. M., & McCarthy, D. J. (2008). ethical turnarounds and transformational leadership: a global imperative for CSR. *Thunderbird International Business Review 50*, 303–314.

Raelin, J. A. (2007). Toward an epistemology of practice. *Academy of Management Learning and Education, 6*(4), 495–519. doi:10.5465/AMLE.2007.27694950

Ramamoorhty, N., Kulkarni, S., Gupta, A., & Flood, P. (2007). Individualism-collectivism orientation and employee attitudes: A comparison of employees from the high-technology sector in India and Ireland. *Journal of International Management, 13*, 187–203.

Rasche, A. (2010). *The principles for responsible management (PRME)—history, purpose and implementation.* Paper submitted to the Academy of Management Annual Meeting, Montreal 2010.

Raufflet, E., Gurgel, C. (2007). Bridging business and society: the Abrinq Foundation in Brazil. *Journal of Business Ethics, 73*(1), 119–128.

Reichel, J., & Rudnicka, A. (2008). Teaching responsibility or responsible teaching. Afterthoughts in the context of the Principles of Responsible Management Education. In: W. Gasparski (Ed.). *Responsible management education* (pp. 74–81). Warsaw: Wydawnictwa Akademickie i Profesjonalne.

Rendtorff, J. (2009). Basic ethical principles applied to service industries. *Service Industries Journal, 29*(1), 9–19. doi:10.1080/02642060802116404

Rendtorff, J. D. (2010). The concept of corruption: Moral and political perspectives. In Stachowicz-Stanusch, A. (Ed.), *Organizational immunity to corruption: Building theoretical and research foundations* (pp. 111–117). Charlotte, NC: Information Age Publishing.

Rexeisen, R. J., & Al-Khatib, J. (2009). Assurance of learning and study abroad: a case study. *Journal of Teaching In International Business, 20*(3), 192–207. doi:10.1080/08975930903099077

Rice, J. A. (2007). Bridging the gap: contextualizing professional ethics in collaborative writing projects. *Business Communication Quarterly, 70*(4), 470–475.

Ritter, B. (2006). Can business ethics be trained? A study of the ethical decision-making process in business students. *Journal of Business Ethics, 68*(2), 153–164. doi:10.1007/s10551-006-9062-0

Rivera-Batiz, F. (2001). International Financial Liberalization, Corruption and Economic Growth. *Review of International Economics.* Wiley Online Library, pp. 1–23.

Roberts, K. (2011). Curbing Corruption: Strict new U.K. Bribery Act escalates liability risks for U.S. Companies. Retrieved on 1/06/13 from http://business.highbeam.com/438571/article-1G1-260070790/curbing-corruption-strict-new-uk-bribery-act-escalates.

Roberts, S. J., & Roach, T. (2009). Social networking Web sites and human resource personnel: Suggestions for job searches. *Business Communication Quarterly 72*, 110–114.

Rock, M. T., & Bonnett, H. (2004). The comparative politics of corruption: accounting for the east asian paradox in empirical studies of corruption, growth and investment. *World Development, 32*(6), 999–1017.

Rodriquez, P., Uhlenbruck, K., & Eden, L. (2005). Special Topic Forum on Do Governments Matter? Government Corruption and the Entry Strategies of Multinationals. *The Academy of Management Review, 30*(2), 383.

Rogers, C. R. (1969). *Freedom to learn.* Columbus, OH: Charles E. Merrill Publishing Company.

Rond, M. D. (1996). Business ethics, where do we stand? Towards a new inquiry, *Management Decision, 34*(4), 54–61.

Rose-Ackerman, S. (1997). The political economy of corruption—causes and consequences. In Elliott, K. A. (Eds.), *Corruption and the global economy* (pp. 31–60). Washington, DC: Institute for International Economics.

Rottschaefer, W. A. (1997). *The biology and psychology of moral agency.* New York: Cambridge University Press.

Sachs, J. (2005). *Who beats corruption?* Project Syndicate. http://www.project-syndicate.org/commentary/who-beats-corruption-

Salem, P. (2003). *The Impact of Corruption on Human Development in the Arab World: A Concept Paper.* UNDP and Lebanese Transparency Association.

Sampford, C. J. G. (2006). *Measuring corruption.* Aldershot, England and Burlington, VT: Ashgate.

Samuelson, J. (2006). The new rigor: beyond the right answer. *Academy of Management Learning & Education, 5*(3), 356–365. doi:10.5465/AMLE.2006.22697024

Sanyal, R. (2000). An experiential approach to teaching ethics in international business. *Teaching Business Ethics, 4*(2), 137–149.

Scherer, A. G., & G. Palazzo (2011). The new political role of business in a globalized world: a review of a new perspective on CSR and its implications for the firm, governance, and democracy. *Journal of Management Studies, 48*(4), 899–931.

Scholtens, B., & Dam, L. (2007). Cultural values and international differences in business ethics. *Journal of Business Ethics, 75*(3), 273–284.

Schwartz, S. H. (1994). Beyond individualism/collectivism: New cultural dimensions of values. In U. Kim, H. C. Triandis, Ç. Kâgitçibasi, S.-C. Choi, & G. Yoon (Eds.), *Individualism and collectivism: Theory, method, and applications* (pp. 85–119). Thousand Oaks, CA: Sage.

Schwartzman, S. (1998). Higher Education in Brazil?: The Stakeholders. *World Bank Human Development Department LCSHD Paper Series No. 28.*

Sedaghat, A. M., Mintz, S. M., & Wright, G. M. (2011). Using video-based instruction to integrate ethics into the curriculum. *American Journal of Business Education, 4*(9), 57–76.

Seipel, M. O., Johnson, J. D., & Walton, E. (2011). Desired characteristics for MSW students and social work employees: Cognitive versus personal attributes. *Journal of Social Work Education, 47*(3), 445–461.

Seleim, A., & Bontis, N. (2009). The relationship between culture and corruption: A cross-national study. *Journal of Intellectual Capital, 10*(1), 165–184.

Shareef, R. (2008). Teaching public sector ethics to graduate students: the public values/public failure decision-making model. *Journal of Public Affairs Education, 14*(3), 285–295.

Shareef, R. (2010). What business schools can learn from public management and vice versa. *Journal of Public Affairs Education, 16*(4), 645–652.

Shin, J. C., & Harman, G. (2009). New challenges for higher education: global and Asia-Pacific perspectives. *Asia Pacific Education Review 10*(1), 1–13.

Shleifer, A., & Vishny, R. W. (1993). Corruption. *Quarterly Journal of Economics, 108*, 599–617.

Simola, S. (2010). Use of a "coping-modeling, problem-solving" program in business ethics education. *Journal of Business Ethics, 96*(3), 383–401. doi:10.1007/s10551-010-0473-6

Sims, R. R., & Felton, E. L. (2006). Designing and delivering business ethics teaching and learning. *Journal of Business Ethics 63*(3), 297–312.

Sims, R. R. (2002). Business ethics teaching for effective learning. *Teaching Business Ethics, 6*(4), 393–393.

Singh, H. P., Jindal, S., & Samim, S. A. (2011). Business ethics: Relevance, influence, issues and practices in international business scenario. *Proceedings of the First International Conference on Interdisciplinary Research and Development, Thailand, 59.1-.5.*

Smith, M. L., Smith, K. T., & Mulig, E. V. (2005). Application and assessment of an ethics presentation for accounting and business classes. *Journal of Business Ethics, 61*(2), 153–164. doi: http://dx.doi.org/10.1007/s10551-005-0851-7

Smith, R. (2005). Greenberg's pals ship a letter rallying support. *Wall Street Journal*, October 29.

Snoeyenbos, M. H. (1992). Integrating ethics into the business school curriculum, *Journal of Management Development, 11*(4), 11–20.

Solberg, J., Strong, K. C., & McGuire, C. (1995). Living (not learning) ethics. *Journal of Business Ethics, 14*(1), 71–81.

Solitander, N., Fougère, M., Sobczak, M., & H. Herlin (2012). We are the champions. Organizational learning and change for responsible management education. *Journal of Management Education 36*(3), 337–363.

Spector, B. I. (2012). *Detecting corruption in developing countries: Identifying causes/strategies for action.* Sterling, VA: Kumarian Press.

Stachowicz-Stanusch A. (2011a). The implementation of Principles for Responsible Management Education in practice—research results. *Journal of Intercultural Management 3*(2), 241–257.

Stachowicz-Stanusch, A. (2011b). The impact of business education on students' moral competency: an exploratory study from Poland. *Vision 15*(2), 161–174.

Stachowicz-Stanusch, A. (2012). *Academic ethos management: building the Foundation for integrity in management education.* New York: Business Expert Press.

Stachowicz-Stanusch, A. *Organizational immunity to corruption: Building theoretical and research foundations.* Charlotte, NC: Information Age Publishing.

Starkey, K., Hatchuel, A., & Tempest, S. (2004). Rethinking the business school. *Journal of Management Studies 41*(8), 1521–1530.

Stevens, M. L., Armstrong Elizabeth, A., & Arum, R. (2008). Sieve, incubator, temple, Hub: Empirical and theoretical advances in the sociology of higher education. *The Annual Review of Sociology, 34*, 127–151.

Strautmanis, J. (2008). Employees' values orientation in the context of corporate social responsibility, *Baltic Journal of Management, 3*(3), 346–358.

Stubbs, W., & Cocklin, C., (2008). Teaching sustainability to business students: shifting mindsets, *International Journal of Sustainability in Higher Education, 9*(3), 206–221.

Sucharow, L. (2012, July). *Wall Street Fleet Street Main Street: Corporate Integrity at a Crossroads*, a US & UK Financial Services Industry Survey. Retrieved on September 17, 2012 from Labaton Sucharow.

Sullivan, D. W. (2010). The impact of the Sarbanes-Oxley Act of 2002 on the teaching of ethics in core MBA curriculums in Ohio. *American Journal of Business Education, 3*(5), 61–69.

Swamy, K. (2011). Financial management analysis of money laundering, corruption and unethical business practices: Case studies of India, Nigeria and Russia. *Journal of Financial Management and Analysis, 24*(1), 39–51.

Swanson D. L., & Fisher, D. G. (Eds.) (2008). *Advancing Business Ethics Education*, Charlotte, N. C. Information Age.

Swanson, D. L. (2005). The buck stops here: why business schools must reclaim business ethics education. *Journal of Academic Ethics, 2*(1), 43–61.

Tabish, S. Z. S., & Jah, K. N. (2012). The impact of anti-corruption strategies on corruption free performance in public construction projects. *Construction Management and Economics, 30*(1), 21–35.

Taher, A. M. M., Chen, J., & Yao, W. (2011). Key predictors of creative MBA students' performance: Personality type and learning approaches, *Journal of Technology Management in China, 6*(1), 43–68

Tang, T. L. P., Chen, Y. J., & Sutarso, T. (2008). Bad apples in bad (business) barrels: The love of money, Machiavellianism, risk tolerance, and unethical behavior. *Management Decision 46*(1–2), 243–263.

Tata, J. (2005). The influence of national culture on the perceived fairness of grading procedures: A comparison of the United States and China. *Journal of Psychology, 139*(5), 401–412.

Telushkin, J. (2003). *The ten commandments of character: Essential advice for living an honorable, ethical, honest life*. New York: Bell Tower.

Templin, C. R., & Christensen, D. (2009). Teaching and assessing ethics as a learning objective: One school's journey. *American Journal of Business Education, 2*(8), 65–74.

The Economist (2008, September 18). The financial crisis: Wall Street's bad dream. *The Economist.* Retrieved September 1, 2012 from http://www.econ-omist.com/node/12273023/print

Thorne LeClair, D., & Ferrel, L. (2000). Innovation in experiential business ethics training. *Journal of Business Ethics, 23,* 313–322.

Tillich, P. (1952). *The courage to be.* New Haven, CT: Yale University Press.

Titus, C. S. (2006). *Resilience and the virtue of fortitude: Aquinas in dialogue with the psychosocial sciences.* Washington, DC: CUA Press.

Transparency International (2004). Special Edition Toolkit: Teaching integrity to youth. *Transparency international's corruption fighter's toolkit.* Retrieved from http://www.transparency.org/whatwedo/tools/corruption_fighters_toolkit_special_edition_teaching_integrity_to_youth

Transparency International (2012a). *Scandals show urgent need for bank reform.* Retrieved August 30, 2012, from http://www.transparency.org/new/feature/scandals_show_urgent_need_for_bank_reform

Transparency International (2012b). *Putting corruption out of business.* Retrieved September 12, 2012, from http://www.transparency.org

Transparency International India (2011). *2011—A crisis in Government* [Press release]. Retrieved from http://www.transparencyindia.org/resource/press_release/Corruption%20Perception%20Index%202011.pdf

Transparency International. (2012). *Corruption perceptions index.* Retrieved from http://cpi.transparency.org/cpi2012/results/

Transparency International. Corruption Perception Index Report 2011. Accessed from http://cpi.transparency.org/cpi2011/in_detail/

Treisman, D. (1999). *The causes of corruption a cross-national study.* Stockholm: Östekonomiska Institutet.

Trent, C. L. S. (2008). *State dominance and political corruption?: testing the efficacy of an alternate configuration of institutional-anomie theory cross-nationally.* Retrieved May 26, 2012, from http://purl.fcla.edu/usf/dc/et/SFE0002545

Tripathi, S. (2012). "Teaching–research synchronization in business schools: a conceptual framework for aligning the research value chain" in Amann, W., Kerretts-Makau, M., Fenton, P., Zackariasson, P., & Tripathi, S. (Eds.), *New perspectives on management education.* Excel Books, New Delhi, 2012.

Tropman, J. E. (2008). Organizational theory. In B. A. Thyer, K. M. Sowers, and C. N. Dulmus (Eds.), *Comprehensive handbook of social work and social welfare: Human behavior in the social environment* (pp. 463–502). Hoboken, NJ: Wiley.

Tugend, A. (2012, September 22). Doing the right thing, whatever that is. *New York Times,* p. B5.

U4 Guidelines (2009). *"Guiding principles for adult learning: Examples of anti-corruption training sessions,"* CHR Michelsen Institute October 2007, No. 13, p. 6 (Retrieved from http://www.u4.no on September 15, 2012)

Vaara, E., & E. Faÿ (2012). Reproduction and change on the global scale: a Bour-dieusian perspective on management education. *Journal of Management Studies, 49*(6), 1023–1051.

Vaill, P. B. (1996). *Learning as a way of being: Strategies for survival in a world of permanent white water.* San Francisco, CA: Jossey-Bass.

Valenzuela-Manalo, M. (2011). Developing a Business Ethics Curriculum for the Bachelor of Science in Accountancy (BSA) Students of De La Salle University (DLSU)-Manila. *Journal of Modern Accounting & Auditing, 7*(11), 1179–1189.

Van Hise, J., & Massey, D. W. (2010). Applying the Ignatian pedagogical paradigm to the creation of an accounting ethics course. *Journal of Business Ethics, 96*(3), 453–465. doi:http://dx.doi.org/10.1007/s10551-010-0477-2

Vargas, Hernàndez, J. G. (2010). The multiple faces of corruption: Typology, forms, and levels. In Stachowicz-Stanusch, A. (Ed.), *Organizational immunity to corruption: Building theoretical and research foundations* (pp. 111–117). Charlotte, NC: Information Age Publishing.

Viswanathan, M. (2012). Curricular innovations on sustainability and subsistence marketplaces. Philosophical, substantive, and methodological orientations. *Journal of Management Education 36*(3), 389–427.

Vizeu, F. (2011). Rural heritage of early brazilian industrialists?: Its impact on managerial orientation. *Brazilian Adminstration Review, 8*(1), 68–85.

Von Weltzien Høivik, H. (2004). Learning experiences from designing and teaching a mandatory MBA course on ethics and leadership. *Journal of Business Ethics Education 1*(2), 239–256.

Vroom, V. H. (1964). *Work and motivation.* New York: Wiley.

Waldman, J. (1974). Overseas corruption of business—a philosophical perspective. *Business and Society 15*(1), 437–445.

Walker, R., & Arnold, I. (2003). Introducing virtual solutions for course design and delivery in business education: Experiences from two economics courses. In: C. U. Ciborra, R. Mercurio, M. de Marco, M. Martinez, & A. Carignani (Eds.), *Proceedings of the 11th European Conference on Information Systems* (pp. 2084–2094). ECIS 2003, Naples, Italy 16–21 June.

Wankel, C. (2010). Orienting business students to navigate the shoals of corruption in practice. In Stachowicz-Stanusch, A. (Ed.), *Organizational immunity to corruption: Building theoretical and research foundations* (pp. 53–68). Charlotte, NC: Information Age Publishing.

Wankel, Ch. (Ed.). (2010). *Cutting-edge social media approaches to business education: Teaching with LinkedIn, Facebook, Twitter, Second Life, and Blogs.* Charlotte, NC: Information Age Publishing.

Waples, E. P., & Antes, A. L. (2011). Sensemaking: A fresh framework for ethics education in management. In C. Wankel & A. Stachowicz-Stanusch (Eds.), *Management education for integrity: Ethically educating tomorrow's business leaders* (pp. 15–48). Bingley, UK: Emerald.

Warren, B. W., & Rosenthal, D. (2006). Teaching Business Ethics—Is it a Lost Cause? *International Journal of Management, 23*(3), 679–698.

WEC (2011). *Business skills for a changing world: An assessment of what global companies need from business skills*, World Environment Center (Retrievable from http://netimpact.org/learning-resources/research/business-skills-for-a-changing-world on January 12, 2013).

Weick, K. E., Obstfeld, D., & Sutcliff, K. M. (1999). Organizing for high reliability: processes of collective mindfulness. *Research in Organizational Behavior, 21*, 81–123.

Welford, R., Chan, C., & Man, M. (2007). *Priorities for corporate social responsibility: A survey of businesses and their stakeholders*. Centre of Urban Planning and Environmental Management, University of Hong Kong.

Welsch, H. (2004). Corruption, Growth and the Environment—A Cross Country Analysis. *Environment and Development Economics, 9*(5), 663–693.

Wharton (2007). *In India, will corruption slow growth or will growth slow corruption?* India Knowledge@Wharton: http://knowledge.wharton.upenn.edu/india/article.cfm?articleid=4214

Wilhelm, W. J. (2010). Ethical reasoning instruction in non-ethics business courses: a non-intrusive approach. *Delta Pi Epsilon Journal, 52*(3), 152–167.

Wilkinson, R., & Pickett, K. (2009). *The spirit level: Why equality is better for everyone*. London: Penguin Books.

Williams, J. W., & Beare, M. E. (1999). The business of bribery: Globalization, economic liberalization, and the "problem" of corruption. *Crime, Law and Social Change, 32*(2), 115–146.

Wood, J. A., Longenecker, J. G., McKinney, J. A., & Moore, C. W. (1998). Ethical attitudes of students and business professionals: A study of moral reasoning. *Journal of Business Ethics 7*, 249–257.

World Economic Forum. *Partnering against corruption initiative*. http://www.weforum.org/issues/partnering-against-corruption-initiative, accessed May 22, 2012.

Wright, M. (1973). The professional conduct of civil servants. *Public Administration, 51*, 1–15.

Xaxx, J. (2012). *How much does employee theft cost employers?* Retrieved September 12, 2012, from eHow.com http://www.ehow.com/info_8013582_much-employee-theft-cost-employers.html#ixzz26NOt5gdu

Yeh, R., M., L. J., Moreo, P. J., R, B., & Perry, K. M. (2005). Hospitality educators' perceptions of ethics education and the implications for hospitality educators, practitioners, and students. *Journal of Hospitality & Tourism Education, 17*(2), 25–35.

Yin, R.K. (2009). *Case study research: Design and methods*, 4th ed. London: Sage Publication.

Zarrouk, J. (2003). A survey of barriers to trade and investment in Arab countries. In Ahmed Galal, A. and Hoekman, B. M. (Eds.), *Arab economic integration: between hope and reality*. Eds. (pp. 48–60). Washington, DC: Brookings Institution Press.

Zauderer, D. G. (1992). Integrity: An essential executive quality. *Business Forum*, Fall, 12–18.

Index

Endorsements

A timely and highly relevant book that constructively contributes to better management. Teaching Anticorruption practically outlines how humanistic management can become a reality.

—Michael Pirson
Associate Professor and Director of Center for
Humanistic Management Fordham University
New York

Teaching Anticorruption illustrates how scholars and educators have started questioning traditional management education and provides great perspectives on how the topic of anti-corruption can be taught. Not only is the book a very timely response to recent recent corporate scandals, it is also a great collection of empirical and theoretical insights for rethinking the curricula of business schools. This book will be an asset to any business school that wants to focus on incorporating anti-corruption topics into the coursework.

—Jonas Haertle
Head, PRME Secretariat
UN Global Compact Office
New York

OTHER TITLES IN OUR PRINCIPLES OF RESPONSIBLE MANAGEMENT EDUCATION (PRME) COLLECTION

Oliver Laasch, Monterrey Institute of Technology, Collection Editor

- *Business Integrity in Practice: Insights from International Case Studies* by Agata Stachowicz-Stanusch and Wolfgang Amann
- *Academic Ethos Management: Building the Foundation for Integrity in Management Education* by Agata Stachowicz-Stanusch
- *Responsible Management: Understanding Human Nature, Ethics, and Sustainability* by Kemi Ogunyemi
- *Fostering Spirituality in the Workplace: A Leader's Guide to Sustainability* by Priscilla Berry
- *Educating for Values-Driven Leadership: Giving Voice to Values Across the Curriculum* by Mary Gentile, Editor (with 14 contributing authors)
- *A Practical Guide to Educating for Responsibility in Management and Business* by Ross McDonald
- *Marketing to the Low-Income Consumer (forthcoming in December 2013)* by Paulo Cesar Motta and Mahima Achuthan

Announcing the Business Expert Press Digital Library

Concise E-books Business Students
Need for Classroom and Research

This book can also be purchased in an e-book collection by your library as

- a one-time purchase,
- that is owned forever,
- allows for simultaneous readers,
- has no restrictions on printing, and
- can be downloaded as PDFs from within the library community.

Our digital library collections are a great solution to beat the rising cost of textbooks. e-books can be loaded into their course management systems or onto student's e-book readers.

The **Business Expert Press** digital libraries are very affordable, with no obligation to buy in future years. For more information, please visit **www.businessexpertpress.com/librarians**. To set up a trial in the United States, please contact **Adam Chesler** at *adam.chesler@ businessexpertpress.com* for all other regions, contact **Nicole Lee** at *nicole.lee@igroupnet.com*.

www.ingramcontent.com/pod-product-compliance
Lightning Source LLC
Chambersburg PA
CBHW060326200326
41519CB00011BA/1845